LOWBUSH MOOSE
(And Other Alaskan Recipes)

Gordon R. Nelson

ALASKA NORTHWEST PUBLISHING COMPANY
Anchorage, Alaska

LOWBUSH MOOSE

Library of Congress cataloging in publication data:
Nelson. Gordon R.   1922-
    Lowbush moose (and other Alaskan recipes)
    Includes index.
    1. Cookery, American—Alaska.   I.   Title.
TX715.N429   641.5'9798   78-16515
ISBN 0-88240-112-2

Fifth printing 1984

Design by Dianne Hofbeck
Layout by Sandra Norling
Illustrations by Val Paul Taylor

Alaska Northwest Publishing Company
Box 4-EEE, Anchorage, Alaska 99509
Printed in U.S.A.

To Alaska
the land and the sea around it
for the good life they have provided four generations of Nelsons
and so many other Alaskans

CONTENTS

HOW TO WRITE A BOOK AND LIKE IT

Cooking has got to be a very old art, and there have been some interesting theories about how man discovered the various methods of cooking, including that one about the pig pen burning down. You know the story—man first discovered roast pork in the ashes of a pig pen. Someone always improves the myth a bit by adding an annual festival: a pig pen burning climaxed with roast pork.

Who am I to be writing a book on the subject of cooking?

I like to cook. But I guess the real reason is that for 10 years before my retirement from the Alaska State Troopers I had a stock answer for anyone who asked what I was going to do after retiring. I'd say, "I'm going to write a book."

The image of me wisely sitting down to write a book seemed to please people. They would smile, nod their heads, and say, "That's nice," or "Oh boy, I bet you could!" Everyone seemed to assume that I could do it.

One day I found that I was retired. It seemed that book-writing time had rolled around, but I had no idea of writing. Fishing, yes, but not writing.

If I hadn't run into someone that I had known before retirement, this book would never have been written. But one day, in the back of an Anchorage drug store, I ran into an acquaintance named Al. Al looked me right in the eye and without any concern about embarrassing me asked, "How is the book coming?"

Those years of loose talk all came home to me. Without a doubt, I was doomed to meet people throughout Alaska who would ask me that same question. Did they really think that I could write a book? Yes, they did.

For days after that I sat with a blank piece of paper in my lap and a well-chewed pencil in my hand. Nothing happened. Then I realized I did not want to do an autobiography. Would you be interested in 20 volumes of my life? No? Well, I don't want to write 20 volumes, either.

The mental effort that went into the decision not to write my autobiography was enough to make anyone hungry. So I laid down my pencil and wandered into the kitchen. I looked in the refrigerator and found nothing interesting. Then I turned to my cooking notebook and started paging through it. I hesitated a moment on the recipe for baked bean sandwiches as my mind drifted back to the sandwiches that my mother used to make.

I had turned several more pages when the idea came to me: Why not write a book about cooking? To pursue the thought further, I made a peanut butter sandwich and sat down to review my notebook.

As the various notes and recipes came before my eyes my mind would skip to the incidents relating to my acquisition of these bits of paper. Some of the recipes were given to me. Others were the results of experimentation. The memories of hunting or catching some of the ingredients also drifted into my thoughts. It was the accumulation of memories that gave me the idea to write this book.

I won't claim I've been cooking for all of my 50-odd years, but I will say that I began at quite a tender age to pay attention to what good cooks do. By now I consider myself to be reasonably skilled in the kitchen.

The people who have not liked my cooking are few in number. I stand six feet tall, weigh 250 pounds, and can develop a steely glint in my light blue eyes. I know that you would like my cooking.

I can remember once serving boiled seagull on a stick and receiving nothing but raves of praise. The fact that the lucky recipients hadn't eaten for almost 48 hours was, I realize, a contributing factor. See— taste buds can be conditioned to accept almost anything.

I've usually not stayed hungry long in Alaska. The environment provides food for anyone who will try to find it. However, the will to survive must be strong enough to allow the individual to eat whatever is available, without cooking if necessary.

On several occasions I've eaten some members of the animal world as well as sea creatures that are not usually thought of as gourmet delights. Emergencies have produced some truly exotic recipes. All too often the cooking in these cases consisted of broiling over an open fire, boiling in a can found on a beach, or burying food in a mud pack under a fire. Sea water, if available, was usually the only seasoning and sometimes half the stew.

The dark and stormy night that my brother Ken and I spent on Hawkins Island near Cordova long years ago comes to mind. Our father had dropped us off on the island one September morning so that we could hunt deer while he went elsewhere and did those things that fathers do. At noon we spotted a deer and Ken dropped it with one clean shot. We were quite far inland and it took us nearly five hours to butcher and pack the animal to the beach.

The weather was cold. We built a fire on the beach in the shelter of a giant driftwood log and huddled close to the fire as we watched the wind pile six-foot and then eight-foot waves onto the shore. By 6 o'clock it was evident that we were not going to get off that beach that night.

Ken, being the older, decided to take care of making dinner. He placed half the deer liver across our driftwood log and

began stabbing it with his hunting knife. Then he placed the piece of mutilated liver in a tidal pool to soak. He explained to me that this would take out some of the wild taste and flavor the liver with salt. The liver soaked while we made ourselves a camp.

Later, sheltered by the log and some planks and brush from the beach, we roasted medium-size chunks of liver over our fire. The pieces were well seared on the outside and a bit rare on the inside, but delicious to a couple of hungry young men. If only we'd had a frying pan, some onions and maybe a few slices of bacon. . . .

While we were busy cooking and consuming that liver we watched the riding lights of Dad's boat well offshore. They dipped and bobbed in the sea as he waited for a change in the weather.

After our meal Ken and I dug into the sand and gravel, pulled a cover of dried seaweed and brush over ourselves, and even slept a few hours. With the coming of daylight the sea returned to normal and Dad rowed the skiff ashore. We were soon en route to Cordova. The mighty hunters had survived the hardships and were bringing home the meat.

The stories and comments in this book are mine, so you'll not likely have heard them before. On second thought, I'd better qualify that statement. Some of my friends and acquaintances might have heard my adventures before. Who knows, some of them might even find themselves in the stories. If you find a story you would like to be in, be my guest. Claim it and tell it as your own. I'll never identify who's who.

As for my recipes, I've given and traded much of my collection around the state. I like sharing them and I hope you enjoy trying them.

STEAMED CLAMS

All along the beaches of Southeastern, and for that matter Western, Alaska I have found that hiding in the sand are millions of clams. When the old tide book says there will be very low or minus tides, we pull on our boots and go clamming. Around Juneau the clam I cherished most was the steamer. Steamers are the little clams, 1 or 2 inches across. You might have to buy yours but, wherever they come from, here's how to cook them.

48 live steamer clams
1/2 pound butter

Thoroughly wash the clamshells. Just with water and a scrubbrush; forget the soap! You will need a kettle with a tight cover. I have one that holds about 8 quarts and works fine. With a smaller pot you simply steam fewer clams at a time. Put a couple of cups of water in your kettle, boil, add a dozen clams, cover, steam for 5 minutes.

During this 5 minutes melt the butter, which you'll need as soon as the clams are done.

Remove the clams with a strainer, discarding any that are not open because they were dead before cooking. Start steaming the next batch.

Serve the butter in individual dishes. The clams, still in the shell, are put on the table in bowls. It is better to bring the crew of eaters right to the kitchen to eat the clams while they are hot. Free each clam from the shell, dip it in the melted butter, and pop it in your mouth.

At a single sitting my group of 6 cleaned up 280 clams. That is the actual clamshell count. Yes, we counted only whole shells. Yield: 2 servings, assuming you've got light eaters.

CLAMS AND GAS BOAT SPUDS

In the summer of 1933 I reached the age of 11. Now I could go to work, and that is what I did when the salmon cannery opened for the season. My job was in the warehouse, casing cans of salmon. The tall one-pound cans came to our part of the cannery in big racks from the cooker. The other workers and I removed the cans from the rack and placed 48 cans in each case. The cases were then sealed and loaded on pallets for shipment.

When the fishing was good all the canning lines of the cannery would be running. The processed racks of cans came at us hot and heavy, in a never-ending stream. When this happened the warehouse crew worked long and hard. The wages for my work were 10 cents an hour and in addition I got a free lunch in the cannery mess hall.

Eating in the cannery mess hall was a real experience. At first I was only eating lunch there, but even for lunch there were at least two kinds of meat, rice, potatoes, two vegetables, bread, butter, milk, coffee, tea, lemonade, cake, pie and sometimes ice cream. This was true for every lunch and you could eat all you wanted. Although small and young, I did justice to the opportunity.

Then the real truth about mess halls was revealed to me. The first time I worked overtime, I got to eat my evening meal in the mess hall. I had just sat down at the table when one of the waitresses placed in front of me a plate that contained the largest rib steak in the world. It drooped over the edges of the standard-size dinner plate. It was so big that my first thought was that I was supposed to carve it or something. But more steaks kept coming until everyone at our table had one of his own.

That piece of beef was the biggest chunk of beef I had ever seen outside a butcher shop. Only a few venison roasts at our house had been bigger. I can still remember cutting into the tender, medium-rare, juicy, wonderful thick steak. I ate until everything but bone was gone. I didn't waste time and eating space with the other things on the table. Finally I was finished and sat there savoring my meal. That last bite had been just a trifle too much.

I felt a touch on my shoulder. It was one of the waitresses saying, "Would you like another steak?" In her hands was a platter with five or more steaks equally as large. Seconds were available. With a great deal of regret I said, "No, thank you."

I doubt if I was of much more use to the

CLARIFIED BUTTER

What's clarified butter doing in this chapter? This is the first place it appears, as you'll discover when you go on to learn about Clam Sauce. How to clarify butter is something you'll need to know throughout this book, so I might as well include the instructions here.

Clarifying butter is really nothing more than removing milk solids from butterfat, which is the main ingredient of butter. But do this only when you have the time to pay close attention to the job. Otherwise you'll just ruin a pound of butter.

Place 1 pound of butter in a saucepan of at least 1-quart capacity. Put this over low heat and melt the butter. Watch the butter and remember you're only melting it at this point.

In 5 to 7 minutes a white substance will rise to the top of the melted butter. Now increase the heat slightly until the white substance foams. Skim off the foam and discard. Set the pan aside to cool.

Pour the clarified butter (what's left in the pan) into a jar through a piece of cheesecloth to remove any sediment. Like any butter product the clarified liquid should be kept refrigerated. Yes, it's worth the trouble.

SWEET-TOOTH CLAMS

Wouldn't you know it: in our family there was a youngster who didn't like clams. This recipe was designed to tempt a child into trying the wonderful clam.

12 live steamer clams
1/2 cup or more juice saved from
    steaming the clams
3 tablespoons honey
1 teaspoon soy sauce
Salt and black pepper

Steam the clams in boiling water for 5 minutes. Drain the clams and save at least 1/2 cup of the juice. Remove clams from the shell and keep warm.

In a saucepan combine the clam juice, honey and soy sauce. Stir this mixture over heat until it is reduced to a syrup. Season to taste. Now add the clams to the syrup and stir until all the clams are glazed. Transfer to a serving platter and serve either warm or cold. I've even served clams this way as a surprise hors d'oeuvre, scattering them around on a serving plate. Interesting reactions.

cannery that evening, though my hands continued to move cans around. Certainly all I could think of was that steak. An older boy on the crew assured me that the dinner was always like that. Now, there just had to be a way to get to eat in the mess hall every evening. I talked to everyone about working hours. The result of my research was to discover that the can-loft crew always worked late and ate in the mess hall at dinnertime. The loft had to have a half-day's cans made up before they quit at night.

All I had to do was get transferred to the can-loft crew and the gates of the mess hall would open wide for me. My dad had always told me, "Hard work is its own reward." So I turned over a new leaf and became the hardest-working kid in the warehouse. I also made it known that I wanted to try working in the can-loft crew, and within a week I was transferred upstairs. I lived and dined in splendor for three weeks. Then the season ended and I was laid off. But there was still a surprise to come. My hard work had been noticed, and besides all the good food I had earned I received a five-cents-an-hour raise for the entire last month. Maybe Dad had known what he was talking about.

I spent much of the fall and winter remembering the mess hall dinners and trying to develop a sure-fire plan to get back on the can-loft crew the next summer. At home now we were back to seafood and venison. And lots of beans, salted fish and crab to fill in those winter meals.

With the coming of spring a new interest developed. The time came for the crews to get the cannery tenders ready for fishing season. The tenders and the fish barges had all been drawn out of the water and stored some distance down the beach for the winter.

As both my dad and brother had each signed up to captain a tender that year, they were active in getting the ships ready. I was invited to travel down to the haul-out site and help. Armed with a paintbrush and a can of paint, I was turned loose to crawl down under the ships on the ways and paint the bottoms where the men couldn't reach. I considered this fun and was happy to be on the crews.

Each spring the canneries all got together and sent a crew out on the Copper River Flats, near Cordova, to find the channels and mark them. The winter storms and ice seemed to cut new channels each year. Once the new channels were found pilings were driven to mark them. In some cases the men just used anchored oil drums as markers. I was picked to go along on this expedition.

Remembering my experience of the previous summer, I made myself useful aboard the two tenders and the pile-driver barge. I soon learned that the cook on each tender tried to outdo every other tender cook, since they each represented a different cannery. As Dad's tender was my home, I found myself supporting that cook, although it took me a while to understand him. He was Chinese and he spoke very broken English. However, it didn't take him long to understand that he not only had a helper but a willing one. Chores were passed my way, but that wasn't all that came my way. The second-best steak ended up on my plate. (The captain got the best one.) I imagine there were members of the crew who thought it was because I was the skipper's son that I got the second-best steak. But Chang and I knew different.

My hard work did not go unnoticed on this trip, either, and when we returned to the cannery the superintendent offered me a job aboard the tender as a deck hand. I jumped at the chance. The cannery couldn't hire me to work on a tender because I was too young—although it was perfectly legal to put me to work in the cannery itself—so Dad was given an extra $100 for the three months I would be aboard. As the working Nelsons pooled their money anyway, this was OK with me. Besides, with my friend Chang, the cook, aboard I would have worked for nothing but the food.

I wish I could say that Chang taught me a lot about cooking, but he didn't. He cooked strictly *Amelican*. Simple and ample quantities were his goal. Just fuel for hard-working bodies.

When fall rolled around we put the tenders to bed for the winter, hauling them out of the water and storing them away. My job ended and school was all I had to look forward to for the next several months. My dad and brother went crab-fishing in a smaller ship, the *Pep*. Winter settled down on Cordova.

I was now an old hand on boats after a

summer's work as a deck hand and I wanted to go out with Dad and Ken on their crab boat. I mentioned this often in case someone should forget me. During my Christmas vacation, I was allowed to join the crew of the *Pep*.

I soon found that a week aboard this little 32-foot craft was greatly different from my summer experience. The size of the *Pep* became evident only when you were out at sea. She was small, and over half her deck space was used for handling crab traps and for storing the catch. The living space was the front 15 feet of the hull. Into this area were crowded the wheelhouse, the engine, an oil stove, a sink, a battery-powered radio receiver, two bunks and a bench with a fold-down table.

I could stand up in the forward part of the cabin, but neither of the men could stand except in the wheelhouse part.

Then there was the winter weather. It either rained or snowed all the time I was out on the *Pep*. The wind blew constantly, simply changing directions occasionally.

I was also to discover that pulling crab traps was wet work, even with oilskins on. If you didn't get splashed wet, you got wet inside the oilskins from sweat. When the weather was calm and the stove in the cabin was going full blast, we could not quite catch up on our clothes-drying. If the weather was rough, the stove didn't burn and we stayed completely wet. At least we were dressed entirely in wool, and that stayed warm even when wet.

On the second day out I discovered that when we had finished eating the large pot of beans Mother had given to us, the quality of food aboard the *Pep* dropped way down. The male Nelsons had always seemed especially hungry upon their return from a trip. Now I knew why: they ran a starvation ship.

Maybe a piece of side pork and a poorly fried pair of boat eggs for breakfast. (Boat eggs were eggs shipped from Seattle by boat—not what you'd call fresh.) Then peanut butter sandwiches for lunch and maybe even for dinner. It wasn't that there was a scarcity of food—just of cooks.

On the third day, right after our noon peanut butter sandwich, I took over the cooking. I started by reinventing Gas Boat Spuds. I know I had seen them somewhere before, but this was the name that the family assigned to the dish after this trip. I should explain that the *Pep* was powered by a gasoline engine, hence she was a gas boat.

I started by firing up the little Shipmate stove, setting the anti-sliding rails in place, and securing our largest frying pan on the stove. Then I cut six long slices of salty side pork and left them sliding around in the frying pan as the ship rolled slightly.

I would pop up on deck and work a few minutes, stowing crab or filling bait sacks with clams. Then I'd jump down in the cabin and check on the frying pan.

During a lull in the work, while we ran over to another string of traps, I peeled and diced enough potatoes to fill the frying pan. I put the cooked salt pork in the oven and dumped the potatoes into the quarter-inch of pork fat in the frying pan. Leaving a heavy cover on the pan, I returned topside. It was necessary to return and stir the potatoes once in a while, but I fitted this into my work schedule.

When the last trap was pulled and we were running to our live box float, I could watch the spuds full-time. When the ship was secure for the night, Dad and Ken

GAS BOAT SPUDS

I've already told of how Gas Boat Spuds were first created by me in my youth. Since then the recipe has been somewhat changed for family use. I like to think of it as a refined recipe.

1 cup onions, chopped
1/4 cup shortening or vegetable oil
3 large potatoes, peeled and diced in
*   1/4-inch cubes*
1/2 teaspoon salt
1/4 teaspoon black pepper
8 eggs

In a large frying pan sauté onions in the shortening until transparent. Add the potatoes and seasonings, stir everything together, and cover. Cook over a medium heat, stirring every 5 minutes, until potatoes are done.

Separate 4 of the eggs and reserve the unbroken yolks. Lightly mix the 4 whole eggs with the 4 whites. Pour this mixture over the potatoes, replace the cover, and cook until the eggs are done.

Divide the spuds into 4 servings. Ease an unbroken egg yolk onto each portion and serve.

This recipe is great with thick slices of fried ham. Or you can dice the ham and add it to the potatoes just before adding the eggs, and make a wonderful one-dish meal.

Note: Try this with chopped steamed clams instead of the diced ham. Or anything else that sounds good. Have fun! Yield: 4 servings.

CHILKAT CLAM STEW

To me the steamer clam and the little-neck clam are a couple of nature's wonders, right in the same class as oysters, king crab and Dungeness crab. I love to eat those steamers when they're right out of the shell, hot and dipped in melted butter. But I found that steamer clam stew was good, too. If this sounds like oyster stew, it's a cousin at least.

24 live steamer clams
1 pint heavy cream
Salt and black pepper

Bring a quart of water to a boil, add the clams, and steam for 4 to 5 minutes. Drain clams and remove them from the shells. Discard any clam that didn't open; it was dead before going into the water. Carefully strain and save the liquid from the clams, discarding the last few tablespoonfuls, as that's where the sand will be.

Rinse out the cooking pan and put in it the clams, 3/4 cup of clam juice and the cream. Salt and pepper the stew to taste, heat to just below the boiling point, and remove from heat at once.

Serve by putting a tablespoon of butter into each deep soup bowl and then ladling the stew on top of the butter. Come on, go all out—serve oyster crackers, too. Yield: 2 servings.

HOT CLAM HORS D'OEUVRES

During the time we lived in Juneau, we seemed to have many parties, and the following recipe was the hit of one of them. We used fresh clams but this is also good with canned clams. I'll give the latter recipe.

2 8-ounce cans minced clams
2/3 cup Swiss cheese, grated
2 tablespoons green onion, chopped
1/2 cup mayonnaise or salad dressing
4 drops Tabasco
48 toast squares made from 12 quartered,
    trimmed slices from a sandwich loaf
Paprika
Fresh parsley

Stir together the clams, cheese, onion, salad dressing and Tabasco and spread about 2 teaspoons of the mixture on each piece of toast. Arrange the toast squares on a lightly greased cookie sheet.

Now set a rack in your broiler about 3 inches from the heat. Slide the cookie sheet onto the rack. Watch the hors d'oeuvres carefully as the cheese should melt in 2 to 4 minutes. Remove, garnish with paprika and sprigs of parsley, and serve at once. I would suggest that you have ingredients ready for making a second batch.

came down to supper. I handed them each a plate heaped with spuds and cooked whites of eggs mixed in, while the yellow yolks accented the dish. Two pieces of side pork were laid across the top. A simple and very filling meal, washed down with coffee.

Someone might think it could have been the howling wind, wet snow or the many other miseries that made the meal so good. That is not so! I've tried Gas Boat Spuds several hundred times since that night, and they were always as good as the first time.

The result of this meal and the others that I cooked for the next few days was that I only just escaped being shanghaied aboard a crabber as a cook at the age of 12. It was my mother's firm hand and, I suspect, voice that steadied things. Dad and Ken went back to their starvation ship with a pot of her beans in their hands and three loaves of her bread under their arms.

A stray thought just occurred to me. I have never seen a crab cooked aboard a crab boat. There was all that wonderful eating, just for reaching out a hand, and the crews ate peanut butter sandwiches. Salmon fishermen eat salmon aboard ship. Cowboys eat beef. It puzzles me. I guess to a crab fisherman those spiny crawling things are just to catch and sell.

When the spring of 1935 rolled around I had my first experience digging razor clams. It was too early to begin working on boats and I was at loose ends.

Our next door neighbor, Pete, had a feud going with his clam-digging partner, so he asked me to go along to the beach and help him dig clams. Just for a couple of tides until his partner cooled off.

We ran down the bay to Pete's camp in his skiff and kicker (outboard motor). The camp consisted of a tent on a small frame. Inside was a stove, a table, two chairs and two cots. Settling in consisted of dropping your sleeping bag on a cot.

At 5 a.m. Pete rolled out of his sack and yelled at me to get up. As I staggered around on cold feet getting dressed, Pete handed me a large corned beef sandwich and a cup of hot but obviously old coffee.

Within a few minutes we were moving out in his skiff toward the clam beaches. Pete handed me the shovel known in these parts as a clam gun and described how to catch the razor clam.

To dig the clam you first have to find it, but that's not difficult because the clam makes a distinctive little hole in the sand. Then you have to sneak up to the hole, drive the shovel down beside the clam, and catch it before it can dig itself too far down.

Boy, can razor clams ever dig! My first two tries resulted in my getting two clam necks. The next three times I was successful in cutting three clams in half. Then I had the knack of it. Pete simply said, "Vatch de tide," and went to work on another part of the beach.

As the tide came back in, we boxed up the clams and loaded the boxes in the skiff. All except about eight beautiful clams which Pete set aside. We ran out to the tender, sold our clams, picked up some bread, and went back to the beach to wait for the next low tide.

Back in camp Pete cleaned the clams he

had saved. Then he mixed up a batter, rolled the clams in it, and dropped them into about a quarter-inch of bacon grease in a frying pan. In a couple minutes we each had a plateful of fried clams such as I have seldom seen since.

At least clam-diggers eat clams. We proved it that day.

Six years ago, while we were living in Juneau, the coming of March made me really clam-hungry. In fact, I'd been hungry for fresh clams since the previous August.

I just happened to be reading the tide book and discovered that the upcoming Sunday morning would have a minus-three-foot tide at 9 a.m. As daylight was due about the same time, I decided to go clam-digging that morning. The little steamer clams from among the rocks on the beaches would be my target.

I was up at 7 in the morning; I fueled the old body with a good breakfast and grabbed my buckets and digging tools. It was cool that day so I dressed warmly. I took along my insulated rubber boots, wool gloves and fisherman's rubber gloves to wear over my wool ones.

I arrived at the clam beach, 30 miles north of Juneau, in one hour. I walked down to the beach in the early dawn light. Dressed as I was, I didn't feel the cold.

I waded out in the bay, filled my buckets about half-full of sea water, and set them just above the tide level. Then I went to work digging clams out from under the rocks. I was soon down on my knees scratching out clams and throwing them into one or the other of my buckets. I worked

steadily for about 15 minutes and then my hands and feet began to get cold. I had two buckets half-full of clams, but what was more interesting was the nice circle of ice built up around the rim of both buckets. Each time I threw in a clam the water splashed up to the rim of the bucket. Each splash had frozen to the rim and now I had a quarter-inch of ice around the top of each bucket. This was salty sea water that was freezing to the buckets. Suddenly I was very cold.

I stumbled back to my truck with my clams and equipment. The thermometer taped to my radio aerial indicated that the temperature was 20 below zero. That is too damned cold to dig clams. It was cold up here beyond Juneau.

With the heater going full out, I drove back to Juneau where I was going to make the world's best clam chowder. That's not bragging, it's just fact. Hundreds of hungry individuals from many lands have testified to the fact.

I'll make a clam chowder at the drop of a hat. A bucket of clams can always start me, and during an off season I have been known to get excited enough to start with clams from cans.

A handy aspect of my clam chowder recipe is that it can be expanded to include many other items such as fresh mushrooms and even corn.

My eldest son, when away in the army, wrote home for my recipe so that he could show those people in the Lower 48 how to live. Which is what you'll learn too if you wander farther into this book.

NELSON CLAM CHOWDER

My recipe for clam chowder is world-famous. Really! One man who has had it is in Cambodia and another is in Africa. Europe, however, may have to hear of it from this document along with you.

The type of clam used in chowder is not critical. I've found that fresh or canned clams work almost equally well, so you can use whatever is available. I'm giving you the reduced recipe, not the one we usually use, which requires an especially large kettle.

24 small steamer clams or 2 8-ounce cans
*   of chopped clams*
2 cups juice from steaming the clams
*   or juice from canned clams and*
*   enough water to make 2 cups*
2 onions, chopped
4 tablespoons butter
2 potatoes, peeled and diced in 1/4-inch
*   cubes*
2 slices bacon, cut in 1/8-inch pieces
2 carrots, peeled and sliced thin
1 teaspoon salt
Black pepper to taste
1 tablespoon soy sauce
1 13-ounce can evaporated milk or 1-1/2
*   cups fresh milk*

Steam open the clams and remove them from the shells, saving the juice and supplementing it with water if necessary. Or open the 2 cans of chopped clams, save the liquid, and supplement with water.

Sauté the onions in a tablespoon of the butter in your chowder pot, which in my case is my faithful Dutch oven. When the onions are transparent add the clam juice, potatoes, bacon, carrots, salt, pepper and soy sauce. Simmer until the carrots are just tender.

Add the milk, clams, and remaining butter to the pot. Bring the chowder almost to a boil, take it off the heat, and let it set for 5 minutes.

Serve in a tureen if you're going formal or set the pot in the middle of the table if things are informal. Large soup bowls and an endless supply of sourdough bread, and you have a meal to remember. Yield: 4 generous servings, or 6 if this is only a first course.

Before I leave this recipe I should mention some of the things that you can use to expand the chowder if you desire. You can always add more clams and milk, but some of the following are good too.

1 4-ounce can mushrooms, lightly sautéed
1 16-ounce can corn
1 cup celery, chopped fine and sautéed
*   with the onions*
1 cup chopped ham, added to pot when
*   juice is added*
Heavy cream instead of milk

WINE-SEASONED CLAMS

As my love of clams matured I found myself tasting clams prepared in a variety of ways. This one is as far from fried clams or clam chowder as you can imagine. It is designed simply to enhance the flavor of the clam rather than using the clam to flavor other foods.

1/2 cup dry white wine (I've used
    dandelion wine. Or try sake.)
24 live steamer or littleneck clams
4 lettuce leaves
1 lemon cut in wedges

Boil a quart or so of water. Add the wine, put the clams into the boiling liquid, and let them steam for 4 or 5 minutes. Remove and drain.

Cover a serving plate with the lettuce. Remove the clams from the shells and place the clams on the bed of lettuce. Decorate the plate with lemon wedges and serve immediately. Yield: 1 serving.

CLAM HOTCAKES

This is a recipe that I dreamed up one Sunday morning while mixing up a batch of sourdough hotcakes. At the time it amounted to adding a can of clams to the batter just before the soda was added. But I realize that not everyone runs a sourdough pot. So I'll give it to you as regular hotcakes. Try it either way.

1/2 teaspoon onion powder
1/2 teaspoon salt
1 cup all-purpose flour
1 tablespoon sugar
2 teaspoons baking powder
1 egg, beaten
Liquid from canned clams
Fresh or evaporated milk to combine with
    clam liquid to fill 3/4 cup
1 8-ounce can minced clams

Combine the first 5 ingredients, thoroughly stir in the egg and liquids, and add the clams. Adjust the batter to your preferred thickness with additional liquid or flour.

Fry the hotcakes on a hot griddle, turning once. Serve with butter and syrup or with mushroom sauce or gravy.

SPAGHETTI WITH CLAM SAUCE

It may be that I have given the impression that I like clams. This recipe should prove it once and for all.

5 cloves garlic, minced
4 tablespoons clarified butter (see
    page 6)
Juice from canned or steamed clams
1 6-ounce can tomato paste
1 16-ounce can tomatoes and liquid from
    the can
1 teaspoon dried parsley
1 teaspoon oregano
2 8-ounce cans chopped clams or
    enough steamed and chopped fresh
    clams to fill about 2 cups
1 teaspoon salt
1 pound spaghetti
1/4 cup Parmesan cheese

Sauté the garlic in 2 tablespoons of butter until lightly browned. Add the clam juice, tomato paste, tomatoes and liquid, parsley and oregano. Stir well and simmer until reduced by about half. Then add the clams to this sauce and remove from the stove. Just before serving, reheat the sauce.

Now we'll cook the spaghetti. Into a large pot pour about a gallon of water and add the salt. Bring the water to a boil and add the spaghetti, making sure that each strand is moistened as it enters the water. Boil for 8 to 12 minutes until the spaghetti is tender. Throw a couple of cupfuls of cold water in the pot to prevent further cooking, stir rapidly, and pour the spaghetti into a colander to drain. While the pot is still hot put the 2 remaining tablespoons of butter in the pot and swish it around. The drained spaghetti now goes back into the pot to be stirred until each strand is coated with butter.

Serve the spaghetti on a platter, and the sauce in a bowl. Diners can dish up their own servings and sprinkle it all with Parmesan cheese. I suggest garlic bread and wine be served with this. Yield: 4 servings.

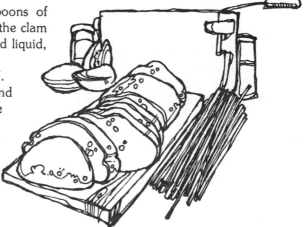

JOHNNY'S JAMBALAYA

During the social disorder we knew as World War II, I spent 2 years with a soldier from Louisiana. His accent was nerve-racking, his complaints about Alaska difficult to bear, and his insistence that we Northerners cooked nothing edible was like a knife turning in a wound. As you can understand, it was with some reluctance on both sides that we became friends. Monumental, however, was our cooperation in creating a jambalaya. While not a cook himself, my Southern friend remembered, I hoped, most of the ingredients that we needed to gather together at my girlfriend's house for this project.

I would like to say that this is his recipe, but it isn't, as he didn't have one. It's mine, but has been named after Johnny the Reb. Regardless, my kids love the jambalaya.

1/2 pound bacon, cut in 1/2-inch pieces
1 large onion, chopped
1 green pepper, cut in 3/4-inch strips
1 cup long-grain rice, uncooked
1 clove garlic, sliced
1 26-ounce can chopped tomatoes, with
   liquid
1 teaspoon salt
1/4 teaspoon black pepper
1/2 teaspoon thyme
2-1/2 cups chicken stock
1/2 pound cooked ham, cut in 1/2-inch
   strips
1 pound medium-size raw shrimp, shelled
   and deveined
1 tablespoon fresh parsley, chopped

I remember that Johnny was insistent that the order and timing of the cooking was critical, so follow carefully.

I use an 8-quart, flat-bottomed Dutch oven, but the recipe can be squeezed into a 4-quart container. Fry the bacon until all the fat is rendered. Lift out the bacon, drain, and save. Sauté the onion in the bacon fat until transparent. Add the green pepper, sauté, and after 4 minutes add the rice. Stir the rice and vegetables over a medium heat until the rice appears opaque. Now it's time to add the garlic, tomatoes, salt, pepper, thyme and reserved bacon. Stir ingredients together and add the stock.

Bring the mixture to a boil, add the ham, and stir again. Cover the Dutch oven and bake at 400° for 15 minutes, then add the shrimp, pushing them well down. Return the mixture to the oven for another 10 minutes. If at any time the jambalaya appears dry add more broth.

Serve jambalaya heaped on a warm platter garnished with parsley. I love to serve either hot biscuits or corn bread with this dish. Yield: 5 or 6 servings.

SHRIMP AND OTHER DEEP SEA CREATURES

During the part of my boyhood that my family spent in Petersburg, my older brother Ken was engineer on the shrimp trawler *Charles W.* This little ship spent her days dragging a trawl—a cone-shaped net—along the sea bottom off South-eastern Alaska. Knowledge of the secret locations where shrimp could be found was hidden in the skipper's head.

The *Charles W.* was only 50 or 60 feet long but to me she was huge. However, I was only seven at the time. I can especially remember the great sorting table in the middle of the ship's forward deck.

Every living creature that crawled, hop-ped, swam or ran across the bottom of the sea would be swept into our trawl as it passed along the bottom. When the trawl was pulled up beside the ship, small netfuls of the trawl's contents would be scooped onto the sorting table.

I was fascinated with the vast heaps of shrimp on the table but even more fas-cinated by the other creatures that I saw. There were hundreds of tiny flatfish: sole, flounder and halibut; dozens of crabs of many species; jellyfish that evaporated if left on deck; and the sculpin, red snappers, tomcod, and a half-dozen other fish that flopped on the table.

The shrimp were sorted into wooden boxes and almost everything else went back into the sea. Some items, however, were kept for the crew and friends. Tender young chicken halibut, fat red snappers, and even octopus were saved. I can still remember how the Japanese cannery workers prized the octopus.

There was one octopus that they never had a chance to enjoy. Someone found a small octopus on the sorting table and threw it down on the ship's deck. The call went out for the kid, as I was known aboard the *Charles W.*

"Hey, kid! Throw that overboard! Put it in the deck bucket and throw it over the side!" came a voice from on high.

I was always a game youngster so I tried. The little octopus was about two feet across when spread out, and it had the usual number of arms. I was too close to the action for it to be funny, but the degree of laughter from above indicated that the sight of a kid with two arms trying to get an

TEN-POUND SHRIMP DIP

The half-carload of potato chips that I ate with this wonderful shrimp dip added at least 10 pounds to my body. Pounds that I didn't and don't need. One of the greatest sorrows in my life as a dieter is giving up this dip. I can only say to the person who gave me the recipe, "Shame on you, Ruthie, you're a shrimp dip pusher!" To you I say, "Come on, try it—you'll like it!"

1/4 pound small cooked shrimp or
*   contents of 1 7-1/2-ounce can*
8 ounces cream cheese
3 tablespoons mayonnaise
1 tablespoon milk
1/8 teaspoon garlic salt

Put the ingredients in a blender and blend for 30 seconds, then spoon into a bowl. Serve the dip with the bowl resting in a bed of ice. Anything that can be used to lift the dip can be served with it: potato chips, corn chips, celery and—my favorite—cauliflower chunks.

LATTA POTTED SHRIMP

After my parents passed on, a number of my mother's recipes came to me. A review of those recipes brought back many a memory. One recipe especially attracted my attention. The paper on which it was written was old, dry and yellow. A notation on the page led me to believe that it had come from Canada, most likely with my great-grandmother Latta when she traveled from Nova Scotia to marry a Nelson. That was a bit over 100 years ago, so the paper had a right to be as I found it. This is that recipe.

1/2 pound clarified butter (see page 6)
1/2 teaspoon mace
1/2 teaspoon nutmeg
1/8 teaspoon cayenne
1/2 teaspoon salt
1 pound tiny cooked shrimp, shelled, or
*   contents of 3 7-1/2-ounce cans*

In a saucepan melt 1/4 pound of the butter. Add the mace, nutmeg, cayenne and salt. Stir in the shrimp and continue stirring until the shrimp are well coated.

Spoon the shrimp into 6 individual dishes. Melt the remaining butter and seal the dishes by pouring a layer of butter over each dish. Refrigerate the potted shrimp for 6 to 24 hours.

Serve ice cold with hot toast for breakfast, lunch or as a midnight snack. It is *not* diet food!

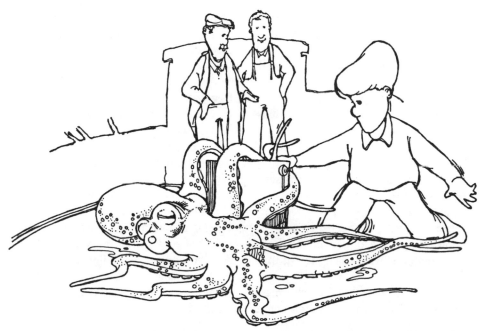

eight-armed octopus off the deck was hilarious.

After much effort my two arms pulled one of its arms loose from the deck. I shoved the bucket under that arm and made a try for arm number two. Then it was suddenly evident that the octopus had the bucket. While I was trying to get my bucket back, the octopus was in a seven-armed ooze toward the side of the ship.

The octopus picked out a scupper in the rail of the ship that was only two inches high and six inches long. The creature never hesitated; it slithered right out the hole and into the sea. I only got the bucket back because the octopus discovered that the pail would not go through the hole. There was a loud cheer from the crew, and the skipper said, "At least you saved the bucket, kid!"

One other trip on the *Charles W.* stands out in my mind. I first became aware of the crew's tension; then the cables to the trawl began to act strange as the trawl was pulled up from the bottom. I think the men aboard knew even then what they had in the trawl. The skipper said, "Get up in the wheelhouse, kid. And stay there until I say you can come out!"

The skipper's word was law, so I climbed on the stool and leaned out the port cabin window.

I was able to get into position to see the trawl as it broke the surface. There was a large thrashing, biting creature in the netting. It was tearing net on every thrash. The word *shark,* with several colorful assorted names before and after it let me know what we had.

I couldn't see just how the crew managed it, but they got a line around the shark's tail. Once they did this, they were able to hoist the shark right out of the trawl. In a minute the shark hung there high over

Shrimp and Other Deep Sea Creatures   19

the men, twisting, turning and biting at everything that came within reach. The men swung the boom from which the shark was suspended across the ship and out over the water.

"Tail him!" the skipper yelled.

The shark was lowered until its tail was even with the side of the ship. With a big knife someone reached out and cut the tail off the creature just under the line holding it. The shark went tailless back into the sea.

It seemed a cruel act, which I did not understand, but even then I had felt and recognized the hate of the fishermen for the shark. They were united in this hate much as a mob is when it will do things that the individual wouldn't do.

I remember the labor that the fishermen then put into salvaging part of their catch and in patching that great trawl before it could fish again. At the time I must have thought the men were angry because of the damage the shark had caused. Now I know that there were other factors, such as the fear of an old enemy, from deep within their minds. The entire incident certainly impressed me.

As I have mentioned, the trawl for that old ship showed me just how much life there really is at the bottom of the ocean. Some 40 years of fishing in those waters since then have done nothing to change my awareness. I cannot remember ever having a fishing line on the bottom for longer than five minutes without something down there messing with the bait. All too often these things were never seen. Some took my bait. Some took my bait and hook. Some held on and even came part-way up from their home in the depths before letting go. Still others came up until I could see them as shadowy figures in the

clear water. I'm sure that there were creatures that I would have liked to have observed more closely. Some I am sure I was better off never meeting.

Among those that I was glad to let go free was my old acquaintance the octopus. In the 35 years since we had last met, it had grown more than I had.

I was once fishing halibut from my 12-foot aluminum skiff when something took my bait. It was big and heavy, for sure. The complete lack of fight led me to envision a rather large tired halibut or a drift log. I must mention that it was one of those rare hot and sunny days in Southeastern Alaska. The sea was a flat calm.

As my line came up from the bottom I leaned over to look into the water at my catch. Suddenly I could see down about 10 feet and there was the octopus. It certainly had grown. Either the distortion of the water, or a mental comparison between the creature and my so-small boat, made the octopus look 12 feet across from armtip to armtip. At that moment I had one of the most practical thoughts of my life. I quit pulling my line.

As I sat there in my tiny boat, I could not help but remember the trouble that I had experienced in getting the bucket away from the octopus the last time we had met. I reached the conclusion that I did not wish to wrestle for the possession of my boat. Not while I was sitting in it.

I leaned over the side looking down into the water. The octopus and I seemed to be watching each other for a few heartbeats. My hand, acting almost on its own, flicked my bait knife and cut the line. The octopus started back down with my hook, line and sinker. Was that a strange ripple in the water, or did I see one of his eyes close

PICKLED SHRIMP PETERSBURG

The only place where I have ever found people pickling shrimp was in Petersburg, when I was a boy. The city at that time was the shrimp capital of the territory. Today either Kodiak or Seward could claim the title if they cared enough to do it. I've only tried this recipe a couple of times—when the shrimp pots were producing more than we could eat fresh. If I had to buy the shrimp at today's prices—well, enough said. But maybe you would like to impress a friend so I'll pass the recipe along.

2 pounds raw medium-size shrimp
1 large onion, peeled and sliced in thin
  rings
2 lemons, sliced thin
1 1-inch piece ginger root, minced
4 bay leaves
2 cups vinegar
2 tablespoons pickling spice
1/8 cup dried parsley
1/2 teaspoon dried mustard
1/4 teaspoon mace
2 teaspoons salt
1 cup vegetable oil

Drop the shrimp into enough boiling salted water to cover and cook for 3 minutes. The shrimp should be pink and firm. Drain and dry on paper towels, then clean and devein the shrimp.

In a deep bowl combine the onion rings, lemon slices, ginger and shrimp. Toss these together and transfer to 2 wide-mouth 1-quart jars. The quantity here should nearly fill the jars. Push 2 bay leaves down into each container.

Now we make the pickling liquid. Into a stainless steel or enamel pan put the vinegar, pickling spice, parsley, mustard, mace and salt. Bring to a boil, stir a few times, remove from the heat, and pour 1/4 cup of liquid at a time into the jars. When the liquid seeps down to the bottom of a jar add the same amount again, until each container is full to within an inch of the top.

Now pour 1/2 inch of vegetable oil on top of the pickling liquid. This will seal out the air and seal in the flavor. Cover the jars and store in the refrigerator for at least 24 hours before serving. The shrimp will keep for 2 weeks, but I've never had any last over a couple of days.

At a party a spread of these with the onion rings makes an attractive and colorful display.

FISH STOCK

To make fish soup you need fish stock. I make stock by simmering fish heads. You can also use fish trimmings, tails or bones. For soups to be made of white fish, I feel the flavor's better if I use the heads of white-fleshed fish only.

6 cups water
1 pound fish scraps
1/2 cup chopped onions
Bay leaf
1 teaspoon salt

Combine ingredients in a pot, bring to a boil and simmer for 30 minutes. Strain through a sieve, saving the liquid and discarding the solids. Your stock is ready.

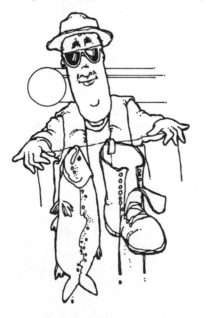

momentarily as the creature drifted out of sight?

If you think this is a lead-in to a recipe for octopus, you are wrong. Would you cook an old acquaintance?

A **few years ago** my son Glen and his buddy Brian accepted the job of diving down and putting a couple of lines aboard a fishing boat sunk in the harbor at Juneau. There was a story, completely undocumented, that over the previous 30 years four or five divers had been lost in the area where Glen and Brian were going to dive. I asked a diver friend about this rumor and was told that there was nothing to it. However, he mentioned that his price for diving in that spot was high. With a bit more questioning I discovered that my friend's price was so high that he had never been hired to dive there.

There is little doubt that the story, whether true or false, was firmly implanted in the young divers' minds as they began their work. The first dive to secure a line to the bow of the sunken boat went smoothly. Then it was time to make the deeper dive to secure a line to the stern. As they drifted down across the open hold of the ship they found that another swimmer had preceded them.

They were face-to-face with a pugnacious head equipped with a mouth full of teeth, and the large mouth was open to a point that the boys could see the molars, too. Behind the head was the rest of the creature, later described as looking like an eight-inch tapered steel pipe.

The signal for "Get the hell out of here!" was passed. Two rubber-clad bodies shot to the surface. The observation point now shifts to where my other son, Ken, who is observant and reliable, was standing on the float.

The two black-clad boys shot out of the water beside the float. They came so far out of the water, Ken said, that they stepped aboard the float with only a slight downward effort. Neither diver argued with this statement.

That evening we paged through the books in my library. Someone pointed out the wolf eel as the most likely creature to have been down there with the boys. The book stated that the wolf eel has an odd preference in foods: sand dollars and sea urchins. The question raised was: Do the sons of sea-faring families classify as sea urchins?

Many times a year Alaskan residents hear about a salt-water fisherman managing to catch a large halibut from a small boat. I would not claim to have the record for the largest caught from the smallest boat, but I'm close to the record in one of the age groups.

The Pacific halibut is most often seen by the angler as a 10-pound to 30-pound fish. But there are some big female halibut out there. The famous barn-door halibut can go to 500 pounds. Hauled up on a dock, it does look as big as a barn door.

My first big halibut was caught while I was sitting in an eight-foot punt. I'll qualify that statement slightly. It was hooked while I was in the punt. It was many a year ago, when I was only 10. While my dad's boat was unloading fish and fueling up I took the punt so that I could go fishing a short

way north of the steamship dock in Cordova.

My fishing gear was primitive by today's standards, but that was 45 years ago. I had 300 feet of halibut cord wrapped around a foot-long board that measured 1" by 6". The hook was a standard commercial halibut hook and my sinker was a nut from a one-inch bolt. My bait was a whole herring. The line was just dropped down to the bottom and left there for whatever might find it.

After the bait had rested a few minutes on the bottom I felt a familiar feeling coming up my line. Something was after the bait. I waited just for a count of 10, and jerked on the line to set the hook. That was the beginning of my troubles. The line started running through my fingers so fast that my fingers were getting hot. The line, unwinding from the board lying in the bottom of the boat, was causing the board to bounce all over the place.

With two-thirds of my line gone overboard, I started trying to find something to tie the line to—quick. I had to stop the fish's run. I flipped the line a turn around one oarlock, which slowed things down a bit. It also tipped the punt sideways until the boat started to ship water over the side.

By letting the line slowly slip to the fish I kept from swamping. I was then able to make two turns of the line around the seat I was sitting on. Next, I quickly flipped the line out of the oarlock and into the sculling notch in the transom. The punt and I began to go sternfirst down the channel.

Now at least I had a chance. I set the oars in the locks and started rowing against my fish. As I sat there rowing I became aware that I had an audience. I had been too busy before to notice, but there were

Shrimp and Other Deep Sea Creatures

HALIBUT BÉARNAISE

Halibut, when fresh, is one of the best-tasting fish in the world. Of all the recipes for cooking it for special occasions, or just when you're in a hurry, here is a recipe that I really recommend. If you would like to live a little, or maybe just impress someone with your cooking ability, try this.

2 medium slices of halibut or 2 1-pound
  fillets
1/4 cup clarified butter (see page 6)
Salt and black pepper
Béarnaise Sauce (see page 133)

Place the fish on a greased broiling pan, baste with the butter, and season. Put under the broiler, cook for 4 minutes, turn, baste, and cook for another 4 minutes. Keep turning and basting until fish is done. Test by flaking.

Serve with warm Béarnaise Sauce for some wonderful eating. Yield: 2 servings.

15 to 20 people standing on the dock watching and yelling advice to me. I said nothing, but rowed and rowed. All I accomplished for an hour was to hold my own. Then gradually I started to gain on the fish. I was moving the punt back toward the dock.

While I was rowing all that time, the steamship *Yukon* came up the channel, swung wide of me, and landed at the Cordova dock. It wasn't long before the word was passed to the passengers that a young man was in a battle out there in the channel. Soon the outboard rail of the ship was lined with people cheering me on.

Slowly I towed whatever was on the end of my line to the dock. I passed under the stern of the *Yukon* and up to the oiling float at the dock's south end. Down the ramp came a group of local men intent on helping me. When I reached the float several hands grabbed the sides of the punt so I could climb up on the float with my fishing line. Now for the first time I had a solid place to stand, and could actually pull in my fish. Slowly I fought to get my line back. No one offered to help pull. Unless I asked for help it was my show.

By this time the stern of the *Yukon* was lined with observers, as was the end of the dock. These people, being higher above the water than I was, and looking down into clear water, saw my fish long before I did. There was a collective gasp from the onlookers as they saw the size of the fish. Then from the end of the float I could see her lying there just under the surface of the water. She was a giant halibut, at least a small barn-door size.

While I had been fighting my fight with the fish, my dad's cannery tender had arrived at the oil float. I hadn't even noticed that it was his, I was so intent. Now it was evident that I needed help if that halibut was to be landed. Dad said, "Shall I tail her?"

With my agreement he went into action. A slipknot was tied on a heavy line. I eased the fish over beside the ship and Dad was able to slowly work the knotted line around the fish's tail. The line was tightened and the fish exploded into action and beat the water to a froth, but the halibut was now ours.

The boom of the tender was swung over and the fish was lifted clear. As it came into sight another sigh went up from the crowd on the dock and ship. Then a cheer followed. As I crossed the float to climb aboard the ship, I got a pat on the back of congratulation from every man on the float. It was truly one of life's greatest moments.

How big was the fish? Mere details, but I'll tell you. She was six feet, six inches in length and weighed 279 pounds. There was a lot of halibut enjoyed by our friends in town for the next few days.

A **few years ago** I had occasion to visit Cordova again, this time in an official capacity as a trooper. I had a couple of days' work to take care of first, but then I had a bit of free time and the fishing bug bit me. It had been at least 25 years since I last wetted a line in that area.

Shrimp and Other Deep Sea Creatures   25

I borrowed a skiff and some fishing gear and ran out behind Spike Island to try for a halibut. In a few minutes I had a nice 30-pounder in the boat.

Then a fast-moving skiff came around the island from town. The young man in the stern swished the skiff up alongside my boat and said, "There's a long distance call for you. Operator 8. You can take it on the dock, Trooper."

I was the only trooper within 75 miles, so he had to have the right man. I thanked him, and pulled my anchor.

At the dock I found the telephone and got through to Operator 8 and then found out it was my top boss in Juneau calling—the Commissioner of Public Safety.

He said, "Hello, Nelson! What the hell are you doing fishing? The whole town of Cordova knows that you were out there behind Spike Island. Now everyone in Juneau knows, too."

So I was done fishing for the day. I made myself a promise to pack some fishing clothes in my travel gear. I guess fishing in full uniform is a bit obvious.

I now had two problems: the job the commissioner was assigning me in Valdez, and a halibut to get home to my wife, Connie, in Anchorage.

With the help of the local butcher, I managed to get my fish boxed so it could go air freight to Anchorage. The box carried my home telephone number so that someone could call to tell Connie to get the fish while it was still fresh. I then turned the box over to the local airline and caught a ride out to the airport so I could catch a plane to Valdez.

After an uneventful flight to Valdez, I was helping the pilot unload the plane. My policy has always been that many hands make work easier for everyone and get the helpers a ride to town. The third piece out of the plane was the box with my halibut. The address said Anchorage, but the box was in Valdez. There would be no flight to Anchorage for two days. The fish would not get there fresh.

In fact my fish was not even fresh now. But I was stubborn. Again the local butcher helped solve my problem. This time the halibut box went into a freezer. The bus driver and the local pilot guaranteed to get the box on the next plane to Anchorage. The pilot would call my wife himself, if necessary. With my problems solved I was off to the highway to work.

Three days later I arrived home with plans to have a nice halibut steak for dinner. As I walked in the door, Connie began telling me how much everyone had enjoyed the fish. She had called another trooper's family to help eat it. Three adults and eleven kids involved had eaten my halibut.

Yes, that's right. I didn't even get a taste of that halibut which cost me so much frustration, time and even reputation.

I fear that too many of my recipes were developed when large quantities of fish were available. Today those same fish often are not only scarce but expensive. As you, the reader, will probably be getting your seafood from the supermarket, I've tried to scale some of my recipes down a bit. I hope you will enjoy the results.

Shrimp and Other Deep Sea Creatures

RENDERED BEEF FAT

You cannot make the next recipe without rendered beef fat. Because beef fat does not leave a fat or greasy taste on things that have been deep-fried, this is a recipe I'll be referring to from time to time. Also, the use of rendered beef fat for frying means you can cook at a higher heat, and without smoke, than with other fats. Believe me, it's worth the effort to render beef fat.

Buy, or talk your butcher out of, 5 or 6 pounds of beef suet. Cut the suet into small pieces, about 1/2-inch square, and put into a pot. I use a Dutch oven. Place the pot on medium heat and let it cook until all the fat is rendered from the suet. Strain the fat and pour it into whatever pot you use for deep-fat frying.

Note: Our dogs have always liked the crisp remainder of the suet.

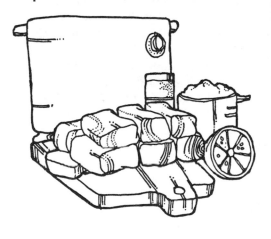

DEEP-FRIED HALIBUT

The world's best deep-fried or French-fried halibut is fried in beef fat. You just cannot make this recipe without it—no substitutes acceptable.

2 eggs, beaten
1 teaspoon lemon juice
1/4 teaspoon onion powder
1 cup flour
1 cup cracker crumbs
8 to 10 pieces of halibut, at least 8 ounces each
Beef fat (see preceding recipe)

The eggs should be beaten alone first, then with the lemon juice and onion powder.

The flour is placed in another bowl, and the cracker crumbs in a third. Now you are ready to coat the fish.

Cut the halibut into pieces about 1" by 2" by 2". You should have a minimum of 8 ounces of fish for each person to be served. More, if your halibut is fresh.

Roll the pieces of fish in flour, then in the egg mixture, then in the cracker crumbs. Place the fish in the wire basket of the French fryer, about 3 pieces at a time. Lower into the hot beef fat and cook for 5 to 6 minutes, or until nicely browned.

Remove, drain, and serve with your favorite sauce. Try some of those in the Soups and Sauces section of this book.

POACHED RED SNAPPER

To properly poach a fish, you should have a special fish-poaching pan—ask any chef. However, because of my family's many moves, we've never invested in such a pan. If enough of you buy this book, I'll finally get one. It was in Juneau that I discovered a school of red snappers and, at about the same time, a large oval roasting pan with a removable rack. We were at once in the fish-poaching business. We ate poached fish often.

This is a 2-step recipe. The first step is making the poaching liquid or Court Bouillon; the second step is the actual poaching.

COURT BOUILLON
(POACHING LIQUID FOR FISH)
2 quarts water
2 cups white wine
3 medium onions, sliced
2 carrots, sliced
4 celery stalks, sliced
1 tablespoon dried parsley
1/2 teaspoon tarragon
1/2 teaspoon thyme
1 tablespoon salt
1/4 teaspoon black pepper
2 bay leaves
1/4 cup vinegar

In a 6-quart enamel or stainless-steel pot combine all the ingredients. (If you use any other kind of pot the vinegar, which is acid, might take some of the lining off the pot.) Bring to a boil, cover, and simmer for 30 minutes. Remove from the heat, strain through a fine sieve into a deep roasting pan or, if available, a fish-poaching pan.

POACHED FISH
Before you get started make sure you have some fresh cheesecloth; you will need a piece a foot longer than your fish.

3 to 4 pounds whole cleaned red snapper
*   or fish of your choice*
Court Bouillon
Fresh parsley and lemon wedges

Wrap the fish in the cheesecloth with a double thickness of cloth on each side of the fish. Tie the ends of the cloth with string.

Lower fish into the poaching liquid, which should be deep enough so there is at least 1 inch of liquid over the fish. Bring to a boil, then simmer for 15 minutes. Remove pot from the heat and let the liquid and fish stand for another 15 minutes.

Lift the fish by the ends of the cheesecloth to a cutting board. Cut the strings, open the cloth, and turn the fish carefully onto a warm serving dish. Gently remove the skin from the top side of the fish. Garnish with parsley and lemon wedges. Or, as an alternative, refrigerate the fish and serve well chilled as a summer dish, removing skin just before serving.

Serve a choice of sauces with this. Yield: 6 to 8 servings.

HALIBUT STEAK SOUP

For some reason, when I was growing up my family never ate fish soup, although we always had plenty of fish around. Maybe that was the reason—we had fish to use up, and no need to stretch it. However, as I myself began to cook, a few fish soups crept into my recipe book. Now to the halibut soup.

5 cups fish stock (see page 22)
2-1/2 pounds halibut, about 1/2 of it cut
    in inch-thick steaks, the rest cut in
    small chunks
1 teaspoon salt
1/4 teaspoon freshly ground
    black pepper
1 cucumber, peeled and diced
2 tablespoons vinegar

Add to the fish stock the fish that has been cut into small pieces and bring to a boil. Simmer for 15 minutes, or until the fish is soft. Now purée the mixture, either through a food mill or with a blender. Return the puréed fish to the pot and add the salt and pepper. Bring the mixture to a boil, add the 4 halibut steaks, and simmer for about 8 minutes. The fish should flake easily with a fork.

Lift the steaks out of the pot and place in wide, deep soup bowls. Quickly add the cucumber and vinegar to the purée, stir, and ladle into the bowls over the steaks.

The biggest problem with this recipe is that I always wish I had doubled it. Yield: These quantities are designed for 4 but I suggest you plan on serving only 2.

SHRIMP AND SOLE

Back in the days when I watched the trawl of the *Charles W.* bring up those little soles and shrimp, I was too young to know what good eating was involved. Now I know about such things. Among my favorite fish are the English sole and the petrale sole, which make excellent eating. Shrimp are always good. To combine sole and shrimp is the challenge of this dish. It's well worth the effort.

4 fillets of sole, about 8 ounces each
Salt
Flour
1 egg
2 tablespoons water
1/2 cup bread crumbs
8 tablespoons clarified butter (see page 6)
1/2 pound tiny shrimp, peeled and
    deveined
Kitchen Bouquet
Lemon wedges

Wash and dry the fillets, then lightly salt them and roll in flour. Beat the egg with the water. Dip the fillets in the egg, coat thoroughly with bread crumbs, and set aside for a few minutes.

Heat 6 tablespoons of butter in a frying pan over medium heat. Sauté the fillets in the butter for 3 to 4 minutes on each side. Transfer to a heated serving dish.

Add the remaining butter to the frying pan and sauté the shrimp for 2 to 3 minutes. Lift the shrimp in a slotted spoon and spread over the fillets.

Now add a few drops of Kitchen Bouquet to the butter in the pan, stir, and pour over the shrimp and sole. Add lemon wedges to the serving dish and place before the eaters. Yield: 4 servings.

COLD SHRIMP SOUP

For a year of my life I was assigned to work in Fairbanks. My first summer there had to be the hottest and driest the Tanana River Valley ever experienced. On July 1 the temperature reached 100°, and this coastal Alaskan almost died of the heat. To me a temperature of 80° is too hot. It was on one of those July days that I was introduced to Cold Shrimp Soup. I had been physically ill from the heat and had no appetite at all. Then a neighbor invited us over to lunch and tempted me with the word *cold*. Would you like to try it?

1 16-ounce can sliced beets
3 tablespoons red wine vinegar
1-1/2 teaspoons sugar
1 cup sour cream
1 pound small cooked shrimp, shelled, or
    contents of 1 7-1/2-ounce can
2 cucumbers, peeled and cut in 1/4-inch
    cubes
4 green onions, sliced in 1/4-inch pieces
4 radishes, sliced thin
4 tablespoons fresh dill, chopped,
    or 1 teaspoon
    dried dill
3 tablespoons
    lemon juice
1 teaspoon salt
3 hard-boiled eggs, sliced

Drain the liquid from the beets into a 2-quart or 3-quart saucepan. Dice the beets into 1/8-inch cubes and put in the pot. Bring the liquid to a boil, hold at a simmer, and add the vinegar and sugar. Stir a couple of times and set aside.

When the liquid is cool remove the beets and set aside. Beat the sour cream into the liquid with a whisk. Now, stirring with a spoon, return the beets to the mixture and stir in all other ingredients except the hard-boiled eggs. Pour the soup into a bowl, cover, and chill.

Serve in bowls with thin slices of hard-boiled egg floating on top. Refreshing! Yield: 4 servings.

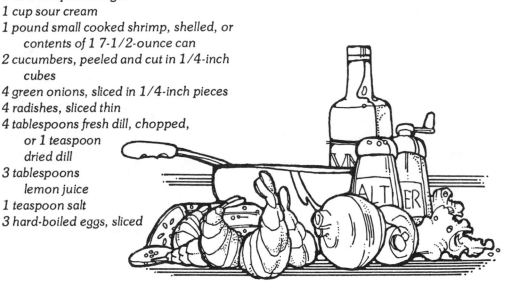

DEEP-FRIED KING CRAB LEGS

Many years ago in the city of Homer there was a small restaurant cuddled up next to the local hotel. They served good food in this restaurant, and the visitors and local residents kept the place busy. The cook at the time of my visits made the best deep-fried king crab legs that I have ever eaten. Only if the cook was out of crab would I eat anything else. She would start the crab legs as soon as I walked in the front door, bless her heart. The following is as close as I can come to her recipe.

2 cups flour
1/4 teaspoon salt
5 tablespoons lukewarm fish stock or water
1 teaspoon dry yeast
5 tablespoons flat beer
1 teaspoon olive oil or salad oil
1 egg white, whipped
4 cooked king crab legs, shelled and cut in
    2-inch pieces
Fat for deep frying, preferably beef fat
    (see page 27)

The batter must be made at least 2 hours before the crab legs will be cooked.

Into a medium-size bowl sift 1 cup of the flour with the salt. In the center of the flour make a well and add the fish stock or water, then the yeast. Let stand without sitrring for 5 minutes. Add the beer and oil and stir until well mixed. Cover with a towel and leave in a warm place for 2 hours. Fold the egg white into the batter just before it is to be used.

Next we go to the crab legs. Dry the chunks of crab and roll them in the remaining flour until thoroughly coated. With tongs coat the pieces with the batter and allow excess to drip off. Place the pieces in your basket for French frying and lower into the fat, which has been heated to 375°. Turn the pieces of crab after 2 minutes and lift them out of the fat after another 2 minutes. Drain and serve with or without a sauce. I like Tartar Sauce with mine (see page 131). Yield: 2 servings.

A COUPLE OF CRAB TALES

Alaska is full of wonderful things to eat. Each section of the state seems to offer some new delight. Having been raised in several parts of Alaska, and later being assigned to other locations, I've had plenty of chances to try many new things in the Alaskan eating experience.

All along the coastal regions from Ketchikan to Kodiak, and on out in the area of the Aleutian Islands, the sea bottom crawls with crabs. The variety available includes box crab, Tanner (snow) crab, king crab and Dungeness crab. The last two are my favorites, with whichever is in front of me being the favorite of the moment. Both provide some wonderful eating!

Whenever I've been living on the coast I've tried to catch my own crab supply as much as possible. I've chased crabs with a skiff in shallow water, fished for them with a ring net, caught them on hook and line, and maintained crab traps.

The crab trap, although simple, was thought out by someone smarter than a crab. It is in effect a cage that you lower down to the ocean bottom where the crabs are. The crabs are lured by bait into a tunnel that tapers to a small hole and they're kept in the cage by confusion. They just can't figure out how they got in there.

I've seen dozens of crab trap designs that people have dreamed up, but the design that my dad used for catching Dungeness crabs 40 years ago will still do the job. If you make the entrance hole just a bit larger the trap will catch king crabs, too. In fact the giant king-crab pots for commercial use are just enlarged versions of the traps for Dungeness crabs.

I make my traps out of the steel used to reinforce concrete. Basically each trap is a box about 18" by 30" by 48". The top, the bottom and the long sides are covered with fence-wire mesh. In each end of the trap are tunnels of netting terminating inside at loops of wire. The loops are just big enough to allow a crab to enter. In an area between the loops is the bait. The crab walks up the tunnel of netting and enters the hole, all to get at those fish heads. Once in, he'll stay there until I dump him out of a loose wire section in the top.

A strong line connects the trap to a float riding on top of the water. Today you paint your name, address and fishing license number on this float.

You leave your trap on the bottom where experience or maybe a friend has told you the crabs are thick. Well, they were last week. Sometimes the trap is left out only hours and sometimes a day or two. It has been my experience in recent years that the real trick is to get back to your trap before someone else does.

When I was young the pulling of another man's crab trap—trap robbing—could get you shot. It was in the same category as stealing a man's horse in the old west. It just wasn't a profitable occupation. Justice was quick and often fatal.

Some men were known to hide on the beach near their traps, with Winchester rifles in hand. About the time the trap robber pulled the wrong trap aboard his boat a shot would ring out. It is said that if you stuff a human body in a crab trap and forget to attach a line to the trap, the body will never be found.

Anyway, having been brought up in Alaska with this knowledge, I have never pulled another man's trap. But people today often do. It's bad enough that they steal your crabs, but to drop an unbaited trap back down is worse. I have had some long hard pulls to find a trap empty of crab. I've even lost a few traps when other people just changed their buoys for mine and went on fishing my trap. Usually someplace else.

In spite of these hazards there is no greater thrill for me than pulling up a crab trap with two to six nice crabs in it. It will positively make my mouth water.

Hey! A crab-pot story just came to mind. A friend of mine pulled his trap to find it had been robbed. But the thief was possibly just a trader. In the trap was a six-pack of beer. Someone wanted a crab or two and didn't want stealing on his conscience so he offered a swap. It was kind of one-sided, but then, knowing my friend, he would have given the guy the crab for the asking. Anyway, I got a beer out of the deal.

If you should be so inclined with my crab trap, I think a fifth of high-class bourbon would be about right for whatever you might find. Anything less than that would

be considered stealing. I enjoy crabs joining me for dinner too much to offer easy swaps. Besides, have you priced fresh crab lately?

Next to the box trap, the simple ring trap has caught me the most crabs. This is just a ring of reinforcing steel, about three feet in diameter, with a "bowl" of netting under it. The ring is lowered by a bridle of line. Such a trap is simple to operate, with bait tied in the middle of the net and lowered to the bottom. I like to fish in water where you can see the bottom even though I have my own special attachment for a ring trap that allows deeper and longer fishing.

In any event the crabs crawl onto the circle of webbing to get the bait. When you see two or three busy at work on the bait, you pull the ring trap up. The trick is to pull the trap up so fast that the crabs can't get

CRAB AND STEAK BÉARNAISE

I had always wanted to try this expensive combination that the chefs of elegant restaurants dream up to tickle the palates, and dent the wallets, of their patrons. So when the day arrived when I had both cube steak and crab available, this is what I made.

6 cube steaks, about 1-1/2 pounds, or
    tenderloin or sirloin
1/2 cup flour
3/4 teaspoon salt
Black pepper to taste
1/4 cup clarified butter (see page 6)
1/2 cup Sauterne or other dry white wine
1 pound crab meat
1 cup Béarnaise Sauce (see page 133)

Dip each steak in a mixture of the flour, salt and pepper and fry in 2 tablespoons of the butter. Remove steaks to a warm platter when done to your preference. Swish the wine in the frying pan and, when heated, pour over the steaks.

Break up the crab, add the remaining butter to the pan, and fry for about 5 minutes, stirring often. Heat the Béarnaise Sauce.

Now we combine everything. Place a steak on each plate, covering with a teaspoon of the wine sauce, a tablespoon of Béarnaise Sauce and a serving of crab meat. Serve at once with whatever sauce remains. Yield: 6 servings.

KING CRAB BARBEQUE

A couple of years ago I weakened and joined the backyard barbeque crowd. I was saved from becoming an addict by a very rainy summer. However, we did dream up a few recipes while the sun was out. These king crab legs came through rather well.

1/4 cup fresh parsley, chopped fine
1/4 cup lemon juice
1 tablespoon prepared mustard
1/4 teaspoon salt
1/2 cup clarified butter (see page 6)
3 pounds cooked and shelled king crab
    legs

Mix the first 4 ingredients into the butter, which should be warm and liquid. Brush the mixture onto the crab legs and cook about 4 inches over medium coals on the barbeque grill. Turn and baste every 2 minutes for 6 to 8 minutes.

Serve with a tossed green salad and French bread. Yield: 4 servings.

out of the net. You might find a fast or lucky crab once in a while, but usually you get them. In connection with this kind of trap I should add that there are some sneaky-type fishermen who claim to be able to lift a ring net so slowly and carefully that the crab never knows what is going on. To each his own!

In spite of all this fooling around with crab traps the largest king crab I ever got was caught accidentally on a hook and line. I had been lying at anchor in Trollers Cove for the best part of a beautiful sunny day in Southeastern Alaska. It would be a couple of hours yet before I could gather up the kids from the beach, so I thought I'd try for a fresh halibut for dinner. I soon had my bait on the bottom, the rod in the holder and my mind far away. About 15 minutes later I became aware that my reel was going, "Tick, tick, tick," as the line was being slowly pulled off the reel against the drag.

Picking up the rod I could feel that something had my bait, so I set the hook. It was soon evident that I didn't have a fish on the line. I was reeling in against a steady but not heavy pull. Leaning over the side of the boat I could look down into the clear water. The granddaddy of all king crabs came in sight as I reeled.

Now a crab will occasionally get hooked, but more often crabs will just tangle in the line while walking around the bait. Usually they untangle and fall off on the way up or when you try to lift the line from the water. I was going to take no chances with this one. I held the line still in the water about 18 inches under the surface. With my pole in my left hand and my large dip net in my right, I was ready to land this creature. Slowly I eased the net

down into the water as far under the crab as I could. Then with one big effort I brought net, crab and line aboard and into the cockpit of the cruiser.

Boy, that was a big crab. I was shortly engaged in combat with it, first over who was going to get to keep the net. The crab was sure that possession was 99 percent of the law and it had no intention of giving up the landing net. The creature pulled and twisted the net with its claws. I pulled and tried to untangle the net. Every time I got close to the crab I got raked with a sharp spine. As we battled, the fishline fell off into the boat. So my catch had only been tangled. I removed the line from the mixture of crab and net and stepped up into the motor well to study the situation from a safe distance.

Suddenly the light came on and I reached down, lifted the net and turned it over. My friend didn't like that, being upside down, so the crab untangled itself from the net and dropped into the cockpit. Once it had all its legs gathered up, the crab started looking for a way out of the boat.

It was going up the side toward freedom when I jumped back into the battle. Seizing a leg, I flipped the crab over on its back and with one foot pushed it back under the motor well. I quickly plugged the exit with a fish box. "Dinner" wasn't going anyplace. He rattled around in there for some time.

Actually, the crab really didn't get the name Dinner until all the kids were back aboard. Then we referred to it by that name right up until we ate it, and as you see we still do.

By the time we reached the dock Dinner was quiet. We were able to get an idea of its size. The arm span was just six inches short of mine, which is six feet. The most important measurement was that my catch was big enough to feed a family of seven with all the crab that any of us could eat. Oh yes, Dinner was available for the next day's lunch in a crab salad. Dinner was much enjoyed.

I've just one more story about crab from the far distant past. It goes way back to 1932, in fact. My family had moved from Petersburg to Cordova, on Prince William Sound. This small community of about 1,200 people was the southern terminus of the Copper River and Northwestern Railroad. It was here that the copper from the great Kennecott Mine reached the sea. The railroad provided half of the economic base of the community; the fishing and canning of seafood provided the remainder.

Our family was involved in the fishing and canning part. Both my father and older brother ran cannery tenders during the summer and fished crab during the winters.

The summer of 1932 was my last summer of complete freedom, although I didn't know it then. From the next summer on, for the next 40 years, I would be busy making a living.

At the age of 10 I was really quite self-sufficient. With my father and brother gone most of the time, and my mother working long hours in the cannery, I was on my own and I had to be self-sufficient.

It was during this summer that I developed my first recipe: Sea-water Boiled Crab. In truth, I was not alone in this effort,

CRAB SPREADER

It seems that all too often these days I am trying to make a small amount of crab go a long way. A batch of this recipe and some crackers recently kept a group of our guests from starving to death until dinner was served.

8 ounces fresh crab meat or contents of
*   1 7-ounce can*
1 tablespoon lemon juice
1/2 cup sour cream
1/4 cup mayonnaise
1/4 teaspoon salt
Paprika

Place the crab in a bowl, sprinkle with the lemon juice, and let stand for 15 minutes. Then add the sour cream, mayonnaise and salt and stir until well mixed.

Spread small amounts on crackers or toast squares. Sprinkle with paprika as a final touch.

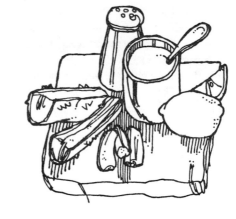

CRAB DIP

In this, the day of the potato chip, don't forget to try leftover crab as a dip. This recipe is simple and very good.

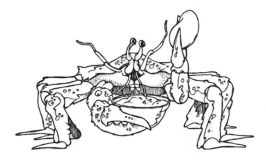

8 ounces cream cheese
1/4 cup mayonnaise
3 tablespoons milk
1/4 teaspoon salt
1/8 teaspoon garlic powder
1/4 teaspoon Tabasco
8 ounces fresh crab meat or contents of
    1 7-ounce can, finely flaked

Mix together the cream cheese, mayonnaise, milk, salt and garlic powder. Add Tabasco and stir until smooth. Add the flaked crab meat and stir well.

Serve with potato chips or whatever you prefer for dips. This is also good as a sauce for French-fried potatoes.

AUKE BAY CRAB BAKE

I found that the nice thing about having a large lump of leftover crab meat is that there are so many things to do with it. It combines well with a number of foods and can be fried, baked or broiled and always tastes good. This recipe combines baking and broiling, and has a special advantage: in our house at least, it ended once and for all the argument about who got the most crab meat.

2 eggs
1 cup white or brown cooked rice
2 tablespoons mayonnaise
2 tablespoons soy sauce
1/2 teaspoon salt
1/4 teaspoon black pepper
1 pound crab meat
1/4 cup green pepper, minced
1/4 cup red pepper, minced
3 tablespoons butter

In a deep bowl beat the eggs lightly with a whisk. Add the rice, mayonnaise, soy sauce, salt and pepper, and whisk smooth. Now mix in the crab meat and the green and red peppers.

Butter 6 individual baking dishes and put a mound of crab meat in each dish. Add 1/2 tablespoon butter to the top of each mound. Bake in a 375° oven for 15 to 20 minutes. Then place under the broiler for 30 seconds to brown the tops.

Serve in the baking dishes and have your favorite sauce available. For myself, I like the buttered crab just as it is. Yield: 6 servings.

for I had a buddy, a young man named Teddy. We had much the same interests and were nearly inseparable, as you will find out.

We had discovered that Dungeness crabs came in with the tide to feed on the clam and salmon scraps by the cannery. Over the years, the clam-shell dump beside the cannery had resulted in a large shallow area south of the building. We could drift across this area in less than two feet of water and spear the crabs. A nail in the end of an old broom handle was our spear.

One of us would man the oars and the other would lie across the bow of the skiff and spear crabs. A quick punch of the nail through the shell and a rapid swing into the boat was the technique used. When we had six or eight crabs aboard, we'd head for the beach.

The first time we caught a crab with this wonderful idea, we carried the crab home in a sack. We found that no one in either family had time to bother cooking our catch. They were all too busy making a living in the short summer working period. If we wanted crab, we would have to cook it ourselves. So we created our camp.

The camp was just a spot on the beach near where we were catching crabs. Between a large outcropping of rock and a big drift log we built a shelter of driftwood and a fireplace. A scrap of boilerplate steel 18" by 30", raised up on large boulders, was our stove. A five-gallon kerosene can with the top cut out was our cooking pot. The can had been around so long that there was no taste left.

The crabs were piled on an old sack until water was boiling in the cooking can. When the half-canful of sea water was boiling hard, we would dump in the crabs. We knew that they required 20 minutes to boil. Somehow we discovered that it took 10 minutes to walk to the cannery, so this was our timer. Teddy would walk to the cannery and back while I watched the fire and the cooking crabs. Yes, I know there are better methods, like counting. The problem we discovered with counting— 1,001, 1,002 and so on—was that it resulted in underdone crab. Only once, though, and then Teddy went back to walking. Why Teddy? He was nine.

We cut up our crabs on a double-bit ax that was driven in a nearby drift log. Incidentally, our camp was located where the tide removed the waste twice a day.

How did the crab taste? It's the question I'm most often asked when telling this story. I have to admit that my vocabulary cannot do justice to the wonderful taste of those crabs, even after 40 years of good eating. They were excellent! We never did catch and cook enough to fill Teddy and me. We always finished all the crab in one sitting. We two growing boys could eat.

Before I leave this first cooking experience, I must add that it led to my first date with a member of the opposite sex.

I was 10 and she was 12. Shall we call her Mary, as I have never been one to gossip about my dates. She was, of course, beautiful. I remember reddish hair and green eyes. There was evidence that she was going to be a woman, and she knew it. I was shy, but not so shy that I would go hide in a corner when girls were around. At least I would stand up and answer questions directly asked of me.

Mary had watched Teddy and me from her upstairs window. Her family's house overlooked our beach and was about a quarter-mile away. She wondered what we were catching and what we did with them. When we met on the boardwalk near her home she stopped me and asked. One thing led to another and I ended up inviting her to our camp for some fresh crab. At least I think that I invited her.

Suddenly I had arranged my first date for the following day. As I wandered away, I thought how strange it was that neither Mary nor I had mentioned Teddy as being necessary to the crab feed.

During the following morning I was successful in losing Teddy for the day. I went straight to our camp and boat. Mary couldn't go out in the boat with me because her mother might see her from their house. I had to go out and catch the crabs alone. I missed Teddy's help.

When I returned to the camp I chopped some wood and built a fire. While the water was heating I tended the fire all alone. Mary merely sat and talked. Not only did I miss Teddy's help, but I knew that I was going to have to take that walk to the cannery to time the boiling.

Mary saved the day, though, by showing me her new watch and offering to time the cooking. I got to listen to Mary talk for the 20 minutes. Teddy was usually quiet.

This date on the beach was one of many firsts for me, but the most notable thing about it was the way Mary could eat crab. She was not one of those picky types when it came to eating. She had no fear of being known as a fussy eater. For 40 years I've been comparing other women's gusto for eating to Mary's. Very few measure up.

After we cleaned up all the crab, we sat and gazed into the flames of the fire for a while. The conversation must have been very limited, as I can't remember any of it. I do remember that when 5 p.m. rolled around she said that she had to go home to dinner. I didn't get up, so she stepped close and quickly kissed me, smiled, and turned to run home. I let her go.

When I next saw Teddy there was a strained moment or two until I told him about my date. I'll admit to enlarging on the truth a bit, but it was merely to entertain Teddy. I didn't have another date or think much about girls for two more years, but that is another tale.

One more story about crabs and traps. My efforts to build a better trap for crabs have not all been successful. But one was unique. To the standard trap frame I added a wire lead-in tunnel with an opening that measured about 5" by 18". Tricky wires were supposed to drop down and prevent the escape of the crabs. I was sure that this trap would outcatch all others.

My son and I went fishing the day after I finished the trap. We dropped it in a likely spot at 8 o'clock in the morning. On the way home we stopped at 3 o'clock in the afternoon to check the trap and see if I'd caught us a good meal.

Just as I was pulling alongside my buoy, it started moving through the water. I actually had to restart my motor and chase the buoy for about 200 yards before I could catch it and pull the line aboard. Something was very odd here.

When I started trying to pull the trap, I found that it must weigh at least 200 pounds. I would pull a bit, tie off the line, and rest. Then I'd go back and pull up a few more feet. I had visions of a trap so full of crab that the crabs had walked the trap across the bottom of the sea. How else could it move?

A few minutes later the trap broke the surface and the mystery was solved. I had a 45-pound halibut in the trap. Now this was nice—I enjoy eating halibut—but I had built a trap for crabs.

My son Wayne called the shot when he said, "Dad, you've developed the world's only self-baiting crab trap!"

To those of you who live by the sea and know the wonderful eating provided by crab, I wish *bon appetit!*

For those of you who must depend on the supermarket to provide your crab, I offer the following recipes so that you too might enjoy that wonderful taste.

CRAB SPUDDLERS

Comes the day when you have both crab meat and mashed potatoes among your leftovers, you have it made. You can make Crab Spuddlers. My kids loved them.

2 cups mashed potatoes, real or instant
8 ounces fresh crab meat or contents of
    1 7-ounce can
1 tablespoon onion, minced
1-1/2 teaspoons Worcestershire sauce
1/8 teaspoon garlic powder
1 egg, slightly beaten
1/2 cup bread crumbs
Dash of black pepper
Fat for deep-fat frying, preferably beef fat
    (see page 27)

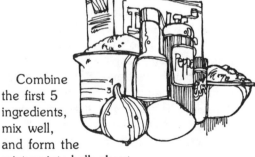

Combine the first 5 ingredients, mix well, and form the mixture into balls about an inch thick. Dip the balls in the egg and then roll them in the seasoned crumbs. Fry in a deep-fat fryer at 375° until brown.

Serve either as a main course or as an hors d'oeuvre. Yield: 6 to 8 balls.

CRAB SOUFFLÉ

Over the years of enjoying crab I've also enjoyed experimenting with different ways of cooking it. It was only a matter of time before I accepted the challenge of making a crab soufflé. This recipe is the result of that effort, and it tastes wonderful.

3 tablespoons butter
3 tablespoons flour
1-1/3 cups milk
2 tablespoons lemon juice
1/4 teaspoon dry mustard
1/2 teaspoon salt
4 egg yolks, beaten
8 ounces fresh crab meat or
contents of 1 7-ounce can
5 egg whites at room
temperature

Any soufflé of mine starts with a white sauce. In a small saucepan melt the butter. Stir in the flour to make a roux. Add the milk gradually, keeping the pan over a medium high heat and stirring continually to prevent the mixture from boiling. When the sauce is thick add the lemon juice, mustard and salt. Set the sauce aside until it is quite cool and then put it in a medium-size bowl.

Stir in the egg yolks, then the crab. Now beat the egg whites until they are stiff and gently mix about a quarter of them into the crab mixture. Fold in the remainder of the egg whites. Thorough mixing is not necessary or desirable, as that would crush the egg whites and cause them not to rise. Turn the mixture into a well-buttered casserole or soufflé dish; the mixture should fill about two thirds of the container. Bake in a 350° oven for 35 minutes.

Serve immediately. Accompanied by a green salad this makes a delightful lunch or supper. Cut the soufflé gently, using 2 back-to-back forks rather than a knife. Yield: 2 to 3 servings.

TENAKEE CRAB CAKES

Over the years I have cooked crab meat many ways, and in the days when my children and I were catching our own crabs we always ended up with large leftover lumps of meat. The legs went the first day and I needed recipes for second-day crab meat. Such a day led me to this recipe.

1 egg
1 tablespoon mayonnaise
1 teaspoon prepared mustard
2 tablespoons onion, minced
1/8 teaspoon cayenne
1/8 teaspoon Tabasco
1/2 teaspoon salt
1/4 teaspoon black pepper
3 tablespoons bread crumbs
1 pound fresh or canned crab meat
Fat for deep frying, preferably beef fat
    (see page 27)
Lemon slices

Beat the egg in a deep bowl. Add the next 7 ingredients and whisk together. When the mixture is smooth, add the crumbs and crab meat and mix well. Form into 8 to 10 balls, flatten them slightly, and refrigerate for an hour.

Heat the fat in a deep-fat fryer to 375°. Place 4 or 5 crab cakes in the basket and cook them for 3 or 4 minutes until golden brown, turning once if necessary. Drain cakes on paper towels and keep them warm while the second batch is cooked.

Serve with lemon slices. A tartar or cocktail sauce should be available. Yield: 8 to 10 cakes—enough for 2 people.

CRAB HELL

If you want to give a deviled egg fancier a thrill, this is the ultimate. If your guests don't eat everything in sight within 10 minutes, call me. I'll be right over to finish up whatever is left.

12 hard-boiled eggs
1/2 cup mayonnaise
2 tablespoons prepared mustard
1/4 teaspoon salt
1/8 teaspoon black pepper
8 ounces fresh crab meat or contents of
    1 7-ounce can
Paprika

Cut each egg in halves the long way. Remove the yolks, mash them, add the mayonnaise, mustard, salt and pepper, and mix well. Break the crab meat into small flakes and add that. Heap the egg whites with the resulting mixture and garnish with paprika.

Serve any time that deviled eggs would be appropriate or, as I said, to really treat your friends.

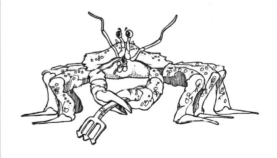

HOMEMADE BREAD

Bread-baking does require certain skills. Some of these skills can be learned at home, some in school and some while watching other cooks. You must have the skill of reading so you can follow the recipe as well as the skills of following directions, remembering procedures, assembling ingredients, judging size, being patient while dough rises, and being able to resist eating hot bread. Other than the above, bread-making is easy. Just gather these items:

1/2 cup milk
3 tablespoons sugar
2 tablespoons salt
3 tablespoons shortening
1-1/2 cups warm water
1 package dry or fresh yeast
5-1/2 cups all-purpose flour

Scald the milk. Then stir in the sugar, salt and shortening. Cool to lukewarm. Rinse a large bowl in hot water to warm it. Pour the warm water (105° to 115°) into the bowl. Sprinkle the yeast on the surface of the water, wait 5 minutes, stir, and add the milk mixture.

Next add 3 cups of the flour to the bowl and beat until the mixture is smooth. Add the remaining flour slowly. You should now have a soft dough. Turn this onto a floured board and knead until it is firm and elastic. Allow a minimum of 10 minutes to do the kneading. Form the dough into a ball and place in a greased bowl, turning the dough once, and cover with a cloth. Set the bowl in a warm, draftfree location and let the dough rise until doubled in bulk, which should take about an hour.

Turn the dough out on the board, punch it down, cover with a towel, and let it rest for 10 to 15 minutes.

Then cut the dough in half. Form each piece into a loaf and place in a greased bread pan measuring 3" by 5" by 9". Cover and let it rise for another hour, or until doubled in bulk again.

Bake at 400° for 30 minutes or until golden brown. Remove from pans and set on a rack to cool. Hide until dinner!

THE BREAD PHENOMENON AND SOURDOUGH

Bread-baking women, men, too, have long wondered about one of the great mysteries of the cooking world: the phenomenon of evaporating bread. The disappearance of freshly baked loaves of bread within the first hour of their removal from the oven has long been a phenomenon worth study. I suspect my mother was aware of this when I was growing up.

The first time I noticed that the mystery was taking place in my own home was several years ago in Juneau. I decided, about the time that I removed four freshly baked loaves from the oven, to begin a program of research toward finding a solution to this mystery. Leaving the bread unguarded in the kitchen, I went into the living room to find a pencil and some note paper. One must take notes if one is going to approach an investigation with scientific accuracy.

I had just found the writing materials when the front doorbell clanged. I answered it and then logged the time spent in discussion with the postman as six minutes.

When I returned to the kitchen the bread rack somehow looked wrong. A careful count revealed that there were three loaves of bread on the rack and one buttery bread knife on the counter.

Suspecting foul play, I began an inventory of the building's occupants. My wife, who was sitting in the living room, looked up and asked, "What's up?" I asked if she had been in the kitchen and received a negative answer. In the den I found my youngest daughter and a friend playing. Not a crumb in sight. I could hear the soft strumming of a guitar from upstairs, so I knew that my oldest son was up there. So it was back to the kitchen, only to find the mystery deepening. There remained only two loaves of bread, but there were two buttery bread knives. While I was thinking about this latest development, I made myself an onion sandwich, using some warm bread.

I have to admit that if there is a large sweet onion around, that helps contribute to the reduction of the bread supply. Try a slice of warm homemade bread with real butter and thin-sliced raw onion on top. To quote my son, "Far out!"

TLC BISCUITS

In these days of packaged mixes it's hard to remember that all baking-powder biscuits used to be made from scratch. To tell the truth, I can remember some excellent homemade biscuits, but some awful ones, too. However, a particular batch of homemade biscuits stands out in my memory; a very pretty young lady baked them for me. I will quickly add that the young lady was one of my daughters. She used this recipe and a large helping of tender loving care.

2 cups all-purpose flour
2 teaspoons double-acting baking powder
1 teaspoon salt
8 tablespoons butter
2/3 cup milk

Into a large bowl sift together the flour, baking powder and salt. Add the butter a tablespoon at a time, mixing it in with your hands so that the ingredients combine to look like coarse corn meal. Then pour the milk into the bowl and mix with a wooden spoon to form a smooth, soft dough, which should be firm enough to gather into a ball.

Place the ball of dough on a floured surface and pat or roll it into a 1/2-inch-thick circle. With a biscuit cutter cut biscuits about 2-1/2 inches across. Place the biscuits on a greased baking sheet. You can gather up the trimmings of dough, roll them into a ball, pat flat, and cut out some more biscuits.

Bake at 400° for about 20 minutes. The biscuits should be puffed up and golden brown. Serve with butter, honey or jam as a side dish for a meal or as a base for strawberry shortcake.

The missing loaves had to have been taken somewhere but they sure weren't leaving much evidence behind. The time had come for a stake-out.

I carefully moved into the pantry, out of sight, using the ironing board as a temporary blind.

Suddenly the back door opened noisily. In came my middle son and middle daughter, along with six of their friends. As they crowded around the refrigerator someone bumped the pantry door. It closed with a bang, upsetting my ironing-board blind and turning the pantry into a darkroom. I stumbled over something, lifted the ironing board off myself, and fumbled for the doorknob. The door was locked.

I beat on the door with considerable effort, but the noise level in the kitchen must have prevented my being heard. It was some time before my middle son heard me and opened the door. He gave me an odd look but kept his mouth shut. Smart kid!

Back in the kitchen I made the discovery that the room was now empty both of young people and of bread. Yes, your guess is correct. I now had four buttery bread knives lying on the counter.

A little later, in the living room with my second drink in hand, I reviewed my notes. Carefully analyzing the evidence, I arrived at the conclusion that there had been no evaporation of bread. However, the evidence clearly indicated that bread fresh from the oven is unstable. If subjected to a number of factors, such as loud noises, currents of air caused by moving bodies, or overcrowding, it will, through catalytic action, convert itself into buttery bread knives.

My continuing test program over the years has revealed nothing to cast doubt on my theory. The only way to prevent the phenomenon is to lock up the fresh bread to retard the circulation of air around it. So protected, it will often last until dinner. You still doubt me? Come over sometime and see my collection of bread knives.

Homemade bread rates just about at the top of my list of good things to eat. When conditions are right, I enjoy baking bread as well as eating it. I came by the bread-baking habit honestly, since it's a throwback to my childhood.

The winter of 1932-33 is one of my most memorable, for it was during that winter that the world of baking opened up to me. My mother always baked our bread and the sight of her kneading dough was a familiar one.

With the coming of this particular winter Mother developed arthritis in her hands. Kneading dough became a very painful job for her. As the family had to have bread, a substitute dough kneader was necessary. Because my brother and dad disappeared for days at a time on their boats, I was the only prospect left. So, with Mother's supervision, I was initiated into the world of bakers and baking. By spring I knew the feeling of dough through all its stages. In fact, I found that I could make bread like Mother made. This skill, learned early in life, has never left me. Even today I'll whip up a batch of bread.

But let us return to the winter of 1932-33 and my initiation into baking. That winter the family was living in one of five small houses perched on a hill not too far from the cannery that owned them. As all the adults of our family worked for the cannery we rated a roof over our heads.

In the other four houses lived people of varied heritages. Swedish, Norwegian, Finnish and Russian were the second languages often heard. We were the only 100 percent Americans around; actually, our mixed heritage was English, Irish, Danish and French-Canadian, but English was our only language, so I guess we were 100 percent American.

When Christmas drew close I found myself, as part of the Nelson baking team, engaged in the Olympics of holiday baking. It was a wonderful period of my life and certainly allowed me an insight into other cultures at an early age. Lessons learned during that winter served me well

through the next 40 years of dealing with people. Our team didn't win the contest; all five families were winners.

During the many winters to follow my knowledge of cooking grew, but the press of work, school and growing older never let me participate in a baking contest again. Except as a judge, I quickly add. The other gain from that great winter was my willingness to bake any recipe that appeals to me, a willingness that has served me well.

For a while my mother operated a café in Cordova called Tonette's. I have both good and bad memories of this period. Our living quarters were behind the café, and for the first time I had a bedroom of my own. Years of sleeping on the couch or sharing a bedroom came to an end.

Now that I had a room of my own, I could start having friends over to spend the night. My ability to invite friends to spend the night in back of a café noted for its cakes and pies rapidly made me a popular young man. My friends envisioned eating themselves into bed each night.

The rule of the house was that I did certain chores each evening, and having guests did not eliminate the chores. The work usually required about an hour of my time. I washed some pots, pans and dishes, and did some straightening up. Not hard work, just character building.

If my guest of the evening pitched in and helped me, even a little, we could have our pick of whatever was on the pie and cake racks as a bedtime snack. But should the guest sit on his butt and wait for me to finish, we were lucky to get a glass of milk and a cookie.

This rule certainly had me picking and choosing my friends. It's funny how the ones I really liked best were those who always pitched in and helped. I soon understood the message that Mother was trying to get across.

The café also provided my first contact with an obnoxious drunk. This man wandered in one evening fairly late when Mother was working alone, doing both the cooking and serving. When I came out of the back room to begin my chores I heard this man, sitting at the counter, talking loud and throwing a foul word into his speech about every third word.

When Mother's voice suddenly changed from a pleasant tone to one of deep concern, I started out to help her, picking up the meat cleaver as I passed the butcher block. I was a hundred pounds of fury, growing madder every step.

When I came through the swinging doors I saw that the foul-mouthed man was just leaving, backward, with my dad on his left arm and my brother on his right. They had walked in at the right time and engaged in some positive action. I never saw that man again and wondered how he could disappear completely in such a small town.

Later I learned he had been blue ticketed, which meant that he was put aboard the next steamship leaving town, and told not to return.

Pie-baking time was early in the morning at Tonette's Café. Mother used all

KARENUT BREAD

My wife has a friend to whom she always seems to be saying, "Karen, you're a nut." I agree, she is, but when it comes to recipes, well, that's a different story. Here's proof.

1 cup Grape-nuts
2 cups sour milk (made by adding 1
    teaspoon vinegar to each cup fresh
    milk and leaving it to rest a few minutes
    before using)
2 eggs
1-1/2 cups sugar
3 tablespoons shortening
2-3/4 cups all-purpose flour
1 teaspoon baking soda
2 teaspoons baking powder
1 teaspoon salt

Let the Grape-nuts stand in the sour milk for 30 minutes.

Beat the eggs, add the sugar, and then add the shortening. After mixing well stir in the Grape-nuts mixture.

Sift together the flour, soda, baking powder and salt. Add to the other mixture and mix well. Pour into a pair of well-greased bread pans.

Bake at 350° for an hour. Let the bread rest a day before eating.

the help she could get, so I spent many hours rolling crusts, pouring fillings, and endlessly using the eggbeater. Try using one of those torture machines for 30 minutes straight. Then you'll see why I rate the electric mixer right next to the light bulb. All the work was worth it, though, when we had all those big beautiful pies setting around cooling. The house specialties were apple, cherry, lemon and custard pies. In season banana cream pie was another favorite.

Right after the breakfast rush, and before the noon trade, Mother usually baked two big round layer cakes. This she did on her own without my help. The only time I could help her with the cakes was on Saturday and Sunday, and then only if it rained too hard for fishing. Even when I did help, it meant turning that damned eggbeater. As I recall, I didn't volunteer very often.

I think my involvement in turning out pies and cakes wholesale affected me, as I have never enjoyed that type of baking, although I like bread baking.

Speaking of baking bread, Mother at first tried baking bread to serve in the café, but it became too time-consuming for the return. The customers would pay extra for pie and cake, but they expected bread free with their dinners. They got it, too, but it soon turned out to be bakery bread. The worst part of this was that the family also had to eat bakery bread.

Thinking of bakery bread reminds me of my first trip as a deckhand aboard a cannery tender. In those days the cannery furnished free bread and water to the fishermen who brought their fish to the tender. As each fishing boat came alongside the tender, I would hand the fishermen the water hose and ask how many loaves of bread they wanted.

The bread was in big long crusty loaves, unwrapped, and stacked on end in wooden boxes. It was just as it came from the oven.

The first time one of the Greek fishermen came alongside he wanted the limit of four loaves. I handed them to him. He threw the loaves up on his cabin top and started pitching fish aboard the tender. Once he had unloaded and received his ticket showing how many fish he had delivered, he dropped his lines and let his boat drift away.

As there was no one else alongside, I stood there watching him. He picked up one loaf of bread and placed it under his arm. Then he doubled up his other hand into a fist and punched it through the loaf of bread lengthwise. The entire center section of the loaf went over the side, to the delight of the seagulls. Then he tore off a big hunk of the remaining crust and started chewing on it.

I caught my dad's eye and I must have looked surprised. He grinned and said, "Greeks don't like anything but crust!"

I saw this happen dozens of times in the next few years. I never did get used to all of that good bread being wasted. I hated to give these men the number of loaves that they were entitled to, but I did. I understand that now the fishermen have to buy their own bread, but I've never gone back to see if the new rule affected their habit.

Who knows, maybe the fishermen have gone to baking their own bread—sourdough, and all crust.

SOURDOUGH STARTER

They tell me that there are sourdough starters in Alaska that are over 100 years old. Well, mine isn't over a week old. It's just too much bother to keep a starter going when it's so easy to start a batch with today's yeast. A friend of mine has the same feeling. She compares keeping a starter alive to keeping a bird. You're always feeding it, watering it, and cleaning up after it. I'll buy that!

I keep my starter in the refrigerator in a gallon mayonnaise jar, but a nice neat crock with a cover would be fine, too. OK, let's start a batch of sourdough.

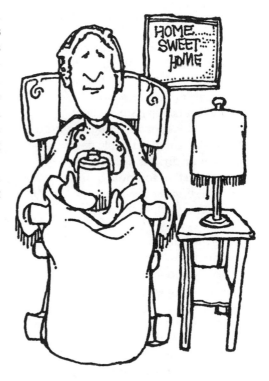

2-1/2 cups lukewarm water
1 package active yeast
3 cups all-purpose or whole wheat flour

Pour the water into a large bowl, sprinkle the yeast on top of the water, and wait 5 minutes. Gradually add the flour, stirring in a little at a time. When all the flour is in, beat the mixture vigorously until it is smooth. Pour the batter into your jar or crock and cover lightly with aluminum foil. Set in a warm place for 24 hours. If the yeast is active, you'll have a good, bubbling starter. You can now claim it is 100 years old and who's to question you?

When you wish to use the sourdough take out what you need but leave at least a cupful of batter in the jar. Add a cup of flour and 3/4 cup of water to the jar and stir. Put the jar back in the refrigerator, where it will keep several weeks. Whenever you wish to use some sourdough go through this procedure to replenish your starter. You can go on like this for that entire 100 years, should you live that long.

See, if you talk about Alaska and eating in the same book, you are going to mention sourdough. It was so important to the early residents that the very name *sourdough* was given to anyone who had lived here for a time.

The most often listed criteria for being a sourdough are: Live through a freezeup and a breakup in the area known as Alaska; shoot a bear and eat of its flesh. Another way of qualifing is to have lived in Alaska for 30 years. I'm a sourdough!

The use of sourdough on the trail and in camp in the old days was an art. It is necessary to realize that sourdough starter will survive only if kept warm. On the trail the only source of warmth is the human body. So the maintaining of sourdough became a very personal thing that could even be likened to the relationship of a mother and unborn child. On the trail a man carried the bag or jar of sourdough right in his parka.

In the evening he added flour and water to the starter in the quantities needed, taking the starter to bed in his sleeping bag to keep it warm and ready for use for breakfast.

In the morning he used a hole in the open flour sack as a bowl and mixed his sourdough hotcake batter. But always he returned a small amount of the mix to the bag or jar in his parka to keep it alive for the next day.

Today's sourdough hotcakes are a far cry from those trail hotcakes. Trail hotcakes were little more than flour, salt and

The Bread Phenomenon and Sourdough

water. Today we add eggs, sugar, milk and even fruit if we so desire. The light fluffy sourdough pancakes at our breakfast table are a joy to behold and fantastic to taste, but they might be a surprise to those men who carried sourdough starters inside their jackets.

When I was growing up, my family used sourdough only for hotcakes, so I did not get a chance to learn to make buns and bread with sourdough until much later in life.

As for using sourdough aboard our boats, it was impossible because of temperature problems. In most cases we had a fire in the galley stove only when anchored or in very calm weather. Therefore the temperature of the living space could go from 30° to 80° and back several times a day. Sourdough simply could not survive that. I suppose we could have carried it around inside our jackets, but it just wasn't worth it.

If we ran out of homemade bread we could whip up a batch of biscuits or even corn bread.

I'm going to pass along a few recipes for sourdough, homemade bread and a cake or two. To dwell much on baking is a waste of time. There are many elaborately detailed books on baking available, with which a sourdough need not compete.

SOURDOUGH HOTCAKES

So let's back up to the point where you removed some sourdough and left the cup of starter in the jar. The part you took out is what we'll make hotcakes out of. My experience indicates that you don't have to measure the amount of sourdough very accurately.

3 cups sourdough (see page 51)
1 egg, beaten, or 2 eggs if you want richer batter
1 cup fresh or reconstituted milk
1 tablespoon shortening, oil, bacon grease or melted butter
1 teaspoon sugar or honey
1/2 teaspoon salt
1 teaspoon baking soda

In a large mixing bowl add to the batter all ingredients except the soda and mix thoroughly. Just before you are ready to start your hotcakes, sprinkle the soda on top of the batter and fold it into the mixture. You will soon notice an interesting expansion of the batter. Spoon this fluffy mixture onto a hot griddle to make hotcakes of the size you prefer. Turn hotcakes once when bubbles appear on the top.

Serve with gobs of creamery butter and your favorite syrup.

SOURDOUGH MOOSE CRÊPES

The sourdough pancake, with a moose and mushroom filling, you cannot find offered in the finest restaurants in the world. But with a little effort you can become one of the few hundred individuals in all mankind to enjoy this delight.

FIRST, THE CRÊPES:
2 cups sourdough (see page 51)
1 tablespoon sugar
1 teaspoon salt
1 egg, beaten
3 tablespoons butter
1 teaspoon soda
1 tablespoon water

In a medium-size bowl mix the sourdough, sugar, salt and egg. The mixture should be fairly thin; add water if needed.

Melt the butter in an 8-inch frying pan, preferably a pan with sloping sides for convenience in turning the crêpes. When the butter is melted pour it into the batter and stir thoroughly. Now dissolve the soda in the water and fold gently into the batter.

Ladle enough batter into the frying pan to form a thin pancake. Tilt the pan so batter will cover the entire bottom. When bubbles appear in the crêpe turn it and cook the second side. Stack the finished pancakes on a warm plate.

NOW THE FILLING:
2 tablespoons clarified butter
    (see page 6)
1 small onion, minced
1/2 pound mooseburger or ground beef
1/4 pound fresh mushrooms, chopped
1 egg, beaten
1 tablespoon Worcestershire sauce
Salt and black pepper

In the frying pan heat the butter and sauté the onion pieces until transparent. Add the ground meat, crumbled into tiny pieces, and cook until brown. Now add the mushrooms and cook for about 3 minutes.

Put the meat mixture into a bowl and stir in the beaten egg, the Worcestershire sauce and salt and pepper.

Fill each pancake with 3 tablespoons of the meat mixture, rolling each pancake around the meat. Set the rolled pancakes on an oval heatproof platter.

THE SAUCE:
3 tablespoons clarified butter
    (see page 6)
2 tablespoons flour
1 cup beef stock
1 tablespoon fresh parsley, chopped
1 cup buttermilk or sour milk (made by
    adding 1 teaspoon vinegar to 1 cup
    fresh milk and leaving it to rest a few
    minutes before using)

Melt the butter in the frying pan, stir in the flour, and remove from the heat. Stir in the beef stock, return to the heat, and, as the gravy thickens, continue to stir while adding the parsley and milk. When the gravy is done, pour over the crêpes and save the remainder for those who want more. Yield: 4 servings.

SOURDOUGH BREAD

There are hundreds of recipes in Alaska for sourdough bread and, since the recipes have had 100 years of experimentation, most are good. This recipe has been around for a long time. We like it.

Making sourdough bread requires planning. You are not going to jump out of your chair and rush into the kitchen and make this bread. You have to start it the day before you plan to eat it.

FIRST DAY
1 cup sourdough (see page 51)
2 cups lukewarm water
2-1/2 cups flour

Place the starter in a large bowl and add the water and flour. Set the bowl, well covered, in a warm place and leave it there for 24 hours.

SECOND DAY
4 cups all-purpose flour
1 teaspoon salt
1/2 teaspoon baking soda
3 tablespoons sugar
3 tablespoons vegetable oil
Butter

Into the bowl of bubbling dough that you prepared the previous day place all ingredients except the butter. Mix until the batter is smooth and the flour is completely absorbed. By now you should be able to lift the dough out of the bowl in one piece. If you can't, work in another 1/2 cup of flour until the dough is firm.

Now lift the dough onto a well-floured board and knead the dough for 10 minutes; then shape it into a ball and drop it into a buttered bowl, turn it once, and cover with a towel. Put in a warm place for about 2-1/2 hours.

Turn the dough out on the board again, punch it down, cut in half, and roll and shape the pieces into long loaves. Place the loaves on a buttered cookie sheet, drape with a towel and set in a warm place to rise again. In about an hour the loaves should double in size and be ready to bake.

Bake at 375° for an hour. Slide the finished loaves onto a rack to cool, but try and serve while they are still warm.

"SMILE" SPLIT PEA SOUP

While I was writing about bread and sourdough and the memories they represent, my mind drifted back to my childhood. I spent considerable time aboard a cannery tender named *Smile*. During the 1930s she worked both in the Kodiak and in the Cordova areas. I know that this seems an odd name to hang on a ship, and certainly no one could ever explain how she received the name. Her sister ship had a nice solid name—*Pioneer* or something like that.

The important part of my story about the *Smile* was a recipe tacked to her galley wall. The recipe was for split pea soup, and this soup had made the *Smile* famous. Well, at least well known in the small circle of seamen who served on or visited the ship. I dearly loved that soup and committed the recipe to memory. If my memory is reliable, this is *Smile* Split Pea Soup.

2 cups green or yellow split peas
5 cups water
5 chicken bouillon cubes
1/4 teaspoon thyme
2 tablespoons oil or butter
1/4 pound bacon, diced in 1/4-inch
    pieces
2 medium onions, chopped
2 medium carrots, ground, grated or
    chopped
1 teaspoon salt
1/4 teaspoon black pepper

Wash the peas and remove those pebbles that sneak in. Then put the split peas in a 6-quart saucepan with the water. If you have a regular soup pot, use it. The bouillon cubes and thyme are now added. Bring the mixture to a boil and simmer for an hour.

In the oil or butter sauté the bacon pieces to render the fat. Remove the bacon bits to a small bowl and save. Cook the onions and carrots in the bacon fat for 5 minutes and then add them to the cooking peas. Cook the soup for another 30 minutes. The peas should now be tender but not mushy.

Thin the soup with water to the desired consistency and add the salt and pepper. Serve in deep soup bowls, with the fried bacon bits sprinkled on the top. Just hope there are seconds left in the pot.

There is another step you can take if you wish to fancy up the soup a bit. Pass the soup through a food mill or sieve to make a purée. Serve in the same manner, but add a large pat of butter to each bowl.

Either way it's a fine soup, and even though you may be getting tired of my saying it, this goes well with homemade bread or with chunks of French bread.

BEANS, BEAUTIFUL BEANS

I **wonder how many** individuals can remember their first meal. Was it mother's milk, strained spinach or hot dogs? I have a food memory that reaches well back into my childhood. In fact my family has accused me of remembering things that never happened. What a nice thing to say to someone who hopes to be a writer!

Anyway, my memory goes back to the time when beans and homemade bread entered my life. The two are really so closely entwined that I don't know which was first. My mother was responsible for both. Come to think of it, the memory of those beautiful baked beans and warm loaves of bread that Mother made might just beat out mother's milk as a warm and wonderful experience.

I think it is time that we explored the subject of beans just a bit more. My mother certainly knew how to get the most out of a batch of beans. As I have it computed, my introduction to beans took place back in the early 30s, the depression years. I know that many times the lowly bean was the only thing Mother had to work with when putting meals on the table. Her beans were definitely seasoned with love along with side pork, molasses and salt.

The first bean day was when dinner con-

sisted of a big bowl of beans at everyone's place. And a platter heaping with home-made bread. Mother always made a large pot of beans and could feed another five people in an emergency. She would say, "Stay to dinner. I'll add another quart of water to the bean soup." Really, she did not have to, as many of our guests knew. Our home always seemed to be a gathering place.

On the second bean day Mother added some sweetening—sugar and molasses—to the beans left in the pot. This mixture she poured into a large flat pan that she popped into the oven to bake. The dark brown top that grew as the beans baked was beautiful. They were the most wonderful baked beans that I have ever eaten.

Then came the day for the very closed affair between Mother and me. It was the third bean day. She always saved enough of those wonderful baked beans to make bean sandwiches for my school lunch. Her bread and those beans still linger on my taste buds.

When I could bring myself to part with even half a sandwich, I could trade it for anything the other kids had in their lunches. Do you know, I was able to trade half of a bean sandwich for the first banana

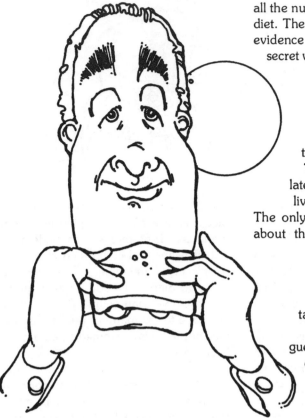

all the nutrients that were missing from our diet. The cod liver oil bottle was always in evidence in our house. It was Mother's secret weapon to assure my good health.

Poor Mother tried everything possible to make cod liver oil palatable to me. In the process of adding the fish oil to juices and foods, she came close to destroying my interest in eating. There are still times now, 40 years later, when I can taste a touch of cod liver oil in my morning orange juice. The only halfway decent thing I can say about the oil is that it seems to have worked. I'm healthy.

I mentioned earlier thinking about first food memories. After a great deal of mental searching, talking to elders, and looking at old photograph albums, I'll make a guess. I think my first food memories come from when I was age seven, in 1929. Does that date fully explain the beans?

Regardless of the causes of, and changes in, food habits over the years, I still like beans, all kinds, and often. No, I will have to qualify that just a small bit. With great regret I admit that it is only occasionally that I eat beans now. Age does seem to affect one's ability to work off the calories in the foods one once consumed with youthful vigor.

It would appear that I had better get on with my explanations of how to cook beans. I did say that I was not going to write an autobiography, didn't I?

that I ever tasted. I wasn't too impressed with the banana, but was it ever a sign of status to have actually eaten one.

Remember now, bananas in those days had to make quite a trip to reach Alaska. By steamship from Central America to the East Coast, by train across the continent to the West Coast, and then by ship to Alaska. But then, all produce coming to the territory in those days was limited and expensive. Apples, oranges, potatoes and onions we could often afford. But salad vegetables and bananas were simply not available to us. They were in the markets— just not in our monetary range.

But then, my mother had a substitute for

BEAN SOUP

This is the recipe for Mother Nelson's first-day beans. It will feed a family of 4 or make a first course for a larger group. I should add that today's technology has resulted in quick-cooking beans; if you buy that kind eliminate the soaking.

1 pound navy beans, white beans, pea
    beans or Great Northern beans
2 quarts water
1/4 pound salt pork, bacon or ham hock,
    cut in 1-inch cubes
1/2 teaspoon salt
6 whole peppercorns
1 bay leaf
1 medium onion, chopped

Wash the dry beans carefully and pick out any small stones or off-color beans. Yes, it seems that you still find both even in packaged beans. Drain the beans, then put them in a soup pot, cover with the water, and either soak overnight or boil the beans for 5 minutes and set aside for an hour to soak.

After the beans have soaked, add the meat, salt, peppercorns and bay leaf to the pot, cover, and simmer for 3 hours, adding more water if necessary to keep the beans covered. Add the onion during the last hour of cooking.

Taste a few beans to see if they are done. If they are, take out 1/2 cup of beans. Resist eating them. Mash these beans and then stir them into the rest of the pot. Now check for seasoning and add a bit of salt if it's required. If the peppercorns show up, take them out. If they haven't done their work by now, it's too late.

Serve the beans in deep soup bowls with homemade bread. If such bread is not available try large chunks of crisp French bread, which is the second best thing for sopping up bean juice.

SECOND-DAY BEANS

This recipe can only be made if you have doubled the bean soup recipe, or didn't eat the batch you made the day before. I know, that idea is ridiculous. I suppose that you could make both recipes the same day, but start early.

2 tablespoons
    brown sugar
1 tablespoon Worcestershire sauce
Bean Soup made from 1 pound beans
    (*preceding recipe*)
1/3 cup molasses

Stir the brown sugar and Worcestershire sauce into cold, or at least cool, bean soup. Pour the mixture into a flat baking pan. The beans should be about 1-1/2 inches deep in the pan. Now dribble the molasses over the top of the mixture.

Bake uncovered at 350° for 2 hours. The time is not critical as the beans are already cooked. Anytime after 1-1/2 hours, when the beans are nicely browned, you can remove them from the oven.

Serve this hot for dinner, with good bread, as with the soup. But Second-Day Beans are also very good cold. Yield: 8 servings.

BAKED BEAN SANDWICHES

As any of you who cook, snack, or are waited on know, the possibilities for any sandwich are limited only by the imagination of the creator, although enthusiasm also is often critical to the development of new ideas. So start with the essentials, and take off from there.

2 slices of bread, preferably homemade
Butter
4 tablespoons Second-Day Beans
    (*preceding recipe*)

Spread the butter on the bread, spread the beans on the lower slice, add the top slice. That's it, you've made a gourmet special.

Too simple, you say! Well, all right, get fancy. Add one or more of the following between the baked beans and that top slice of bread: thinly sliced onion rings, ketchup, chili sauce, mustard, slices of dill pickle or cucumber chip pickle, any cheese or what-have-you in your kitchen.

You may not have Second-Day Beans around often to experiment with, so enjoy them while you can. Our 6 kids and dozens of their friends have enjoyed this delight. This is a taste that could fade into history unless we all take positive action and continue the tradition.

POT-BAKED BEANS

I don't pretend to know how the recipe for Boston baked beans reached Alaska. But it did, although here they are known just as pot beans. Certainly every family in my youth seemed to be the proud owners of a bean pot. The slow electric cookers that flood the market today are the descendants of the bean pot. Maybe you could make Pot-Baked Beans in your electric cooker, but I still like the bean pot. Here's my recipe.

1 pound dry white beans
1-1/2 quarts cold water
1 teaspoon salt
1/3 cup brown sugar
1 teaspoon dry mustard
1/4 cup molasses
1 medium onion, sliced thin
1/4 pound salt pork, bacon or ham,
    sliced thin

Thoroughly wash the dry beans, bring to a boil in the water, simmer 5 minutes, and let stand for an hour.

Add the salt to the beans, cover and simmer for another hour. Drain the beans and save the liquid, which should be about 1-3/4 quarts. If some of the liquid has evaporated add water at this point. Then add the brown sugar, mustard and molasses.

Now you need a 2-quart bean pot, a covered casserole or your electric cooker. Fill the container with alternating layers of pork, beans, onion and liquid until the pot is full. Try to end up with pork as the top layer.

Cover the pot and bake at 300° for 5 to 7 hours. Add water along the way if needed. Every time you check the pot it should drive the gang in the living room wild. It will smell *so* good. And it will eat just as good as it smells.

CHILI SAUCE

As my family increased over the years, eventually totaling 8, we were always looking for or developing recipes for large groups. This recipe has always been a favorite. I will first tell you how to make Chili Sauce, which is excellent by itself, but I'll admit that we more often used this recipe and the next—for pinto beans—mixed together for family meals.

5 tablespoons shortening, oil or clarified
    butter (see page 6)
3-1/2 pounds round steak, moose or
    caribou, cubed in 3/4-inch pieces
2 cups onion, chopped
4 cloves garlic, minced
4 tablespoons chili powder of whatever
    strength you prefer

1-1/2 teaspoons oregano
1-1/2 teaspoons cumin
1 teaspoon cayenne
2 tablespoons salt
1 teaspoon sugar
1 6-ounce can tomato paste
1 26-ounce can whole tomatoes
2 cups beef broth

Place 3 tablespoons of shortening in a large pot or Dutch oven. Then add and sear the meat, turning it constantly until browned. Transfer the meat to a bowl.

Add the rest of the shortening to the pot and sauté the onion and garlic until wilted. Add to this the chili powder, oregano, cumin and cayenne, and stir until all the onion is coated. Next, the meat goes back into the pot followed by the remaining ingredients.

Cover the pot and simmer for an hour. Then give it another hour to simmer uncovered. Stir once in a while.

Serve this with bread, preferably good old homemade bread. This chili-meat combination will stand by itself as the main dish of a good meal. But if you are like us, you'll have trouble resisting the temptation to add beans. Yield: about 10 servings.

BEANS TO ACCOMPANY CHILI SAUCE

Because beans prepared in this manner are so often eaten with the preceding sauce, don't get the idea they aren't good alone. I've made these beans just for themselves, although I might add a few extras like ham, bacon, onion or additional spices.

2 pounds pinto beans
1 teaspoon salt

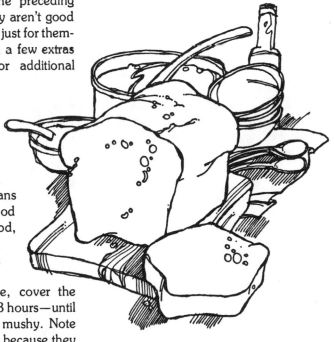

Wash the beans and pick out the small pebbles and bad beans. It's best to soak the beans overnight, but the quick method is all right, too. For that method, place the beans in 4 quarts of water, boil for 5 minutes, and let stand for an hour.

Once the soaking's done, cover the beans and simmer for about 3 hours—until they become mealy but not mushy. Note that the minimal seasoning is because they will be combined with the Chili Sauce. When the beans are done to the degree you approve of, drain them and add to the sauce.

Serve in soup bowls with bread for a hearty meal. For those who like food really hot I put a bottle of Tabasco or some other commercially prepared hot sauce on the table.

MALLARD DUCK AND CABBAGE

The Matanuska Valley is famous for its cabbage, as I might mention now and then. The valley is also visited by many migratory birds each spring and fall. The area is like a feeding station, what with the grain in the fields and the many inviting lakes to swim around on. I used to find lots of nice mallards there each fall, and this is a recipe I often used to roast my catch. The combination of cabbage and duck makes excellent eating. You can substitute a domestic duck if you like, but either way try this combination.

1/4 pound slab bacon, cut in 1/4-inch
    cubes
1 large duck, about 5 pounds
1 1-pound cabbage
2 tablespoons onion, preferably green
    onion, chopped
1 clove garlic
1/2 teaspoon thyme
1/2 teaspoon fennel
1/4 teaspoon sage
1/4 teaspoon marjoram
1-1/2 cups sauerkraut juice from a crock
    or can

Fry the bacon in that Dutch oven or in a 4-quart casserole, stirring until the fat is rendered. Remove bacon bits from the grease and save both.

Cut the duck into quarters, dry thoroughly and brown in 2 tablespoons of bacon fat. While the duck is cooking shred the cabbage into 1/8-inch strips. Remove duck to a side plate.

Drain all grease from the pan and then add to the Dutch oven or casserole the remaining bacon grease, the cabbage, onion, garlic and spices. Cook uncovered at a moderate heat, stirring often, until the cabbage is limp. Then stir in the sauerkraut juice. Lay the pieces of duck on top of the cabbage and scatter the bacon bits over it all.

Cover and roast at 425° for 15 minutes. Reduce the heat to 325° and roast for at least an hour. If you suspect you might have a tough bird, roast slower and longer, starting with a 325° oven and keeping it that way. Test with a fork; if juice is transparent, not pink, the duck is done.

Tip the Dutch oven or casserole to one side and drain off the fat before serving this dish. Arrange the cabbage on a heated platter and place the pieces of duck around it. Yield: 4 servings.

GUNNYSACK GOOSE

In the fall of 1935 I first went hunting with my own gun. All my life I had lived with a gun readily available in a closet, in the corner of a room or hanging on a wall. I was taught to respect a gun and never to point it, either on purpose or by accident, at any person. Dad always said, "Never point a gun at anyone unless you *intend* to kill him!" Think on that a minute.

I don't know your reaction to Dad's statement, but to me it was my most important lesson in gun-handling. I was a successful policeman in a wild and woolly country for 21 years without ever pointing a gun at a single person. There was never a time during those years that I was in the slightest doubt of one point: If all else failed I would draw my weapon, point it at an individual, and kill, if events demanded this be done. I fully believe that this positive knowledge made itself felt by others and prevented me from ever having to use a gun against another person.

I am not talking about disarming policemen. I believe in extensive training in the use of firearms, and in the application of common sense in weapon use.

But let's get back to my first hunt with my own gun. I had bought a single-shot Stevens 12-gauge shotgun with my sum-

mer's earnings. Thus armed I was ready for the war with the ducks and geese.

Near Cordova the great Copper River meets the sea, and over untold years a vast estuary called the Flats has built up. I think all the migratory birds passing into and out of Alaska make a stop on these flats. When I was young, at least, it was one of the best hunting areas in the world.

I went to the Flats with a group of men, including Dad and my brother Ken, aboard a 35-foot fishing boat. We towed three new skiffs to be used for the actual hunting. After a full day's travel we anchored that evening in a slough.

It was during the evening that I first heard the term *gunnysack goose*. I didn't know what the men were discussing but I was not about to reveal my ignorance and ask. My reasoning was that it could be something like a snipe hunt, and I had already been through that experience. I also noticed a frown on Dad's face when the goose was mentioned.

In the morning, early, Ken and I rowed ashore in the dark and he led me to his favorite hunting spot. As the light came I found myself in a thicket of brush in a vast flat area. I couldn't see any game, but the cackle of geese could be heard close by.

KRAUT-STUFFED GOOSE

The goose that most often came my way in my early days of raising a family was the Canada goose, approximately in the 8-pound range. This bird tends to be dry when roasted and certainly has nowhere near the fat of a domestic goose. In this recipe I add some fat in the form of bacon, so if you wanted to try the recipe with a domestic goose reduce the bacon to just enough for your taste.

1/4 pound slab bacon, cut in 1/4-inch
    cubes
2 cups onion, chopped
4 pounds fresh or canned sauerkraut,
    drained
2 cups apples, chopped
1 cup potatoes, chopped
1/2 teaspoon salt
1/8 teaspoon black pepper
1 teaspoon sage
1 6- to 8-pound goose

Fry the bacon pieces to render some fat. Remove and reserve the bacon, add the onion and sauté until transparent. Add the sauerkraut and cook for 10 minutes.

In a large bowl combine the sauerkraut, bacon, onions, apples, potatoes, salt, pepper and sage. Mix thoroughly.

The goose should be washed well inside and out and dried carefully. Salt the inside of the cavity and fill it with the kraut mix-ture. Sew up the opening and truss the bird with string.

The goose should now be placed on the rack of a roasting pan, breast side up. Roast at 325° for 2-1/2 to 3 hours; 20 to 25 minutes a pound is the rule. At least twice during the cooking, baste the bird with the drippings.

When the goose is done, remove it to a serving platter and let set for 15 minutes before attempting to carve it. The dressing should be removed and served in a separate dish. It will likely be the best kraut you ever tried. Yield: 4 servings.

They were all around us, it seemed, in the dips in the terrain.

Suddenly a shot was heard from behind us. This was followed by a great rustle of feathers and wings as a massive flock of geese took off to the north of us. I've often described it to doubting listeners, but I'll try again. The sky actually turned black with Canada geese. I cannot even guess as to the number in that flock. I doubt if *thousands* would be the right description—maybe *hundreds of thousands* would be more accurate.

I remembered to put my one shot into the flock and watched a great goose crumple and fall. I didn't remember to load and shoot again, although my brother shot three times and got three geese.

When I reached my goose I was a thrilled young man. I wasn't thrilled at having killed something; that didn't enter my thoughts. After all, I had killed thousands of clams, crabs and fish. Where is a thrill to killing?

The chase, the taking of game, and the providing of food for my family was the basis of my thrill. At that moment I shared with untold generations something only a successful hunter can feel and understand. I have experienced this feeling many times since.

As this book is not about hunting, I had better get on with the stories. Let's go to Thanksgiving of the same year. The Nelson family was asked to join the Turner family for Thanksgiving dinner. The largest goose I had ever seen was brought to the table. I knew in the first seconds of eating that this was something new, something I had never tasted before. The flesh was lighter in color than that of goose, and the taste was delightful. I could not leave well

enough alone; I had to ask what kind of a bird we were eating.

"Gunnysack goose," came the answer from down the table. Not wishing to show my ignorance again, I smiled and kept my mouth shut.

The next day I caught my brother alone and asked him right out, "What is a gunnysack goose? And why does no one ever discuss hunting them?"

After first telling me that no one ever talked about hunting this bird because hunting it was illegal, Ken then told me that a gunnysack goose was a swan.

I already knew that even though large flocks of swans came through the Flats, we couldn't shoot them. This was not new, but the idea of the gunnysack had me puzzled. I asked about that.

Ken told me that the person hunting illegally would shoot a swan and place it in a gunnysack with several big rocks and then tie the mouth of the sack shut. Then, if a game warden encountered the hunter, the hunter threw the sack into the water. The rocks took the evidence away. This made swan hunting something to be considered, although most men were sportsmen enough to leave the swans alone. Out of the practice had come the name gunnysack goose.

Now I understood that frown on my father's face when the subject came up in hunting camp. But my, how he had enjoyed that Thanksgiving dinner!

I have never taken one of those great birds nor have I had the chance to eat one of them again, so you'll find no recipe for gunnysack goose in this book. However, after the taste that I had, I can understand why the bird was prized as a food bird and why it was once hunted so heavily that it had to be protected by all nations in the Western Hemisphere.

One summer a few years ago I worked with a man named Clement Z. Brooks, Clem for short. All summer long he talked about bird hunting. He liked to hunt ducks and geese but he talked especially about what he called "upland game." I gradually learned that this included partridge, pheasant, turkey and several species that I had never heard of before.

After a while I had too much of this talk, but first I had to uphold my end of the talking so I mentioned ptarmigan hunting a couple of times. He at once perked up and questioned me at some length. Before I knew it I had agreed to take him for a ptarmigan hunt in the fall.

One September morning found us 10 miles west of Paxson on the Denali Highway, armed to hunt ptarmigan. The vegetation then was high-mountain brush, knee-high, with moss-covered rocks here and there.

Clem was carrying about $1,000 worth of double-barreled 12-gauge shotgun. I was tempted to hide my old 20-gauge pump shotgun whenever his flashed in the sunlight.

It was a beautiful day and we were walking away from the road along a wide ridge. About 100 feet from the road we found our first action when two ptarmigan exploded out of the low brush. Their plumage was in the process of turning to winter white. I courteously waited for Clem to shoot, but he did not. Now I admit that these birds come out hard and fast but I somehow had expected a better response from Clem, the man who'd talked so much about hunting upland game.

I explained that those partly white birds had been ptarmigan. Clem allowed that he had thought so, but damn, they were sudden. We agreed to take turns shooting as we flushed birds.

Within a few more feet I kicked out a couple of ptarmigan and got a double with a fast crossing shot followed by a straightaway shot.

While I was out picking up my birds, I kicked up one more. Clem made an excellent crossing shot. He had a bird and a confident smile.

We continued along the ridge, kicking up one and two at a time. I was limiting myself to only one out of each turn, as Clem was having trouble. Every bird that he shot at was going away, and he just could not seem to put shot where the birds were. Clem was beginning to become irritated over his poor shooting.

About noon we sat down behind some willow brush to eat our lunch. Suddenly we could hear a bird coming down the hill behind us. A ptarmigan went right over our heads so fast we could almost hear a sonic boom. What we actually heard, and the reason for the ptarmigan's high speed, was a big hawk going full out after the ptarmigan. The two birds were only in sight for a second or two as they blasted down the hill and out of sight.

Clem turned to me and said, "Why didn't you tell me they could fly faster than sound? Now I'll just shoot at where I expect to hear them." I'm still not sure just what he meant, but he certainly understood what he meant. On our return walk he finished shooting his limit with ease. We soon both had our limits.

HUNTER'S STEW

This is a recipe with many options, depending on where you are standing when you decide to make the stew, what game or meat is available, and who you're trying to impress. I've tried to refine it down to 2 basic recipes, a recipe for using in my own kitchen and another for cooking in camp.

HOME STEW

3 breasts of ptarmigan, grouse or chicken, split in halves
2 26-ounce cans tomatoes
1 large onion, chopped
1/4 teaspoon sage
1 big pinch cayenne
1 clove garlic
1 teaspoon salt
1/4 cup butter
2 cups water
4 medium carrots, cut into 2-inch slices
4 medium potatoes, cut in 1-inch squares

For home stew, put all the ingredients except the potatoes and carrots into a 4-quart pot and bring to a boil. Simmer for 15 minutes, add the carrots, simmer for 30 minutes, and then add the potatoes. Simmer for another 20 minutes or until meat is tender.

CAMP STEW

3 breasts of ptarmigan or grouse, split in halves
2 26-ounce cans tomatoes
1/4 cup dehydrated onion
1/4 teaspoon sage
1 big pinch cayenne
1/2 teaspoon garlic powder
1 teaspoon salt
1/4 cup butter or bacon grease
2 cups water
1 16-ounce can carrots or peas and carrots
1 16-ounce can potatoes

For camp stew just simmer together all ingredients except potatoes and carrots for an hour or until the meat is tender. Then drain the canned potatoes and carrots and add them to the other ingredients. Melt the butter or bacon grease in the frying pan, drain the bird breasts, and brown them.

Serve the vegetables in big deep bowls with the pieces of bird on top. You'll enjoy this at home, but I've always found that it tastes just a little better when you're sitting around a campfire. Yield: enough for 2 hungry hunters, otherwise 4 servings.

There are many recipes for what to do with ptarmigan when you have a number of them but my favorite is ptarmigan stew, and that was what I made for Clem that night. I'm sure that the stew wasn't the only reason why he became addicted to ptarmigan hunting but it was a contributing factor.

Alaska has another bird that Clem would have classed as upland game. It's the grouse or, as commonly known here, the spruce hen.

There may be a dumber bird in existence somewhere, but our spruce hen certainly rates high in stupidity. I've seen a grouse sit on a branch of a tree while several fellows, taking turns, shot at it 14 times with a 22-caliber pistol. I know because I was one of the shooters. The front sight of the pistol had been damaged in a fall and that prevented us from hitting the bird. Well, that's my story. Before someone could compound the story further by firing the 15th shot I threw a stick at the bird and it suddenly became aware that it was in danger and left.

Another time I was driving along the Richardson Highway and spotted two grouse in a gravel pit loading pebbles. (Spruce grouse take small pebbles into their craws to grind up their food the way chickens do.) I stopped and worked around to where I could get a shot at one. When I shot, the closest bird went straight up in the air with its wings beating like mad. It almost went out of sight it was up so high. Then it stopped flying and fell. The bird fell hard because it had died way up there. My shot had taken the top of its

head off and, not being used to using a brain, it had flown that high before dying. The second bird got away while I watched its high-flying buddy.

One day in my youth I followed a flock of spruce hens up a valley and found a "lost" mine. I started up the area in heavy timber to scare up a spruce hen or two. I spooked a flock of them and shot one. The rest of the grouse proved smarter than usual and flew farther up the valley. I followed along behind, every now and then spotting a roosting bird and shooting, as they led me farther and farther into the valley.

The valley ended in a little clearing, and facing me was a cave opening in the rock wall. I just had to go check the cave. As I approached I could see that it was really an old mine shaft that had been driven into the mountain. The timbers around the entrance were badly rotted away.

I stood there wondering what someone had been looking for when this shaft had been dug. I wasn't about to go into the mine and look as I had always been warned about old mines. But I could dig around in the tailing dump on the hillside.

I found three green copper nuggets. These were native copper and next in value to pure copper. One nugget weighed almost three pounds, while the others were not over a pound. If I had found gold I couldn't have been more excited.

I could hardly wait to get home and tell Dad about my find. I can still remember his saying, "Yep! It's copper all right. Nice nuggets, too." But there was no excitement in his voice over my lost mine. Then he told me about many people prospecting in that area in the early days and the many holes they had driven into the mountains. Often copper was found, as in my mine, but not in the quantities necessary for

large-scale mining. So the people's dreams died, just as mine did that day.

I had the copper nuggets for years, until a house fire, and then they were lost.

Where is my lost copper mine? Well, I can best describe it as a few miles north of Cordova, three spruce hens to the east, and across the creek. OK?

While many people hunt and enjoy the spruce hen, it is not my favorite bird. The taste is often strong and the ptarmigan is much better. But in case you stumble onto a couple and shoot them, I'll throw in a couple of recipes.

GROUSE AND NOODLES

As I have mentioned, I prefer other game birds to the grouse, but when only grouse are available this is the recipe that I most often use. Try it with ptarmigan or even chicken.

2 grouse or 1 large ptarmigan or chicken
Water
1 medium onion, chopped
1 cup celery, chopped
3 bay leaves
1 teaspoon cinnamon
1/4 teaspoon cloves, crushed
1/2 teaspoon salt
1/8 teaspoon black pepper
3 cups flat egg noodles
2 tablespoons butter

Place the cleaned birds in a Dutch oven or casserole and add water until the pot is three quarters full. Add the onion, celery, spices, salt and pepper. Cover, bring to a boil, and reduce heat to a simmer, cooking the birds for 2 hours or until tender. Remove the birds from the pot, drain, cool, and strip the meat from the bones.

Strain the cooking liquid to remove all the solids, then return the liquid to the pot, bring to a boil, add the noodles, and cook until tender.

While the noodles are cooking, brown the boned meat lightly in the butter in a frying pan. Drain the noodles, arrange on a platter, and make a circle of grouse or chicken meat around the noodles. Yield: 4 servings.

ORANGE-BRAISED DUCKS

With the exception of the big mallards, I have found most ducks not worth the effort to shoot, clean and cook. However, if you happen to shoot some small ducks, this recipe could save the day. It has saved my reputation as a cook a couple of times.

2 4-pound ducks or 4 2-pound ducks
1/4 cup vegetable oil
2 cups chicken stock
12 whole cloves
1/4 teaspoon cayenne
1 green or red pepper, cut in strips
1 cup orange juice
2 tablespoons lime juice
1/4 teaspoon salt

Dry the ducks inside and out and brown in the vegetable oil in a frying pan. Remove the ducks, pour off the oil, and scrape any brown particles from the frying pan into a Dutch oven or casserole. Put a cup of the chicken stock, the cloves and cayenne into the casserole and stir. Add the ducks and the pepper, cover tightly and braise for an hour, in the oven or on top of the stove. Remove the ducks and pick out the cloves.

Add the orange juice, lime juice and salt to the mixture in the pot, stir, and return the much moved ducks. Baste the ducks, cover and bake at 375° for 30 minutes or until done.

Serve on a heated platter, pouring the cooking sauce into a gravy boat. Yield: 4 servings.

SMOTHERED CHICKEN

Several years ago I stumbled onto sour cream cooking, and the variety of dishes we subsequently prepared using this marvelous ingredient appeared endless. The fad seems to have faded. These days I can take sour cream cooking or leave it— except for a few dishes. This chicken-and-sour-cream recipe has stood the test of time.

1 2- to 3-pound chicken, cut up for frying
3 tablespoons butter
1/2 teaspoon salt
1/4 teaspoon black pepper
2 tablespoons flour
1 cup sour cream
1 teaspoon poppy seeds
2 cups water
2 teaspoons lemon juice

In a large frying pan or Dutch oven brown the chicken in the butter. Season with the salt and pepper and remove the chicken from the pan. Stir the flour into the drippings, then blend in the sour cream, poppy seeds and water. Bring to a boil while stirring. Return the chicken to the pan, cover, and simmer for 45 minutes or until the chicken is tender. Stir in the lemon juice.

Serve on a warm platter with the sauce poured over the chicken. Yield: 4 servings.

BAKE-FRIED CHICKEN

The chicken is a wonderful bird. She eats well, lays eggs, and makes manure for the garden while alive. Dead, she makes wonderful eating, roasted, broiled, fried or however we would cook her. Unlike the wild birds, she can be carefully selected for tenderness, size and anticipated cooking method. I like the chicken! Fried, especially, like this.

2 chickens, cut up for frying
Margarine
1/4 cup flour
1/4 cup corn meal
1/4 cup dried milk
1 tablespoon paprika
Dash of monosodium glutamate
Salt and black pepper
Or, instead of dry ingredients, prepared
   coating for frying chickens

Thoroughly dry the chicken pieces with paper towels.

This recipe requires 2 oven pans about 10" by 16" coated with margarine. My method for coating is to put a cube of margarine in each pan and place the pans in the oven while it is being preheated. I remove the pans when the margarine is melted and tilt the pans to coat the insides.

Mix together all remaining ingredients and pour the mixture, or a commercial coating, into a paper bag. Put the pieces of chicken, 2 or 3 at a time, into the bag, shake a few times, and remove the chicken, knocking off any excess coating. Place the coated chicken pieces in the pans.

Put the pans in a 350° oven for 30 minutes, then turn the pieces of chicken over and bake-fry for another 25 minutes.

Serve the crisp brown chicken immediately on a heated platter. The drippings can be used to make excellent gravy, so have some boiled spuds ready to use it up. Yield: 8 servings.

KERALA CHICKEN STEW

Our life in Juneau resulted in many wonderful memories. Among them is that of our friendship with a man from Kerala, India. We knew him as P.K. because he had found that we Alaskans had some trouble pronouncing his name and with the fact that his last name came first. However, we had no trouble understanding that he was a good friend and companion.

P.K. showed us how to make chicken stew as it was made by his family in Kerala. *Almost* the same, as he admitted to reducing, or Americanizing, the spices a little. When my family is all together someone is bound to suggest that we use P.K.'s recipe for chicken. And it is very nice that we can remember P.K. every time we eat it.

2 medium onions, chopped
2 tablespoons salad oil
2 4- or 5-pound chickens, cut up for frying
1/2 cup coconut milk (purchased in
    powdered form at a health food store)
    or liquid drained from a coconut
1-1/2 teaspoons ginger
1/2 teaspoon cardamon
1/3 teaspoon cinnamon
1/4 teaspoon cloves, crushed
1/4 teaspoon turmeric
1/3 teaspoon black pepper
2 large potatoes, cut in 1/2-inch slices

In a large pot sauté the onions in the salad oil until transparent. Add the chicken, and lightly fry for 5 minutes, stirring often. Add the coconut milk, spices and pepper, cover, and simmer for 2 minutes. Stir well, cover again, and simmer for 10 minutes more. Add the potatoes, stir, cover, and simmer for 20 minutes, stirring once again halfway through the simmering. Now the chicken and potatoes should be done, but test the chicken to be sure.

Serve the chicken pieces in one dish, potatoes in another, and the juice separately. You'll need lots of paper towels or napkins. Yield: 8 servings.

CLARA'S RICE (WITH CHICKEN)

This recipe is being offered at this time for 2 reasons. First to prove to you that not all my recipes are not as old as I am, and second because the notes I took while watching my Aunt Clara make it a couple of months ago just fell out of my notebook. You'll see that this is a modern up-to-date recipe.

2 cups Minute Rice
1 10-ounce can chicken soup
1 10-ounce can mushroom soup
1 10-ounce can onion soup
3 chicken breasts
8 chicken thighs
Paprika

For this recipe you will need just 2 utensils: a baking dish and a spoon. Pour the Minute Rice into the baking dish, empty the cans of soup into the rice and stir until there is some of everything in every corner of the dish.

Now place the pieces of chicken on top of the rice, skin side up, and sprinkle paparika over the chicken. Bake at 275° for 3 hours.

Serve this meal in the dish it cooked in. Fresh broccoli is excellent with this rice. Yes, it's a rice dish—the chicken is just there for the flavoring. You could throw the chicken away and enjoy the rice alone, but don't, because you will find that, aside from making the rice good, it's good chicken. Yield: 6 generous servings.

TROPICAL CHICKEN

The idea of adding fruit, especially tropical fruit such as bananas and pineapple, to main-course dishes has always fascinated me. I've tried many main-dish recipes involving fruit and found few that I liked, but a couple were great. Try this.

1 3- or 4-pound chicken, cut up for frying
1/4 cup butter
1/2 teaspoon salt
1/4 teaspoon black pepper
1-1/2 cups water
3 tablespoons onion, minced
3/4 cup barbeque sauce
1/2 cup molasses
1 9-ounce can crushed pineapple
4 tablespoons cornstarch
1 cup green pepper, sliced
4 bananas, sliced

In a large frying pan brown the chicken pieces in the butter and season with salt and pepper. Add the water, onion, barbeque sauce and molasses. Cover and simmer for 40 minutes. Now remove the chicken. Combine the syrup from the pineapple with the cornstarch and gradually pour this mixture into the pan, stirring constantly. When contents of pan are well mixed, you should have a thickened sauce. Now add the green pepper and the pineapple. Cover and cook for 5 minutes, then stir in the bananas.

Serve by placing chicken pieces on a platter mounded with rice. Pour part of the sauce over the platter and serve the rest in individual bowls. Yield: 4 servings.

TWO-WAY HOT CHICKEN

People from nearly every nation in the world, every culture, religion and geographic area seem to cook chicken. The ways that this ubiquitous bird is prepared for eating must number in the thousands. After our experience with our Indian friend, P.K., my mind was open to trying some ways of preparing chicken that were different from what I'd been used to. This one, hot from the oven and hot from spices, was among the interesting results.

1 2- to 3-pound chicken, cut up for frying
Water to cover chicken pieces
1 tablespoon lemon juice
1 teaspoon salt
4 tablespoons butter
3 large onions, chopped
4 tablespoons chili powder
2 tablespoons tomato paste
4 tablespoons red wine
1/2 teaspoon powdered ginger
1/2 teaspoon black pepper
6 hard-boiled eggs

Place the chicken in your trusty Dutch oven or a 4- to 6-quart pot and cover with water. Add the lemon juice and salt. Bring to a boil, cover, and simmer for 10 minutes. Remove from the stove, lift out and drain the chicken pieces, and save 2 cups of the liquid.

Now put the butter in the Dutch oven and sauté the onions to a light brown. Add the chili powder, tomato paste, and a cup of the chicken liquid and simmer for 5 minutes; then add the wine, ginger, pepper and the other cup of chicken liquid. Return the chicken pieces to the mixture and simmer until done.

Shell the eggs, piercing each one with a knife in 6 places, and drop the eggs into the pot for 3 minutes.

I suggest serving this with the chicken and eggs arranged on a platter heaped with rice. The cooking liquid can be used as a sauce, thickened if desired. Yield: 4 servings.

STUFFING THE BIRD

As far back as I can remember the male members of my family have been dragging home dead game and geese. When I was married, I discovered that during our 2-year courtship my new wife, Connie, and I had hunted in a lot of Alaska. I also discovered that Connie was not thrilled at all by bringing home the fruit of the hunt. She didn't want to have anything to do with the stuff, so I was the appointed game-cleaner and cook. It became necessary for me to research my mother's and my mother's friends' cooking notes if the birds I had bagged were to be enjoyed. I have since discovered that the stuffings I found will work equally well in chicken or turkeys. Just adjust the amounts to fit the bird.

MICHIGAN WILD RICE STUFFING— MY MOTHER'S FAVORITE
1 teaspoon salt
1 cup wild rice (OK, it's expensive, so
    how about 1/4 cup wild and
    3/4 brown)
2 cups onion, chopped
1/4 cup celery, chopped
3 tablespoons butter
1/8 teaspoon cayenne or 1 teaspoon
    chili powder

Put the salt in about 3 cups of water in a large saucepan and bring to a boil. Slowly add the rice, then simmer for 30 minutes or until the rice is tender.

While the rice is cooking, sauté the onion and celery in the butter until transparent. Stir in the cayenne.

Drain the rice, stir in the celery and onion, and stuff your bird. As it roasts this mixture will mellow the creature into something out of this world.

CLAM STUFFING
1 cup onion, chopped
1/4 cup celery, chopped
3 tablespoons butter
1 cup clams, minced, or contents of 1
    8-ounce can
2 cups bread crumbs
1/2 cup seedless raisins
1/4 teaspoon dried parsley
1 teaspoon sage
1/2 teaspoon salt
1/4 teaspoon black pepper
2 eggs, beaten

In a large frying pan sauté the onion and celery in the butter until just soft. Add the clams, bread crumbs, raisins, parsley, sage, salt and pepper. Stir all these together and then add the beaten eggs and stir again as it cooks for 5 more minutes.

Now stuff your bird. Incidentally, you can try this recipe with oysters instead of clams. It is equally as good.

MARINATED MOOSE ROAST

Because apple trees are almost non-existent in Alaska, you can be sure that any apple product you see here is shipped in from the Lower 48. I've always been happy that the apple and apple cider seasons come at the same time as the moose-hunting season. That way I can turn a fresh moose roast into a marinated roast, which is really fine eating. Try this recipe with a roast of beef, too.

3 cups apple cider
2 medium onions, cut in chunks
1 good-size carrot, cut in chunks
1-1/2 cups red wine
1/4 teaspoon thyme
1 bay leaf
6 juniper berries or 1 tablespoon gin
10 peppercorns
1/4 teaspoon dried parsley
1 5- or 6-pound rib roast

The first thing you will need is a large enamel or stainless steel pan both for heating the marinade and containing the marinating meat later on.

Put 1/2 cup of the cider, along with the onions and carrot, into a blender. Blend until you have a liquid, and pour that into the pan. Add the rest of the cider and all other ingredients except the meat. Bring the mixture to a boil and simmer for 15 minutes.

Cool this marinade to room temperature and add the meat, which should marinate for 24 hours. Turn the meat every few hours. After the meat has marinated remove it from the liquid and set aside to drain while you strain the solids from the liquid. Save the liquid.

Completely dry the roast, then place it on the rack of a roasting pan.

Put the roast into a 500° oven. After 20 minutes baste the meat with 1/2 cup of the marinade and reduce the heat to 350°. Baste the roast every 15 minutes. It's done when your meat thermometer reads rare, medium or well done, whichever is your choice.

Transfer to a platter and let the meat rest 10 minutes before carving. Yield: 5 servings.

LOWBUSH AND HIGHBUSH MOOSE

In the summer of 1936 my family left Cordova and moved to Anchorage, which at that time consisted of about 3,500 people gathered rather closely round the railroad yards. The first thing that impressed me about Anchorage was the fact that the city was laid out in regular square blocks, with wide streets. I soon discovered that they ran north-south and east-west. You see, up until this time I had lived in towns and cities that had streets that followed such things as the contour of the land, stream beds, railroad tracks, horse trails, Indian trails and the paths that fishermen used from their boats to their homes.

In my 50-odd years I have lived 23 of those years in the city of Anchorage, for four different periods. This, combined with the fact of my graduation from Anchorage High School, class of 1941, would seem to make Anchorage my hometown. At least I call it that. The city has changed over the years. Today it is close to 200,000 people, and they're expanding into the surrounding areas. Anchorage is certainly not the same as when I first saw it.

There used to be a great tall water tower on the northeast side of town. This provid-ed the water supply for all of us. Around the base of the town there was considerable brush, and in 1936 you could still find rabbits in places like that. So one fall day I was thrashing around in this brush and came out under the water tower. As I stepped out into the clearing another young man came from the brush on the other side of the tower. He too was carrying a rifle. We stood looking at each other for a few seconds and then started talking. He was moose-hunting, which I thought odd, as I had seen no moose. He thought that my quest was equally ridiculous, as he had seen not a single rabbit. So, based on this beginning, we continued to talk and became fast friends. His name was Phil and we shared many youthful adventures and a few later ones.

Down on Ship Creek, near where the main gate to Elmendorf Air Force Base is now located, Phil and I built a hunting camp. It was about a 2-1/2-mile walk from our homes by the route we used, which wandered along the old Loop Road beside the creek. We spent most of our weekends during the next few years going to, coming from, or entertaining ourselves at that camp. What we were hunting in the begin-

HERB-STUFFED RABBIT

The Arctic hare can be a dry piece of meat, especially a hare taken in the winter. I've heard it told that you could eat nothing but rabbit, which has no fat, and starve to death. But who wants rabbit that often? A woman in Gakona showed me this way to cook hare; she claimed to have used this method over a campfire on the trail and I see no reason to doubt her. You can even try it with a domestic, from-the-meat-market rabbit.

1/4 teaspoon rosemary
1 teaspoon dried parsley
1/8 teaspoon wine vinegar
1/4 cup butter
1 2- to 3-pound rabbit, cut in pieces

In a small dish crush the rosemary and parsley and add the vinegar and butter. Stir and let blend while you wash and dry the rabbit pieces.

With a sharp paring knife make a slit in the flesh of each piece of rabbit. Put a teaspoon of the herb butter in each pocket. Close the pockets with toothpicks or skewers.

Put the rabbit pieces in a pan and place the pan about 4 inches below a broiler. Turn the pieces after 15 minutes and broil another 15 minutes. Baste with the remaining butter mixture as necessary. Yield: 4 servings.

ning was rabbits, but later our interests changed and the camp area was where we entertained female companions.

When we entered high school we met two girls who were also interested in such things as hiking, cooking out, hunting, fishing and the opposite sex. After considerable milling around and getting acquainted, Phil and I finally decided to show the girls our camp.

We had a lot of fun, just young-people-together type fun. The walking, talking, bits of hunting, outdoors cooking and companionship were enjoyed by all. Our togetherness lasted the best part of two years. As it happened we paired off toward the end of the period, but that is another story.

The girls' first rabbit I remember still. Phil and I had sent the girls walking down through a clearing while he and I thrashed the brush on either side to scare them out a rabbit. The girls were out of sight.

Suddenly there was a shot and then a period of silence. Then another shot, a single high-pitched scream, a silence and then screaming from both girls. I ran toward the sound as the screaming went on and on. I envisioned one of the girls shot, or a bear in their trail.

I burst on the scene to find that the girls had a rabbit down. One girl had the rabbit pressed to the ground with her rifle barrel. The other girl, with great determination, was trying to kill the rabbit. It seemed that either beating it to death with the gun butt, or shooting it again, were alternately passing through their minds. Both girls were completely intent on what they were doing, but all three, the two girls and the rabbit, were screaming. Before I could reach the group another shot was fired and it was all over. The sudden silence was startling. The girls had bagged their first rabbit.

They too were now hunters, and had provided meat for the family, for we were a sort of family. Yes, we cooked and ate their rabbit that Saturday afternoon. I sometimes wonder if the one of those girls who is still living remembers the feeling of that day.

It used to be that when you said *meat* in most of Alaska you meant game meat. In season, it was often moose. At all other times, in the area where I lived, the only meat readily available from the land was lowbush moose—rabbit.

I know there are no rabbits in Alaska except domestic rabbits. Those brown, gray or white things that hop all over the land are Arctic hares. So maybe our name of *lowbush moose* is more accurate than *rabbit*.

The Arctic hare is fairly strong-tasting meat. A bit wild, some say, but eat it anyway. Others soak the meat in salt water overnight, or even for just a few hours. This takes most of the wild taste out of the meat. Try one of the rabbit recipes here if you do take an Arctic hare.

Having discussed the lowbush moose, let's turn to the highbush moose or, to you, just plain moose. The moose is a large dumb animal that looks as if it was designed by three drunk hunters who were trying to improve on the elk. During the winter, spring and summer it would seem that you are stumbling over moose everywhere. They jump out of the trees and land in front of your car, walk through your flower garden with their large feet, and eat all the good stuff in your vegetable garden. But come fall and the hunting season the males, at least (the only sex of moose that can be legally shot these days), evaporate into thin air and can only be found far back in the woods and only in the early morning or late evening, if at all.

Moose like people, and they seem to gather where people live. I have a very simple theory about this fact. Wherever man goes he removes the large vegetation such as trees. Whether this is done deliberately or accidentally is immaterial. When this occurs the plant life comes back as second growth, willows and such. Moose feed on second growth so they move in to eat the things they like. Then people begin to stumble over moose. I'll admit to oversimplification, but I'll stand on my theory.

It doesn't matter why the bull moose is where he is as long as you find him during the hunting season. So my advice is as follows. Go forth into the woods and find a young three-year-old bull that has been in good feed and lazy as hell all summer. On the first day of hunting season you get up early, get to the moose before anyone else, and shoot him. You'll find yourself with a great deal of excellent meat on your hands—not, I hope, too far from your means of transportation.

My wife's first moose was very much like the one I've just described. All summer I had watched him hanging around a farmer's oat field in the Matanuska Valley.

I talked to the farmer and recieved permission to hunt in his field. At the first crack of dawn, on the first day of moose season, Connie and I were standing on the highest point of this field. From there we could see the entire field and an unplanted clearing behind it.

There was a short wait as the light drifted across the field and a few patches of mist developed in the darkest corner. Then three moose seemed to rise out of the ground. We had managed to get up before the moose that morning. With the glasses I picked out the young bull moose that we wanted and pointed him out to Connie.

I stood to one side with my rifle ready, planning to fire quickly if she missed. The crack of her rifle split the morning air, there was the solid *thunk* of a bullet hitting meat, and down went her moose. We waited a couple of minutes to see if the animal was going to get up. Nothing happened.

We had to walk about 200 yards through head-high oats to reach the moose. Just as we reached the end of the oats Connie's moose jumped to its feet and started to run. I lifted my rifle to my shoulder when Connie's rifle cracked again. The moose went down like someone had hit him on top of the head. When we walked up to him, he was definitely dead. Connie's last shot had taken him right behind the left ear and ended his foolishness. He had already been shot through the heart and was dead anyway; he was just too dumb to know it.

Later we discussed Connie's fabulous shot at a running moose. As far as I knew she had never shot at a moving target in her life. Her explanation was simple. All she saw when that animal jumped and ran was a great pile of roasts, steaks and even mooseburger getting away. That was not

acceptable, so she shot it in the head. Talk about thinking positively!

The tender young bull was one of the best-eating moose we ever brought home. The fat across the back was nearly like prime beef. After a few days' hanging in our garage, the moose was made into those roasts, steaks and mooseburger that Connie had envisioned and then it was all tucked away in our freezer. That meat certainly helped feed our family of eight that winter.

Not all moose that are taken are as tender as Connie's first one. I've dragged home moose so tough that you couldn't chew it. The winter season of 1953 found us still without our winter's meat. We were living at Glennallen on the Glen Highway at the time.

My hunting partner and I ventured forth on a cold day in November to find some meat. It was 30° below zero at noon that day. Just as it was getting dark we found and shot a very large, old bull moose. We just had time to clean and cut the animal into pack loads before it became too dark to see. We covered the pile of meat with the hide and left it for the night.

The trip back to the car was through three feet of loose snow for a mile, and uphill besides. It was 45° below when we reached home that night. A hot buttered rum, a bite to eat, and I was happy to climb into bed.

By the end of the next day we had the moose hanging in my garage. I cut off some nice steaks from the loin and we started cooking. The steak as it broiled smelled delicious. But the steak that

BLODGETT LAKE BURGERS

While my family was spending part of a summer on Blodgett Lake in the Matanuska Valley, we were introduced to another way to make ground moose or ground beef taste good. An elderly man of Finnish background invited the whole family over to his place for lunch. He served a beautiful salad of lettuce, onions and radishes from his garden along with something he called Minnesota Beef Burgers.

To make these burgers he started by frying a sliced medium onion in about 3 tablespoons butter. When the onion was barely transparent he crumbled 2 pounds of hamburger into the pan, salted and peppered it, and stirred so that the meat cooked in small pieces.

When the meat was done he served it on buttered halves of hamburger buns. All of us enjoyed this style of beef, which the kids later named Blodgett Lake Burgers. Yield: 4 to 6 servings.

BOUQUET OF MOOSE

During the period of our lives when we were both working, Connie and I developed some shortcuts for cooking. With the help of well-trained children and automatic timing devices, not to mention luck, we made some interesting meals. Some of those timed meals were all right, but with today's meat prices, I prefer to depend on myself to watch the meat. This recipe takes a minimum of effort.

1 cup vegetable oil or beef fat (see
page 27)
1/4 cup Kitchen Bouquet
1 4-pound roast: a center cut with round
bone in it, either moose or beef
Salt and black pepper
8 unpeeled potatoes, thoroughly washed

In a large frying pan heat the oil or fat until very hot. Meanwhile, brush Kitchen Bouquet on the pot roast and rub in the Kitchen Bouquet along with salt and pepper. Carefully ease the roast into the hot fat, sear the meat, turn it, and sear the other side.

Remove the roast from the frying pan and place on the rack of a roasting pan. Cover and roast at 350° for an hour. Turn the roast over, place the potatoes around it, and roast for 1-1/4 hours more.

Slice the meat and serve on a heated platter with the potatoes arranged around the meat. Yield: 6 servings.

MOOSE AND LIVER HAMBURGERS

During the winter of the tough moose, we tried many ways to dress up the meat a bit. This recipe helped us with those 400 pounds that we had to grind up.

1 pound ground moose or beef
1/2 pound beef liver, ground or chopped
    fine
1/4 cup onion, minced
1 cup quick-cooking oatmeal
1 teaspoon salt

Thoroughly mix the ingredients. Form the mixture into patties about 4 inches across and 3/4 inch thick.

Broil the patties or fry in a pan with some shortening, turning once. Yield: 4 servings.

reached my mouth was so tough that I could not chew it. You could cut the meat with a sharp knife, but chew it you could not. We tried until our jaws ached. We managed to slice it thin and swallow some whole but found this completely unsatisfactory. I remembered a song about a razorback hog that was so tough you couldn't stick a fork in the gravy, but I didn't feel like singing.

The next day we tried boiling, roasting and finally pressure-cooking our moose. There was no way that you could chew it, and this was our winter's meat. We had nearly 800 pounds of it. If we didn't eat this it would be rabbit all winter. So Operation Mooseburger was born.

I drove into Palmer and picked up 50 pounds of beef suet and we borrowed a big commercial meat grinder from one of the lodges. We were ready to begin.

I don't want you to get the idea that the operation was easy. It took four of us, two men and their wives, nearly a week to process the moose. It resisted being boned and it required triple grinding, mixing with the suet, and a final grinding. It did not resist the packaging and freezing. At the end of our week of hard work we had 800 pounds of mooseburger: 400 pounds for each family.

Connie's mother sent a book entitled *365 Ways to Cook Hamburger* for Christmas. We tried at least 200 of them that winter. The mooseburger was tasty—a bit tough, but at least chewable.

I mentioned that moose are dumb, but once in a while a small indication of intelligence shows. Like they figure out that it is easier to walk on streets and on sidewalks, which are cleared of snow, than out there in the woods. So they come into towns in the winter. They like your special shrubbery as a change of diet, too.

After they have been in town for a while they lose all fear of man and dog. In fact they seem to develop a definite hatred for dogs. Oh yes, they do get somewhat irritated at some of the dumb things that men do, too.

One winter in Palmer we had an old cow moose of some 1,000 pounds on the hoof that adopted a family on the edge of town. The family kept finding the moose standing on their porch in the morning.

The husband chased her off so he could go to work and then the wife chased her off so that the kids could go to school and she could go to the store. In the afternoon they chased her off so the kids could come home and, later, so the husband could. This went on for several days until they finally called me.

The husband had had enough of the moose and really was just interested in shooting her. I talked him into trying to simply chase her away. We got her started away from the house just fine. She was

moving quite well until we reached the deep snow, and then we discovered that she did not wish to go snow-wading.

I was standing in four feet of snow about 100 feet from the nearest road when the cow decided she had been pushed as far as she was going. Suddenly she stopped, the hair on her back stood up, and she charged right at me.

I was in trouble. I couldn't get my feet out of the snow fast enough to dodge her charge. I thought of shooting her with my trusty .38, but she was too close. If I hit her, she would just fall on me, and I didn't want 1,000 pounds of moose either lying or standing on me. So I took a chance, and when she got within reach I whipped off my fur hat and slapped her across the eyes with it. She stopped, squealed and turned away, with a very hurt expression on her face. Again I had survived by doing the unexpected.

Later that night she was back on the porch again. We finally got Fish & Game to come up and shoot her with a tranquilizer gun. Then we loaded her on a truck with a crane and drove her 10 miles away. She never came back for a repeat of that ride.

I've selected an assortment of recipes for lowbush and highbush moose critters for the next few pages. As you might guess, I have hundreds more, but enough is enough. Any highbush moose recipe works just fine for beef, too.

MARINATED HARE

Once upon a time there lived a man in the Matanuska Valley who raised rabbits. Rabbits, not hares. He enjoyed eating rabbits and frowned upon the wild Arctic hare as less than desirable. Every once in a while one of his rabbits would escape and disappear into the bushes where the Arctic hares lived. One day the man saw an Arctic hare in its white winter fur, but this one had a large black spot on it. He shot the animal and discovered that it was bigger and fatter than the Arctic hare. He cooked it after marinating it in wine, as he was accumstomed to doing, and found it excellent. The story says he opened his cages and turned all his rabbits loose. The man is long gone, but there is a certain place I've heard of where the Arctic hares are big, fat and tasty even today.

Should you find one of the above, or just buy a rabbit in the market, try this method of cooking it.

1 3- or 4-pound rabbit
1-1/2 cups dry white wine
3 tablespoons vinegar
1/4 cup vegetable oil
1 medium onion, sliced thin
1/2 teaspoon thyme
1 bay leaf
1 teaspoon dried parsley
1/2 teaspoon salt
1/4 teaspoon black pepper
1 tablespoon butter
1/4 pound slab bacon, in 1/4-inch cubes
4 small onions
2 cloves garlic
2 tablespoons flour
1-1/4 cups beef stock

It is the marinade that is the most important part of this recipe, as that is what turns just plain rabbit into something special. Wash and dry the pieces of rabbit and place them in a shallow pan so that all the pieces will be in the marinade.

Combine the wine, vinegar, oil, sliced onion, thyme, bay leaf, parsley, salt and pepper. Mix lightly and pour over the rabbit pieces and refrigerate for 24 hours, turning the pieces at least 3 times.

When it is time to cook the rabbit put the butter in a frying pan and sauté the bacon pieces. Drain the bits of bacon after the fat is rendered and save the bits and the fat.

Remove the rabbit from the marinade, dry the pieces, and fry them in the bacon grease. As the pieces brown, place them in a casserole with the 4 whole onions.

Pour most of the bacon grease out of the frying pan, drop in the garlic, and stir for 2 minutes. Add the flour, remove pan from the heat, and stir in the beef stock and 1/2 cup of the marinade. Stir constantly at this stage. Return the mixture to the heat and stir until the liquid thickens. Pour this sauce over the rabbit, add enough of the remaining marinade to cover the pieces, and scatter bacon bits over the top.

Bring to a boil on the stove and then bake, covered, at 350° for an hour. Serve right from the casserole. Yield: 4 servings.

CHOPPED MOOSE ROQUEFORT

The moose meat that we had was usually quite lean, so if we were grinding it we would add beef suet to it on the second grinding. However, once I discovered this recipe, I always packaged up some of the mooseburger without the suet. If you want one of the greatest eating experiences in the world, but don't have lean moose available, try this recipe with ground round or lean ground beef. The ingredients listed here are for 1 person; you'll need to allow more per person if you're serving big eaters.

1/2 pound lean ground meat
3 tablespoons butter
Salt and black pepper
1 ounce Roquefort or blue cheese,
    crumbled or sliced thin

Make a beef patty by placing 1/4 pound of the meat between 2 pieces of waxed paper and flattening the meat into a thin patty—about 6 inches across. Do the same with the remaining meat. Since each serving is 2 patties, remember when preparing this for several people to end up with an even number of patties.

Pick out a frying pan wide enough to handle 2 patties side by side. Melt the butter in the pan and put in the patties. Salt and pepper them to taste. Cook over a medium heat until the bottom is done, turn, and cover with the cheese. When the patties are done, stack one on top of the other and serve hot from the pan. Or keep the patties in a warm oven and serve them all together.

It almost became a tradition in my family to have fresh broccoli and little, new potatoes in a cream sauce with these meat delights.

Note: You can make these with plain old Cheddar cheese for those who say they cannot stand Roquefort or blue cheese. I have noticed that the younger generation's tastes often do not include Roquefort; they tend to taste with their noses rather than their tongues.

MOOSE LOAF CHISTOCHINA

This recipe was given to me by the wife of my hunting partner in the tough-moose episode. I've used it more with the trusty hamburger, though, than with moose-burger. Either way it's quick and tasty.

1 pound ground meat
1 cup quick-cooking oatmeal
2 eggs, beaten
1 onion, chopped
1 3-ounce can chopped pimentos
1 teaspoon salt
1/4 teaspoon black pepper
1/4 teaspoon nutmeg

Thoroughly mix all ingredients together; some people find it easiest to do this with their hands. Pack the resulting mixture into a greased meat loaf tin or bread pan. Bake for an hour at 350°.

For variation I substitute 1/4 cup of finely chopped green peppers for the pimentos. Yield: 4 servings.

CORNED BEEF AND CABBAGE

The best corned beef I ever found was made up in the back of the butcher shop of a Juneau supermarket. The butcher made it himself, and you had to ask for it because not a single pound ever found its way into the meat case. His regular customers were always aware when another batch was about done. Beside his efforts you needed:

2 to 3 pounds corned beef
4 medium onions
8 good-size carrots, peeled
1 large cabbage, quartered

For this I like to use my big Dutch oven, but a soup pot works just as well. Put the corned beef into the pot and pour in enough cold water to cover the meat. Bring to a boil and skim off the skum that appears on the surface. Reduce the heat, cover and simmer.

Add the onions and carrots when the pot has simmered for 3-1/2 hours; after another 1/2 hour add the cabbage.

After the pot has simmered for a total of 5 hours test the carrots for tenderness. If they're done, you're ready to serve. The beef will be a beautiful red color and very tender. Remove the meat from the pot, drain, trim off most of the fat, and slice against the grain. Surround the slices of meat with the vegetables on a large platter.

This is a filling and tasty single-dish meal, and there's only 1 pot to wash. Yield: 5 or 6 servings.

GAKONA BOILED MOOSE

By spring of each year, if we had any moose meat left, it was usually quite dry as the freezer tends to make it that way. I was always looking for a new way to cook this dried-out meat. So I took a page from the Indians, who seemed to often cook their moose by boiling it. Our first boiled moose was edible but not great. So we read some books and asked around. Suddenly we had at least 10 recipes, all guaranteed not to fail. This is what we finally decided upon after experimenting. Of course it's fine for beef, too.

1 rump roast or whatever cut you have
3 quarts chicken stock
1 teaspoon salt
3 tablespoons butter
2 large onions, sliced
1 medium parsnip, sliced thin
3 carrots, sliced
4 stalks celery, sliced
1 bay leaf
1/2 teaspoon
    dried parsley
6 peppercorns
4 allspice berries

Put the meat, stock and salt into a 6-quart pot or soup kettle. Bring to a boil, skim off the foam, and turn down the heat so the contents of the pot will simmer.

In a frying pan melt the butter, sauté the vegetables, and add them to the pot. Add the bay leaf, parsley, peppercorns and allspice. Cover the pot and simmer for 2 to 3 hours, until the meat is tender. Add water if necessary to keep the meat covered.

Remove the meat, drain, and slice carefully with a very sharp knife. Arrange on a warm platter and serve. The liquid in the pot will make wonderful soup stock.

I like this dish with horseradish. Yield: 1 serving for each 8 ounces of boneless meat.

MOOSE RUMP SAUERBRATEN

Whenever I butcher a moose, or for that matter whenever I see a good rump roast in the butcher shop, I think of sauerbraten. I was introduced to this delightful eating late in life, so now I make up for lost time by preparing sauerbraten as often as the rest of the family will let me.

2 cups cider vinegar
1 medium onion, sliced thin
1 tablespoon salt
1/4 teaspoon black pepper
3 bay leaves
4 cloves
1 4-pound rump roast of moose or beef
Burgundy or Chianti to cover the
*   marinating meat: approximately 3*
*   cups*
Shortening
1/2 cup hot water
1 tablespoon honey

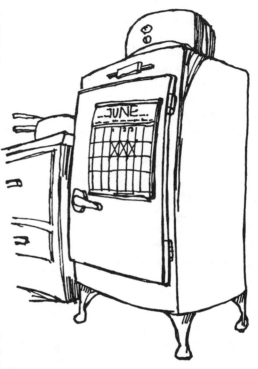

Make a marinade of the vinegar, onion slices, seasoning and spices. Place the roast in a bowl, pour in the marinade, and add enough wine to cover.

The roast should soak in the marinade for 4 days, in the refrigerator, please. Turn the meat at least twice a day. When the time is up the meat will be purple. Bear with it and dry the roast with paper towels.

In a frying pan melt some shortening and quickly brown the meat on all sides.

Now place the roast in a covered roasting pan with 1/2 cup of the marinade, the hot water and the honey. Roast at 350° for 3 hours, adding water if necessary to maintain the level of liquid.

Remove roast from the pan to a serving platter. Make a gravy of the juices in the pan if you desire. Yield: 6 servings.

MOUNTAIN TENDERLOIN

On a hunting trip to the Purchase Creek country north of Willow, where the new state capital will be, I had one of the outstanding camp meals of my life. It was a simple meal: just meat, bread, butter and coffee. Ah, but the meat was tenderloin of moose. Early that day someone in the party had shot a very big moose way back and way up on the mountain. The whole crew had worked hard all day to bring the meat to the meat cache.

The camp boss and cook decreed that the tenderloin of that moose was camp meat. Each tenderloin removed from the moose was 2 feet long and up to 6 inches wide. They were beautiful pieces of meat. Our crew of 5 consumed an entire tenderloin that evening. This recipe for moose or beef will give you just a taste of what we experienced. This is for a single portion only.

1/4 cup salt
1 quart water
2 slices tenderloin, cut 1/2 inch thick
Vegetable oil or beef fat (see page 27)
Butter
Black pepper

In a shallow pan add the salt to the water and stir until completely dissolved. Soak a slice of tenderloin in the salt water for 5 minutes. Meanwhile, begin to heat the oil or beef fat in a frying pan over medium heat. Pick the meat out of the water, shake off the water, and carefully slip the meat into the hot fat. Cook the meat 1 minute, turn it, and cook for 1 minute more.

Remove the meat from the frying pan, place on a warm plate, put a teaspoon of butter on top, sprinkle with pepper, and hand the plate to a hungry man. Have lots of good homemade bread or garlic bread handy. Don't forget, on those occasions when you're preparing this for a crowd, to save and eat the last 2 slices of tenderloin yourself.

The fried tenderloin can be held in a warm oven if you're planning a sit-down dinner. In that case, throw a big tossed green salad into the plans as well.

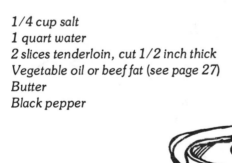

CARIBOU AND FRUIT STEW

As I have mentioned, I was raised with a minimum of fruit available. The idea of putting fruit in meat dishes was new and exotic to me. This recipe was born from the mating of the Alaskan caribou and a shipment of fresh fruit.

2 tablespoons vegetable oil
4 tablespoons butter
3 pounds caribou or beef, cut into 1-inch
    cubes
2 medium onions, chopped
1-1/2 cups dry white wine
1 6-ounce can tomato paste
1 bay leaf
Salt to taste
1/8 teaspoon black pepper
1/2 teaspoon thyme
1 cup beef stock
3 cups sweet potatoes, peeled and diced
3 pears, peeled, cored and diced
3 apples, peeled, cored and diced
1 banana, diced

In that heavy Dutch oven or skillet heat the oil and butter, brown the cubes of meat and remove from the pan. Brown the onions in the remaining oil. Stir in the wine, tomato paste, bay leaf, salt, pepper, thyme and beef stock. Return the meat to the pan, bring to a boil, cover, and simmer for an hour. Add the sweet potatoes and simmer another 1/2 hour.

Now it is time for the fruit. Carefully stir in the pears and apples and cook uncovered for 10 minutes. At the last moment sprinkle the bananas over the top and serve.

If you cooked the stew in a Dutch oven serve it in that; if you did your cooking in a skillet be careful not to crush the fruit when you transfer the food to a serving bowl. Yield: 6 servings.

CARIBOU TO YOU

Let's not start that argument. I know some people say the caribou and the reindeer are the same animal and also that the barren lands caribou and the woodland caribou are different. I just don't care.

If it looks like a caribou, if the hunting season is open on that species, and if I can see the road from where I'm standing, I'll shoot one. For you see, properly cared for, the meat of the caribou is excellent eating.

Many hunters admit to not liking the meat of the caribou and to giving the meat away or having it made into sausage. Certainly, made into sausage, usually hard and hotly spiced, caribou is excellent, especially with lots of beer. And I'll admit that much of the mistreated caribou meat that's made into hamburger would be better off in sausage.

I've seen too many caribou, still undressed, tied on the backs or tops of cars, to eat any such meat that I didn't care for myself.

But my friend, if you have a place, or can arrange for a place, in which to hang the hindquarters of a caribou at a cool temperature for an extended period of time, do so. When the time comes to eat that flesh, you will not think it is the same animal.

I've always tried to hang my meat before butchering. But seldom have I had the right place to properly age the meat. In the fall season the weather's too warm for proper aging but in the winter the meat freezes.

Several years ago Connie's dad shot a caribou just before taking an extended vacation. He mentioned he would give us a hindquarter but in his rush we didn't get together. I just assumed that he had forgotten and I put the meat out of my mind.

About a month later, he called and asked if we didn't want the meat. He had left it hanging to age in a local locker plant for us. I told him yes, we wanted the meat, and rushed down to get it. I was thinking that it must be a frozen quarter and that he was kidding about it aging.

When the man at the locker plant showed me the quarter of meat with my nametag on it my first impression was that the meat was garbage. I can only describe it as moldy. No, I can also describe it as having a fine black fuzz growing on it. The smell was ripe, but somehow different from the smell of rotted meat. Armed with this last thought, and the locker man's statement that it was excellent meat, I gathered the strength to take the quarter home.

Caribou to You   *93*

As I carried the fuzzy meat into the house, Connie got a strong whiff of it and threatened to go out the front door. This always stimulates my competitive spirit, so I placed the meat on the cutting block and grabbed a knife.

The first cut exposed a beautiful dark red meat that was so tender it seemed to roll off the knife. I sliced off a couple of steaks and trimmed off the outer fuzzy edges. With a bit of butter in the frying pan, I seared these two steaks and turned them

out on two plates. Connie's hand came out for a plate when I handed it to her, and who can blame her, because the steaks smelled heavenly.

Very few pieces of meat have I enjoyed more than that aged caribou. It was tender, succulent and certainly not wild-tasting. Connie just sat there smiling.

The rest of that quarter of meat was carefully cut and trimmed and stored in the freezer. We saved it for special occasions. I recall that several of our hunting friends ate some of it and could not identify it as caribou.

If you hunt, be sure to take good care of the meat you get and age it if you can possibly do so.

All my life I have hunted the male animal when after either deer, caribou or moose. The first female I shot, a caribou, was shot in desperation. It had been a busy season for the local trooper, me. We had lost hunters in the woods by the tens, had a couple of accidental gunshot wounds, one hunter dead from a heart attack, and one dead for looking like a moose. Not to mention a couple of light plane crashes and a dozen automobile accidents.

I hadn't had a chance to hunt until the last few days of the season. This set of circumstances found me hunting on the last day of the season three miles from the nearest road. I was now willing to take anything that looked caribouish, and was not wearing a red hat.

I guess I had better throw in here the information that it was legal to take the female caribou in the state at that time. I was about to give up and start back to the car. But first I would sit on an inviting big rock and rest a bit. As I sat there someone started a war to the south of me. There was so much shooting that it appeared there was a major battle going on. Just as the shooting stopped a herd of about 20 caribou came in sight, headed right toward me. I oozed my way off the rock and down behind it.

CARIBOU-ZUCCHINI CUSTARD

With just a little care big beautiful zucchini squash can be grown here in Alaska. The very size of a good crop, not to mention the size of individual zucchini, demands some imaginative recipes. This recipe was the result of that pressure.

1 large onion, chopped
4 tablespoons butter
1 pound ground caribou or beef
1 pound zucchini, diced
1/2 teaspoon salt
1/4 teaspoon black pepper
1/4 cup tomato sauce
2 tablespoons fresh parsley, minced
6 egg yolks, beaten
6 egg whites, beaten stiff

In a medium frying pan sauté the onion in the butter for 5 minutes, then add the meat and brown for 10 minutes.

Add the zucchini and cook over a medium heat for another 10 minutes, stirring continuously. Add the salt, pepper, tomato sauce and parsley and cook 10 minutes more.

Remove the mixture from the heat, let it cool for 10 minutes, then carefully beat in the egg yolks. Fold in the egg whites and spoon the mixture into a 2-quart baking dish. Bake at 375° for 45 minutes, or until set. Yield: 4 servings.

CARIBOU MEATBALLS WITH RICE

This is a recipe that really makes me appreciate the convenience of quick-cooking rice.

1 pound ground caribou or beef
2/3 cup quick-cooking brown rice,
*   uncooked*
1/4 cup onion, minced
1 clove garlic, minced
1/4 teaspoon ground allspice
1/2 teaspoon salt
1 10-1/2-ounce can tomato soup
1 cup water
1 tablespoon Worcestershire sauce

In a medium-size bowl mix the meat, rice, onion, garlic, allspice and salt. When well blended, shape the mixture into balls about the size of Ping-Pong balls.

In a frying pan mix the soup, water and Worcestershire sauce, and bring to a boil. Carefully put the meatballs into the soup mixture, cover, and cook for 45 minutes over medium heat.

Remove the meatballs to a platter and keep warm. I sometimes thicken the soup and turn it into a gravy, which can be poured over the meat or served separately. Yield: 4 generous servings.

The herd was coming fast, in full retreat from the battle, no doubt. I lay there waiting for them to get closer and finally they were just in range. I was carefully examining the herd for the animal that I wanted when all but one caribou turned sharply into a draw and disappeared. That eliminated my hesitation. My sights moved to the remaining caribou and I squeezed the trigger.

I didn't even know it was a cow until I reached her. She was big for a caribou, I know, because it took me two trips to pack her out. Add that up: three miles to the road times two trips out and two back. I walked a dozen miles for that animal, and six of those miles staggering under a load of meat. I have never again hunted that far back without having available some means of transportation.

Few men alive today, if any, took the caribou like my friend Sam. He was an Athabascan Indian, originally from Chitina but living at Gakona when I knew him. As I was new in that part of the country, I asked Sam about hunting caribou. He didn't have a car and wanted to hunt many miles from his home. I had something to offer—transportation—so we made a deal. I would furnish the wheels and he would find me some caribou.

Several mornings later found us about 10 miles west of Glennallen, going into the woods where I had never seen a caribou. I have to admit that the youthful experience of a snipe hunt crossed my mind. Was he just leading me on? But I knew that he needed meat, too.

We were about a mile from the road when Sam led me into a clearing in the trees. It was a half-mile wide and about two miles long. The surface of the clearing was in low willow brush, nothing over 18 inches high. Sam pointed to a small island of raised ground a quarter-mile ahead and suggested that I go there and wait. He indicated that he would sweep around the opening to the east and find the caribou. I could only agree and move out. Once on the high ground I sat down to wait. A full hour passed with nothing happening except that the bugs found me.

Then there was movement way down at the end of the clearing where Sam had gone. With my glasses I spotted a herd of caribou moving slowly toward me, with individual animals appearing to stop and feed as they moved. I crouched down and waited for the herd to get within rifle range. When the caribou were about 150 yards away, their movement quickened. I raised my rifle and swung it to pick out my animal. As my telescope sight passed through the herd I was surprised to find Sam loping along in the middle of the caribou. He wasn't doing anything special to hide himself, just moving with the herd.

I watched Sam look my way, kind of grin, and then shoot the biggest caribou, which was just 30 yards away from him. The sound of the shot startled the herd and it was only fool luck that led me to swing my gun away from Sam and knock down an animal before the rest reached the concealment of the woods.

Just how Sam found the herd, got into it, and moved it toward me, I'll never know. Asking Sam just produced a grin and a shrug of his shoulders. Sam is dead now, and I suspect that his secret went with him. Other Indians just say that Sam was a good hunter and let it go at that.

I think I was fortunate to see Sam at work; I may have been looking back in time to when men first hunted herd animals, and I may have observed the skill that allowed those men to survive. Sam might well have been the last man alive with the skill of those survivors.

Sam showed me another interesting aspect of his life. The family that he headed did not own a frying pan or roasting pan. The only way they ever cooked meat was by boiling it. Moose, caribou, rabbit, duck, goose and even fish all went into the cooking pot. Salt, if available, was added. I have no idea how the results tasted.

We do not have to follow Sam's cooking habits, as we have many ways to cook our meat, fowl and fish. I wish I had Sam's recipe for catching the eatables, though.

PEPPER STEAK CARIBOU

In the good old days, the caribou-hunting season usually added about 100 pounds of steak to our freezer. By the middle of the winter we were always looking for a different way to prepare these steaks. From that need was born this recipe.

2 pounds round steak: caribou, moose or
* beef*
1/4 cup vegetable oil
1 large onion, chopped
1 clove garlic, minced
1 tablespoon soy sauce
1 teaspoon salt
1/2 cup water
1 large green pepper, cut in strips
1 cup fresh mushrooms, sliced, or contents
* of 1 8-ounce can*
1 16-ounce can whole tomatoes
1 tablespoon cornstarch mixed in 3/4 cup
* water*

This recipe requires a Dutch oven or a frying pan with a tight cover.

Cut the steak into slices about 1/2" by 3" and brown them in the frying pan in the oil. Add the onion and garlic and sauté until transparent. Add the soy sauce, salt and water. Cover and cook over low heat for 45 minutes. Then add the green pepper, mushrooms, tomatoes and cornstarch mixture and cook for 10 minutes.

I suggest that you serve this over mashed potatoes or rice, as you will not wish to lose a drop of the gravy. Yield: 4 servings.

CARIBOU-STUFFED CABBAGE ROLLS

The Matanuska Valley cabbage grows nice big leaves for making cabbage rolls and sauerkraut. All this cabbage, added to the availability of caribou meat, certainly gave us the makings for this recipe. Stuffing the cabbage rolls was fun, and so was eating them.

1 pound fresh sauerkraut or contents of 1
    24- or 26-ounce can
10 large cabbage leaves
Grease from 3 slices bacon: about 2 table-
    spoons grease
1 large onion, chopped
2 cloves garlic, chopped
1 pound ground caribou,
    moose or beef
3/4 cup rice, cooked
2 eggs, beaten
2 tablespoons paprika
1/8 teaspoon thyme
1 teaspoon salt
1/8 teaspoon black pepper
1 8-ounce can tomato sauce
1/2 cup water

If the sauerkraut is fresh, soak it in cold water for 10 minutes and drain. If the sauerkraut is canned, just drain it.

Simmer the cabbage leaves for 10 minutes in enough lightly salted water to cover. Remove and dry the leaves, taking care not to break them.

Fry and remove from the pan 3 slices of bacon, or melt 2 tablespoons of previously rendered bacon grease, in a medium-size frying pan and sauté the onion and garlic until transparent.

In a large bowl combine the meat, onion, garlic, rice, eggs, paprika, thyme, salt and pepper, mixing them thoroughly.

Spread the sauerkraut over the bottom of a 5-quart casserole or Dutch oven, making a layer about an inch thick.

In the center of a cabbage leaf place 2 heaping tablespoons of the meat mixture. Fold the leaf into a compact bundle and lay it on the bed of kraut. Continue this way until you run out of meat. You may find that you want to put less meat into the leaves, depending on their size and how they want to be folded. If you have trouble making the rolls stay neat tie them with string or heavy thread but do try to remember to remove the string before serving dinner. You should have a layer of rolls on top of the kraut.

Mix the tomato sauce with the water and pour over the cabbage rolls. Bring the liquid to a boil, cover, and simmer for an hour.

Mound the sauerkraut on a serving dish, with the cabbage rolls arranged around the mound, and serve with your favorite sauce. Just plain sour cream is excellent with these rolls. Yield: 4 large servings.

CARIBOU AND LENTILS

In any discussion about dried foods—beans, peas and such—someone should bring up lentils. I fear many people have forgotten this excellent dried vegetable. Oh, I see a lentil in canned vegetable soup once in a while, but who really notices it? To bring one of my favorite dried foods to the attention of the American people (now watch the price of lentils go up) I offer a recipe you gotta try.

1 medium onion, chopped
2 cloves garlic, sliced thin
1 tablespoon clarified butter (see
    page 6)
2-1/2 cups beef stock
1 bay leaf
2-1/2 cups lentils
Salt and black pepper
6 rounds caribou or beef shank, cut 2
    inches thick

3 tablespoons vegetable oil
1/2 cup green onions, chopped
1/4 cup fresh parsley, chopped, or 1-1/2
    tablespoons dried parsley that has
    been soaked in water

In a 4-quart pan or Dutch oven sauté the onion and garlic in the butter until transparent. Add the beef stock, bay leaf, lentils, salt and pepper. Bring to a boil and simmer, covered, for about 30 minutes. Check the lentils for tenderness. Remove from the heat and keep warm.

While the lentils are cooking brown the shanks in the vegetable oil in a frying pan after seasoning to taste. Place the meat on the rack of a roasting pan and roast at 350° for an hour, basting the shanks with the drippings at least once.

Remove the meat from the pan and pour the drippings into the pot of lentils. Add the chopped green onions and parsley and stir. Then spread the drained lentils on a serving platter, place the rounds of meat on the lentils, and serve. Yield: 4 generous servings.

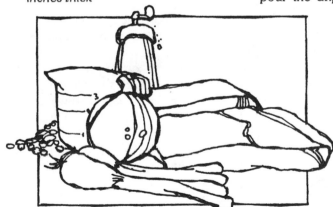

TROUT ANTOINETTE

So you are tired of the traditional ways of cooking trout like frying, broiling and roasting. Yes, they are all good, but there is another way, as this recipe from my mother's collection will show you.

4 medium-size trout, cleaned, but with
 heads left on
1/4 teaspoon salt
Boiling water to cover fish
6 tablespoons butter
1/4 teaspoon paprika
1/4 teaspoon ground allspice

Place the trout in a large frying pan, salt, and pour in the boiling water. Keep the water simmering for 6 minutes. Remove fish and set aside to drain.

In a saucepan melt the butter and add the paprika and allspice.

Skin the fish and lay it on a warm platter. Pour the butter sauce over the fish and serve. Yield: 4 servings.

ILIAMNA BARBEQUE

Iliamna Lake in western Alaska is the largest lake in the state and would be the largest in several other places. This lake has a large population of whitefish along with many other species. One night during the summer of 1963 I was stranded in a fish camp on the shore of this lake. The airplane that was supposed to pick me up was off somewhere else waiting out the weather. So, according to the tradition of true Alaskan hospitality, I was invited to supper by a young couple living in the camp. That night we had barbequed whitefish, and I had a new recipe worth logging in my notebook.

2 tablespoons onion, chopped
1 tablespoon butter
2 tablespoons cider vinegar
1 cup ketchup
3 tablespoons Worcestershire sauce
2 tablespoons brown sugar
1/2 teaspoon salt
1/4 teaspoon black pepper
4 fillets of whitefish, red snapper or perch

Sauté the onion in the butter until transparent. Add the vinegar, ketchup, Worcestershire sauce, brown sugar, salt and pepper. Simmer for 5 minutes.

Place the fish on a plate and paint the sauce on one side. Now arrange the fillets in a shallow greased pan, painted side down, and pour the rest of the sauce over them.

Bake at 425° for 35 to 40 minutes. Yield: 4 servings.

FRESH-WATER FISH

Alaska abounds with fish of all kinds and fresh-water fish are readily available to all who make the effort to find them.

I could write a book about fishing in Alaska and may do so some day, along with hundreds of other fishermen who have the same idea. Certainly I'm not going to tell you *all* my fish stories now, but maybe just a couple.

For instance, just to the north of Cordova, above the old steamship dock, there were a hill and a fresh-water dam. I've not been to that dam in 40 years, so it might well have been a victim of the 1964 earthquake, an event that changed many things in the Cordova area.

Anyway, the lake behind that dam, when I was a young one, was full of pan-size trout. The lake surface was about five acres in area then, and that was a lot of water to me. It was a nice place to spend the afternoon, just me and my fishing pole.

One day I sat there on the dam and caught 16 little trout, none over nine inches. I would have stayed until the pond was empty, but I was expected home.

To leave the dam meant walking over a gorge on a walkway built right on top of the big wooden pipe leading to the Cordova canneries. This walkway was about 350 feet long and never less than 30 feet from the ground.

It was time to go, so I picked up my string of fish and walked to a place on the dam where there was a trickle of water. I cleaned my fish and had my head down for about 10 minutes. When I stood up, there was a big black bear coming down the face of the dam toward me.

The bear had no doubt smelled the fish and was intent on investigating. Suddenly my string of fish became nothing except bear bait in my hand. I fully intended to donate the fish to the bear, but my legs started long before my hand got the message to drop the fish. The result was that the fish dropped on the walkway some 50 feet from where I started.

As I crossed the 200-foot mark on the walkway, I could feel through my feet that something else was on the walkway. A quick glance over my shoulder showed me that the bear had stopped at the fish to smell them. It would seem that fish was all that was on the bear's mind. The blackie had no interest in a skinny boy who could run like an Arctic hare.

As I cleared the end of the walkway, I didn't feel quite so trapped. I stopped to look back and watch the bear enjoy my

TROUT IN SOUR CREAM

One of my best meals of trout consisted of 4- and 6-inch beauties headed, gutted and roasted on a stick over a fire, all within 1-1/2 minutes before eating. But if you are taking yours home to eat, try this.

4 fresh trout, at least 8 inches long
Salt
1/2 cup flour
6 tablespoons clarified butter (see page 6)
1 cup sour cream
1/2 teaspoon lemon juice
Fresh parsley
Lemon wedges

Wash and dry the fish, salting inside and out. Roll in flour until the fish is well covered.

Put 4 tablespoons of butter into a frying pan just big enough to take the fish without bending them. Fry the trout at a fairly high heat for 5 minutes on one side and 4 minutes on the other. Take special care in turning the fish and cook only 2 at a time. Put the cooked fish on a warm serving dish.

Discard the used butter, add 2 more tablespoons to the pan, and add the sour cream. Stir with a wooden spoon to loosen any brown residue in the pan. Cook for 3 minutes but do not boil. At the last second stir the lemon juice into the sauce. Remove from the heat and pour over the trout. Sprigs of parsley and some lemon slices are optional but add a nice touch. Yield: 2 servings.

fish. My fishing pole? I still had it in my hand. You don't give up everything to the bear.

I fished the lake behind that dam many times afterward, but I had learned one important lesson. Never again did I let myself remain so unaware of what was going on around me. Like a bird feeding I now take time out to look up and around me every once in a while.

Only on one other occasion did a bear sneak up on me and hijack my fish. That was years later and the bear involved would have outweighed my little blackie by another 800 pounds. This fellow was a brown bear.

I was fishing the Mendeltna Creek, a quarter of a mile or so upstream from the Glenn Highway Bridge. I had worked myself through a wide stand of alders out on a gravel bar in a curve of the river. I had made a great deal of noise because I experienced some difficulty reaching the spot where I was standing fishing. I was casting across the river into the outside curve of the water. My efforts during some 15 minutes had already produced a nice 10-inch rainbow, which was lying on the gravel near my feet.

I picked another strike out of the river and had an even bigger rainbow on the line when I suddenly smelled bear. The hair on the back of my neck felt like it was standing straight out from my skin. I glanced around and about 50 feet away from me stood the biggest, hungriest-looking bear that ever got close to me.

To get to where it was standing the bear had to have come through the same stand of alder that I had been so noisy in passing. I should have heard the bear, but I hadn't. The murmur of the river must have masked out the sound. Another lesson learned, I hoped not too late.

My visitor stood looking at me, turning its head from side to side. Very carefully I started edging out into the river. I had

visions of making a long shallow dive into the deep water if the intruder charged at me. Slowly the water moved up my legs, then over my boot tops and into the boots. Then up my body, past my belt, and up toward my chest. That water was terribly cold.

I was walking in water just about up to my armpits when I realized that I still had a fish on my line. The fish was jumping and seemed to have distracted the bear.

I was able to wade within about six feet of the bank across from where I'd been.

Still moving slowly and carefully, I pushed off and swam until I could reach the side. The bank was steep and difficult to climb, especially with my boots full of cold, cold water. As I slipped out of sight in the brush I stopped for a second to see the bear sniffing at the trout I had left on the bank. Again I had given a fish to a bear, and it seemed to be a good swap: one fish for one life. I walked rapidly back to the highway—as rapidly as I could with hip boots full of water.

What happened to the second fish? I don't know what happened to it. I reached the car with just a fishing pole and broken fishing line. Each time I had saved my fishing pole and my life. The total cost was a few fish and my dignity, which I discovered is self-renewing. I'm just glad to be writing this.

Up until I was assigned to Glennallen in 1952, I was not acquainted with the Alaska lake trout. I can't tell you why, but I'd missed fishing it.

One day a neighbor stopped by from a fishing trip and asked if we would like a lake trout. Being always fish-hungry, I said yes. He took me out to his car and opened the trunk. The fish he lifted out and handed to me was about the size of a medium king salmon, at least 30 inches long. I was surprised and said so. Then he showed me the two he was taking home. They were both larger than mine. He said that he had taken them while trolling in the Tangle Lakes, on the Denali Highway.

For dinner that night we had excellent lake trout steaks. The yellowish flesh was wonderful, unlike any other fish I had ever

eaten. So our family became another that pursued the lake trout in the depths of its lake-bottom hiding places.

The lake trout can be taken by trolling or by fishing through the ice in the winter. You really have to enjoy eating this fish, though, to stand out on the ice at 50° below zero while you try to catch it. I will not, but try me at 10° below. I may weaken.

A **number of years ago,** during the middle of the winter, I visited a friend who was living up in the country around Tok. I had driven 300 miles, arrived after dark, talked late before a fireplace. I slept well and long that night.

I awoke to the smell of coffee and frying fish. I got up, pulled on my pants, and wandered out to the kitchen-living room area. I looked over Bud's shoulder and found a whitefish cooking in the frying pan.

He pointed to the coffee pot and then the table. I poured me a cup of strong fragrant coffee and slid into the seat at the table. As I hit the bench, a plateful of fried fish touched the table. Bud still hadn't said anything, just grinned. Armed with a fork I attacked the fish, which was delicious. Four bites later, Bud put several chunks of oven-toasted bread on my plate.

When I had polished off everything in sight, it was time to begin the conversation. I asked where he had come by fresh white-fish.

Bud told me that under the ice in the lake he had a net that provided the fish. He also made a couple of comments about the early risers getting the fish. If you wanted to catch fish in the wintertime you couldn't sleep until noon.

So I answered back that here it was now only 10 in the morning, and did he always get up in the middle of the night to go fishing? What kind of a lantern did he use, and yes, pass me another fish.

Some six whitefish later both Bud and I were full. Sitting over coffee, Bud allowed that he would have to run his net again today since I was such a heavy eater. He said we'd run the net just before dark at 2:30 in the afternoon. That way he was hopeful that he could catch enough fish to feed me without ruining my sleeping time.

So at 2 p.m. we walked out on the lake ice to where Bud's net was busy fishing. Bud had about 70 feet of net stretched under the ice between two holes. As the temperature was about 10° below zero, we had to break considerable ice out of both holes. This was even though Bud had fished the net just a few hours earlier. Bud said that if he missed one day he would lose the use of his net until spring.

Because Bud had been fishing the lake for years he knew where to stretch his net to catch the fish. He mentioned that during his first two winters there he had moved the net constantly trying to find the white-

TROUT WITH CARIBOU SAUSAGE

I mentioned that much caribou meat ends up as sausage, so here's a way to use that sausage. But please use a mild sausage or you'll never even taste the fish.

4 fresh trout, about 8 inches long
1/2 cup flour
1/2 teaspoon salt
1/2 teaspoon paprika
Black pepper
1/2 cup clarified butter (see page 6)
Lemon juice
6 ounces caribou sausage, salami or
    pepperoni, sliced thin

Dry the fish carefully. Combine the flour, salt, paprika and a few shakes of pepper in a medium-size paper bag and place the fish in the bag one at a time. Shake the bag to coat the fish, then remove excess flour from each trout.

In a medium-size frying pan fry the fish in the butter for 5 minutes, turn, and fry 4 minutes on the other side. Remove, sprinkle with lemon juice, and keep warm on a heated platter.

Put the pieces of sausage into the pan in which the fish was fried. Cook for 2 or 3 minutes and then pour the remaining butter and sausage over the fish and serve. Yield: 4 servings.

fish. Moving one of these nets is no small chore.

Bud went off on a tall story about how he was going to train a beaver to swim his lines under the ice from hole to hole. But before he was able to do this he found his present fishing location and the net had not been moved since.

The net was equipped with a long line on either end so that it could be pulled out of the water through one hole and then, from the other hole, be pulled back into fishing position. We found eight fish in the net. This seemed to please Bud, who said 10 fish a day was good fishing for the net.

Bud supplied himself with fish all winter and in addition had a small barter business going with several families in Tok. You know, fish for coffee and flour. It helped Bud survive the winters.

Back at the cabin I expected more fish for dinner, but this was not to be. Bud carefully cleaned the fish and laid them out to freeze. For dinner he produced two big beautiful moose steaks, which were also welcome. The next day as I headed back down the highway towards Glennallen I had a package that felt like frozen whitefish to deliver to a woman down the way. I wonder—no, I don't!

In my lifetime of fishing there have been many outstanding days to remember, but one involving grayling has always been one of my favorite memories.

About 190 miles north of Valdez, beneath the Richardson Highway, a small creek crosses under the road. It's known as Gillespie Creek, and is so small it only rates a culvert under the road. Even at flood stage the little stream couldn't rate a bridge.

One spring day I was fish-hungry and was working my way along the highway trying many of the usually productive streams. With no luck. When I reached Gillespie Creek I remembered that it came out of a small lake just a couple hundred yards off the highway. I elected to walk up there and try.

As I approached the lake I could see fish feeding on the surface. Small insects seemed to be hanging a few inches over the lake surface. The air was absolutely still and the only sound was the whisper of tiny wings.

I tied on the smallest black gnat fly that I had and flipped it out toward the lake surface. It never touched the water, as a nice grayling took it right out of the air. The fish gave me a short but spectacular fight, but ended up on my fish stringer. By the time the fish was taken care of the lake had returned to the condition I had found it in.

During the next half-hour the fly fooled another dozen nice grayling. The smallest was 12 inches long and the largest was an amazing 16.

Then the evening breeze arrived and blew the insects away from the lake. The grayling were gone although I tried another dozen or so casts. I was through fishing.

I went on home with fish enough for dinner and for breakfast. I enjoy fresh fish and especially like a couple of fish for breakfast. No, that is not a fin on my back, but I certainly tend to go upstream in the summer.

HOOLIGAN AND HERB BUTTER

The Twentymile River runs into Turnagain Arm, which is part of Cook Inlet. The river's about 39 miles south of Anchorage on the Seward Highway and it's visited each year, sometime in June, by a vast run of a small smeltlike fish known locally as hooligan. The fish make excellent eating, if you know how to cook them. Try this.

1/4 pound clarified butter (see page 6)
1/2 teaspoon salt
1 tablespoon fresh parsley, minced
1 tablespoon chives, minced
1 tablespoon lime juice
Tabasco
Black pepper
2 cups beef fat (see page 27)
24 hooligan or smelt, cleaned but with
*   heads and tails left on*
1 cup flour

Warm the butter and add the salt, parsley, chives, lime juice, a dash of Tabasco and pepper. Stir and keep warm.

In a deep frying pan heat the beef fat to 350°. Wash and dry the fish, sprinkle lightly with salt, and roll in the flour. Shake off excess and slip each fish into the hot fat. Fry 4 minutes on one side and 3 on the other. The fish should be brown and crisp. Remove and drain on paper towels.

Serve on a warm platter with the herb butter in a pitcher so that everyone can season to taste; some prefer hooligan right out of the pan with nothing to distract them from the fish. Yield: 4 servings.

FRIED FISH SOUTHERN STYLE

When, as a boy, I caught a large trout in the 18- to 24-inch range Mother would cook it this way—Southern style. As she never traveled south of Ohio in her life, I don't know where she found the recipe. I've tried it for other fish, both fresh-water and salt-water types, and find it an excellent way to fry either kind.

1 large trout, grayling or whatever
1 teaspoon salt
1/4 teaspoon black pepper
1-1/2 cups white or yellow cornmeal
Shortening, vegetable oil or beef fat
*   (see page 27)*

Clean and wash the fish. Cut it into pieces about 3 inches long, split the pieces, and remove the backbone. Leave the skin on. Lay each piece skin side down and make 3 diagonal slashes about 1/4 inch deep across it. Salt and pepper the pieces and coat them thoroughly with the cornmeal.

In a medium-size frying pan bring 1/2 inch of shortening or fat to a high temperature—at least 350°. Place 2 or 3 pieces of fish in the pan, cook for 4 minutes, turn, and cook about 3 minutes more. The pieces of fish should be nicely browned. Be sure to let the temperature rise to its starting point before adding the next batch of fish. Rapid, thorough cooking is the key to success. Yield: 2 servings.

DILL-CURED SALMON

I've mentioned that the catching and processing of salmon have been a big part of my life. Maybe I should be sick of it, but I still like the fish. The flesh of the king salmon, for example, looks good enough to eat raw.

But, like most people in the United States, I don't like raw fish and find myself reaching for cooking utensils whenever I have fish to eat. But there is one exception to that rule, for a few years ago a woman showed me how to dill-cure a couple pieces of king salmon. It's the closest that I'll get to eating raw fish, and it is at least processed, if not cooked.

4 pounds king salmon cut from center of
    fish
1 large bunch fresh dill, chopped
1/4 cup sugar
1/4 cup salt
2 tablespoons coarsely ground black
    pepper
1 cup cider vinegar

First cut the fish in halves lengthwise and remove the backbone and secondary bones. Place one piece of fish in a deep casserole, skin side down. Cover this piece with the dill. Combine the sugar, salt and pepper in a bowl and sprinkle on the fish. Now add the second piece of fish, flesh side down so that you've made a fish sandwich with the skin outward. Pour the vinegar over the fish and weight the fish to hold it down in the liquid (I use a foil-covered rock).

Place the casserole, covered, in the refrigerator. Take it out and turn the sandwich over every 12 hours for 3 days, basting the fish with the liquid each time you turn it and taking care to get some liquid in between the pieces of fish.

After 3 days remove the fish from the marinade and scrape off all seasoning. Drain the solids from the liquid and store the salmon in it until you wish to start eating the fish, which will keep several days at least.

When you wish to eat a piece of the salmon dry it and place it on a cutting board, skin side down. With your sharpest knife, slice the salmon as thin as possible and cut each slice free from the skin. Lay the slices on a bed of lettuce and serve as an hors d'oeuvre or as part of a main course with lemon or mustard sauce or whatever sauce you prefer. Most likely you will find yourself slicing the second piece of cured salmon before the evening is over.

SALMON FOR FUN AND PROFIT

I imagine that you have been wondering how I could get so far into a book about Alaskan cooking with only a passing mention of our greatest fish, the salmon. There is only one answer: A fish that is an outstanding sport and commercial fish, that is good fried, broiled, baked, boiled and even smoked, deserves a chapter all its own.

I've fished for the wily salmon in about every way you can imagine. I've used my hands, rod and reel, nets, a fish wheel, trolling gear and even a rifle.

The use of a rifle, while strictly illegal, was brought on by frustration and real hunger. The incident, which long ago passed the statute of limitations, would have been excusable under the eat-to-live provisions of the law, maybe.

In 1939 I was working with a survey crew on the Kenai Peninsula. We had been way out on a spike camp for several days. (Spike camp is when you're roughing it— no stove, no tents and in this case, temporarily at least, no food.) The pack horses that had been expected to bring us a new

supply of grub were two days late. We were hungry.

On the way back to camp we had to cross the Anchor River several miles inland from the sea. There in the river were several large king salmon. Every once in a while one of them would make an attempt at crossing a shallow area on a gravel bar. We looked at one another and decided on a salmon dinner and several of us set out to hand-catch a salmon. After a half-hour of effort in this direction all we had accomplished was to get ourselves good and wet, although one of the guys claimed to have at least touched a salmon. It was time for ingenuity.

I had my rifle so I set up the salmon trap. Two of the men waded out to the shallow place that the salmon were trying to cross and stood very still in the icy water. They were the catchers.

I stood on the river bank with my rifle in the ready position. A big king salmon made a try at the ripple of water. I waited until it was well past the two men and shot the fish in the head. The salmon drifted back with the current and one of the fellows just picked it out of the water. A loud cheer went up from six hungry men. I took a gracious bow and smiled to my audience.

We packed the fish, which appeared to be a 25-pounder, in grass and river mud and baked it in a fire pit that evening. Then the seven of us sat around the cracked baking cover and polished off every scrap of salmon.

I've enjoyed taking the silver salmon with a rod and reel all over Southeastern Alaska, the Kodiak area and down around Seward. A better fighting fish in this weight class would be hard to find. I also fished the silver commercially on the Copper River Flats as a youth, but weather and tides made this a hard job for limited return.

While living in Southeastern from 1965 to 1972 I owned a small boat which I had rigged as a commercial troller—just a couple of hand gurdies (winches for hauling in lines) and two side poles. These allowed me to run two trolling wires and up to six leaders.

The two species of salmon that we most often caught from that boat were silvers and kings. I would pick up an occasional marketable humpy, chum or halibut. We also caught a lot of scrap fish as well. These mainly went to feed the eagles that followed our operation with interest.

Whenever I could see a big old bald eagle, either sitting in a tree or circling overhead, I would save my scrap fish. Once I had the lines baited and fishing again, I would throw a scrap fish overboard. I'd watch to see how soon it was before old sharp-eyes would spot the floating fish.

Sooner or later an eagle would notice the dead fish and down it would come. Flaring out close to the water, the eagle would grab the fish and fly off with the catch.

On one particular day I caught a tomcod that had to go 25 pounds. Without thinking I donated it to the eagles, as usual. As I stood watching, a large proud-looking symbol of our country came out of the sky. The eagle flared out beautifully, reached out and sank its claws into the fish, and started to lift. The fish did not lift. The eagle went headfirst into the sea and just about ruined its dignity. There was a second or two there when I thought I would have to go back and save the eagle from drowning, but it got itself unsorted. The bird retracted its claws from the fish, got right side up, and made a "carrier" takeoff from the belly of the floating tomcod. A few powerful flaps of the wings and the eagle was once again a handsome national symbol soaring in the sky. It soon flew to the limb of a tree and settled down, a much wiser bird.

On another day I was trolling on the east side of the south end of Shelter Island near Juneau. It was a nice flat, calm day, with sunshine and everything. As I was making my 15-minute pass down the fishing area everything changed. The sun went away and hid behind a cloud, the wind came up to about 25 knots, a heavy sea began building, and it began to rain hard. I almost forgot to mention that the tide changed, too. I was aware of all this but I didn't care because I was catching fish as fast as I could bring them in. My fish box was full and in addition I had six or eight

POOR MAN'S SMOKED SALMON

The smoked salmon that was so inexpensive in my youth, and the salmon I smoked myself in later years, caused me to develop an appetite for smoked fish that I cannot ignore. However, today's prices for smoked salmon can almost destroy that appetite. I have found that I can hold my craving in check with this recipe.

1 16-ounce can salmon
8 ounces cream cheese
1 tablespoon lemon juice
1 tablespoon onion, minced
1 teaspoon horseradish
1/4 teaspoon commercial smoke flavoring
1/4 teaspoon salt

Drain the salmon and remove the pieces of skin and bones. Flake the fish into a mixing bowl and add the remaining ingredients. Stir together, then chill in the refrigerator for 3 hours.

Remove the chilled mixture from the bowl onto a board and shape into a roll about 2 inches in diameter. Serve on a small serving dish with crackers or toast squares.

For special occasions coat the salmon roll in chopped nuts to dress it up a bit. Or make an excellent dip for potato chips or vegetables by adding 1 cup of heavy cream to the ingredients.

NELSON PLANKED SALMON

I have always liked salmon planked in the old Indian method over or by an open fire. But let's face it, there are all too few occasions to cook this way. So why not develop a recipe to look and taste similar? It just might even be better, unless you are fond of flying ash.

For this recipe I usually fillet a 5- or 6-pound salmon, removing the backbone and leaving the skin on. I use half of this and freeze the rest in water for use later for the same recipe.

6 tablespoons clarified butter (see page 6)
3 tablespoons vegetable oil
2 tablespoons lemon juice
1 tablespoon liquid smoke
1 teaspoon salt
1/4 teaspoon black pepper
1 salmon fillet, approximately 3 pounds

In a saucepan blend together over low heat the butter, oil, lemon juice, liquid smoke, salt and pepper.

On a heavy, oven-safe serving platter or a flat roasting pan that you have painted with some of the mixture from the saucepan, lay the salmon, skin side down. With a pastry brush paint the top side of the fish with the remaining sauce.

Bake at 350° for 40 minutes. Baste the fish every 10 minutes with the sauce. When the fish flakes easily it is done.

Serve right on the cooking platter after pouring off any excess liquid. Yield: 4 servings.

big silvers sliding around underfoot. I was almost glad when I ran out of the end of that school of fish.

But being greedy, like all fishermen, I had to try one more pass through the school in spite of the miserable weather that I now noticed. I started a turn for a pass back through the fish. As my boat came around, my inside pole began ringing the hit bell like mad. This meant that there was something big down there hooked onto one of my leaders.

I quickly cranked up the wire to get at the big fish. I was pulling wire, unhooking leaders, and working my way down to the bottom leader. You must realize that while this was going on, I was also jumping to the steering wheel to correct my direction, as I was now trying to take my boat upwind into about a six-foot sea. I would get things steady and pull a few fathoms of wire and then jump right back to correct the ship again.

Suddenly I reached the end of the bottom lead and there was the granddaddy of all king salmon on the end of that line. At $1 a pound, I was looking at $50 at least. Greed took over again and I forgot everything except getting that fish into the boat. As I pulled the king into the cockpit the trolling motor quit cold.

I looked up to realize that I had let the boat make a complete circle while I was busy elsewhere. What had stopped the motor was the port-side trolling wire wrapping itself around the propeller. This was

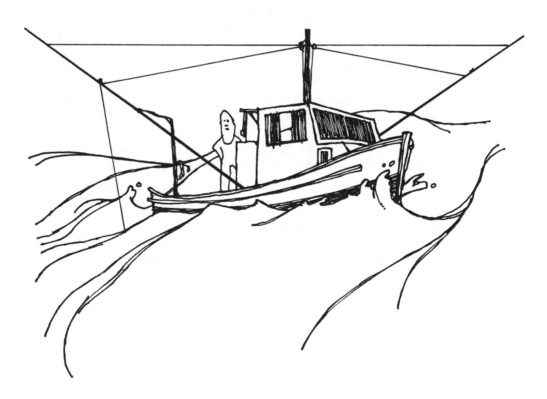

SILVER SALMON SIPLETS

In the good old days when I was living in salmon country, I always seemed to have leftover fish. Nowadays I all too often have to go to the shelf for a can of salmon. So here is a recipe that you might use for leftover salmon, but you also can reach for a can and make it anyway.

2 cups silver salmon or contents of 1
*   16-ounce can*
1 onion, grated
1/4 teaspoon nutmeg
Salt, black pepper and mayonnaise

Remove all bones, skin and dark fat from the fish and then force the fish through a food mill. Add the grated onion and the nutmeg, and salt and pepper to taste. Mix thoroughly, adding just enough mayonnaise so the mixture will hold its shape when formed in 1-inch balls.

Roll the balls in more mayonnaise and arrange on a plate on a bed of lettuce or watercress. Chill and serve as hors d'oeuvres or as an extra dish for supper.

ONIONLESS SALMON LOAF

We had an elderly friend who was fond of salmon loaf, but he had a problem. Onions distressed him to the point that he could not eat anything containing them. To meet this challenge we created Onionless Salmon Loaf for the nights this gentleman joined us for dinner.

2 cups cooked salmon,
*   or contents of 1*
*   16-ounce can,*
*   flaked*
1-1/2 cups
*   bread*
*   crumbs*
1/2 cup green
*   pepper,*
*   minced*
1 10-1/2-ounce
*   can mushroom*
*   soup*

Combine all ingredients and mix lightly. Pack into a greased loaf pan. Bake at 350° for an hour. Turn out on a serving platter.

Sometimes I make a sauce from a second can of mushroom soup and a small amount of milk, a combination that also makes a good gravy for the boiled potatoes that are good with this dish.

3/16-inch steel wire, which is really tough, and bad news for a propeller.

Let me describe the scene for you. My boat was now lying in the trough of the sea and rolling like something out of a county fair entertainment ride. I was not entertained. The wind and the tide were both taking me right in on the reefs at the end of the island. I was without power and I had stainless steel wire wrapped around the propellers of both of my engines. I was also dragging about 90 feet of wire and leaders behind me. I was in a lot of trouble.

I quickly tied the stern docking line around my waist and leaned over the stern of the boat to have a go at untangling the wire from the two outboards hanging there. About five minutes went by, during which I was nearly drowned by several seas breaking into the motor well. I got all but what looked like one twist off the little trolling motor. I stood up and took a look at the reef and figured I still had a couple of minutes to work.

This time I was going to have to reach deep in the water to clear that last twist of wire. The bottom of the motor would be in a foot of water one second and three feet under when the next sea broke. To get the wire loose I was going to have to hold on and work regardless of everything else. This meant letting the next sea cover me, if necessary. That happened twice before the wire slipped free of the motor. With the wire clear I stood up and pulled the starter rope in the little engine. If it started I still might miss the reef.

One quick pull and the little jewel of an outboard got going. I jumped to the wheel and steered the boat straight out away from the reef. It was touch and go for a while but the motor finally pulled us out-side the danger area. Now I could try to free my other motor and my lines.

A few minutes later I ran in to a sheltered bay to sort out my fishing gear, clean a lot of fish and remember what fun it is to fish in Alaska. I love it! There is no fishing in the world that I enjoy more.

Each fishing season the first order of business for my family, when all the children were still at home, was to get the freezer full. We would put up only about eight kings, as this was not our favorite salmon. It was the silver that we liked best and which filled the biggest share of the freezer. We also liked the silver best as a smoking fish, so many silvers found their way into our smokehouse.

As you might have guessed, the halibut we picked up incidental to the salmon-fishing also made it to our freezer until room got scarce. There was always room to squeeze in a few red snapper and some crab or shrimp.

That troller of ours provided us with a lot of good eating all year round. It also paid for its fuel, oil, fishing gear and some other costs. We never did make a great deal of money with the boat because I was busy earning a living during five out of seven days a week. But we certainly had fun.

Salmon is good food, and these are all good recipes, so try one or more of them.

RED CAVIAR

Many years ago I was part of a group that spent an evening in the executive bunkhouse of a cannery with an old Russian gentleman. We had a delightful time eating smoked salmon jowls, drinking vodka, and listening to Russian short wave broadcasts that the old man translated except when he became too angry with what was being said. In return, my friends and I assisted him in damning the Russians—after all it was his vodka.

In the morning he was up bright and early and showed me through the plant where he was supervising the making of salmon-egg caviar. At the end of the processing line the eggs were sealed into what looked like 10-gallon kegs. He lifted out a small paper cupful of these eggs and handed them to me. It was my first experience with red caviar—or any caviar, in fact. The caviar was excellent if a bit salty for my taste.

I guess I was hooked, and here is a recipe I found that almost duplicates the Russian man's sample.

2-1/2 cups salt
1/6 ounce sodium nitrate
1/32 ounce sodium nitrite
(Two items can be purchased at a
    drugstore, but give advance notice)
1 teaspoon ginger
1 teaspoon dry mustard

1 gallon water
6 sacs salmon eggs (contents of 3 female
    salmon)

Stir all the ingredients except the eggs into the water. Now slit the egg sacks and squeeze the individual eggs into the solution. Stir well and let stand for 5 days in a cool place, the refrigerator if possible.

Strain the eggs from the solution and store them in glass jars under continued refrigeration. Serve them as you would any caviar. I like them mixed with a touch of minced raw onion and a drop of lemon juice and spread on bread or toast.

GRILLED SALMON STEAKS

The first time I saw a barbeque grill aboard a 25-foot cruising boat I was intrigued. It was arranged in such a manner that the charcoal grill itself was out over the side of the boat on a swivel fitted into the deck. This had been done not only to make the grill fire-safe, but also to make more room in the cruiser's cockpit for people. Not to mention the fact that it allowed the cook to stand upright.

The final benefit of this device was to allow me to eat the freshest salmon that I had ever experienced. From the ocean to the plate in less than 20 minutes. I'll report to you that it was excellent, but if we could have marinated it as in the following recipe, it would have been even better.

6 steaks from king or silver salmon
1/2 cup salad oil
1/4 cup vinegar
1/4 cup lemon juice
2 tablespoons onion, grated,
*   with juice*
1/2 tablespoon dry mustard
1/4 teaspoon salt

Place the steaks in 1 or 2 shallow dishes or do as I do and use a stainless steel baking pan. Combine the remainder of the ingredients and pour over the fish. Refrigerate for 4 hours, turning the fish over every hour.

When you're ready to cook drain off and save the marinade.

In a well-greased wire broiler basket put the steaks at medium height over a bed of coals. Cook until lightly browned, which should take about 5 minutes. Baste with the marinade, turn, and grill until fish is done. Test to see if the fish will flake to determine the doneness. This is where cooking skill enters the picture because the fish must be cooked but not overdone.

Serve hot from the grill with some marinade available in a small pitcher. Yield: 6 servings.

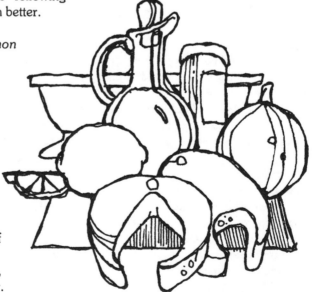

SALMON BAKED IN FOIL

This recipe is a family favorite. We usually bake up to a 10-pound fish, which gives us a meal of hot salmon the first day and a meal of cold salmon the next. Unless the nibblers and salmon sandwich fiends get into the leftovers.

For a special dinner party, we baked a whole 30-pound king salmon in this manner. It required many pieces of heavy aluminum foil to wrap the fish, and I had to make a pan out of sheet aluminum to hold it. Even then we still had to bend the salmon's tail to get it in the oven. The fish was certainly impressive as well as tasty, but I'll never cook another that big.

1 6- to 8-pound king or silver salmon
1/4 cup lemon juice
1/4 teaspoon salt
6 slices bread
2 tablespoons butter
1 medium onion, sliced
1 green pepper, cut in 1/4-inch strips
1 tomato, sliced
1/8 teaspoon thyme
4 slices bacon

You'll also need a piece of 18-inch-wide heavy-duty aluminum foil 6 inches longer than the fish.

Wash and dry the salmon. Brush the entire fish, including the body cavity, with lemon juice and sprinkle with salt.

On the aluminum foil lay the slices of bread and rest the fish on the bread.

In a medium-size frying pan melt the butter and add the onion, pepper, tomato and thyme, stirring until everything is coated with butter. Fill the cavity of the fish with this mixture.

With a sharp knife make 4 diagonal slits across the top side of the salmon. Place a slice of bacon in each slit.

Carefully fold the aluminum foil lengthwise over the fish, folding 2 or 3 times to assure a tight seal. Now shape the foil to the fish, turning the ends back over the fish, again folding at least twice. The salmon should now be sealed in a capsule. Place this bundle in a shallow baking dish and bake at 450° for an hour.

Remove the fish from the oven. Let it rest for 10 minutes, then unfold the foil. Carefully lift the fish from the slices of bread to a serving platter. Discard the bread as it has served its purpose of soaking up extra liquid and fat and preventing the fish from sticking to the foil.

You can serve this fish as is or you may wish to remove the skin from the top. Either way, garnish the salmon with lemon slices and parsley and serve with a selection of sauces. Dress it up as you see fit, but do try some Nelson Seafood Sauce (see page 133) on this salmon. Have fun, and good eating. Yield: 6 to 8 servings.

SALMON PATTIES

If you bake a fair-size salmon and do not invite the entire neighborhood to dinner you will have leftover fish. I love the feeling of having this in the refrigerator, as it opens so many doors to good eating.

One day when we had such a bowl of salmon in the refrigerator a neighbor wandered in for a mug of coffee. We became so engrossed in our own stimulating conversation that we ended up at dinnertime still sitting around the kitchen table. I invited our neighbor to dinner and said all we had was leftover salmon. Yes, she would stay, but only if she could make her favorite salmon patties. She could, and did. I sat there and took notes, which convert to this.

1 16-ounce can salmon or 2 cups leftover salmon
1/3 cup liquid from canned salmon or 1/3 cup fish stock (see page 22) or water
2 tablespoons butter
1/2 cup onion, chopped
2/3 cup bread crumbs
2 eggs, beaten
1 teaspoon dry parsley
1 teaspoon dry mustard

If the salmon is canned, drain it, reserving the liquid, and pick out pieces of skin and bone. Flake the salmon. In a frying pan, heat the butter and sauté the onion until transparent, then put in a bowl with 1/3 cup of the crumbs, the liquid, eggs, parsley, mustard and salmon. Mix well, shape into patties, and roll the patties in the remaining bread crumbs. Fry over medium heat until brown, turn, and brown the second side. Serve hot with your favorite sauce. Yield: 4 servings.

SALMON ANTIPASTO

With a family of 8 and many friends with families as big, we seemed to acquire some recipes that involved large quantities. But then maybe you have a big family, too, or an invitation to a potluck supper. This recipe has always been a success.

1-1/2 cups cider vinegar
1 cup salad oil
2 6-ounce cans tomato paste
1 teaspoon salt
1/2 teaspoon coarsely ground black
pepper
4 celery stalks, sliced thin
1 green pepper, chopped
1 cup onion, sliced in thin rings
1/2 cup water
1 16-ounce can sliced carrots
1 16-ounce can wax beans
1 4-ounce can mushroom pieces and
stems
1 3-ounce can sliced pimentos
1 dill pickle, sliced diagonally
4 cups cooked salmon or other fish, even
tuna, boned

Start by making the dressing. Place the vinegar, oil, tomato paste, salt and pepper in an enamel or stainless-steel pan and stir thoroughly. Heat this sauce to just below the boiling point and set aside to cool.

Next put the celery, green pepper and onion into a pan with the water and boil until tender. Drain and let cool.

Put these vegetables, the canned vegetables and the sliced pickle into a big bowl. Break up and add the fish, but do not stir any of these things while adding. Now pour the cooled dressing over the contents of the bowl and carefully mix until everything is coated. Put the salad in a serving dish and chill until time to serve.

MOOSEBURGER SOUP

The ground moose or beef that you intend to put into this soup should be extra lean. I grind my moose meat without suet when the meat's intended for this recipe. And we grind a lot, in anticipation, when we start this soup.

The basic soup is good in its own right but it is also the basis for other imaginative soups.

BASIC MOOSEBURGER SOUP
2 pounds ground moose or beef
4 tablespoons shortening or butter
4 quarts beef stock or water
2 stalks celery, diced
2 onions, chopped
3 carrots, diced
1 teaspoon salt
1/4 teaspoon black pepper
1 teaspoon dried parsley
2 bay leaves

Crumble the meat into small pieces, put it in a 6-quart soup kettle, and brown it in the shortening. Pour off any fat. Add the liquid, bring to a boil, and simmer for an hour, skimming off any froth. Add the vegetables, seasoning and herbs and simmer for 30 minutes more. Serve as is or use as a base. This soup is quite accommodating; you'll find you can come up with lots of variations. Mine are just to get you started.

VARIATION ONE: Vegetable Chowder
To half of the basic soup add 2 packages of frozen mixed vegetables and simmer for 10 minutes. Then add 1 cup of diced boiled potatoes. Heat for 5 minutes and serve.

VARIATION TWO: Delight Soup
To half of the basic soup add 2 packages of frozen cauliflower and simmer for 10 minutes.

While this is cooking, put 2 cups of cold milk and 2 tablespoons of cornstarch in the top of a double boiler. Heat, stirring constantly, until the mixture starts to thicken. Add 1/4 cup of Parmesan or Romano cheese and stir until blended. Keep warm.

Now pour 1/2 cup of the soup into the cheese mix, stir well, and then add the cheese mix to the soup pot. Stir and remove from the stove. Cool for at least 5 minutes and then stir in the beaten yolks of 2 eggs.

SOUPS AND SAUCES

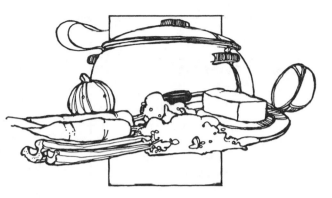

When I first sat down to write this book I had no intention of including this chapter. It just seemed to develop all by itself as I worked my way through my notebooks and recipes. That's the reason you'll find soups in other chapters and even a sauce or two.

The wonderful soups that my mother made were by no means limited only to bean soup. She could make a good-tasting soup out of anything available, and I've included some of the recipes that bring back especially good memories.

My travels around the state for so many years exposed me to kettles containing a wide variety of soups. Whenever I found an excellent soup I would try to get the recipe. All too often I found that these soups were made by touch. You know—take a handful of this, a pinch of that, a bunch of whatever's ripe in the garden, and put it in enough water to fill the pot up to that little mark there where the handle is welded on. Try converting that into a recipe.

Every time a cook uses the no-recipe or touch system that cook is in effect creating a new soup. After all, even the changing of a single ingredient makes a different soup. This is the reason you can find hundreds of recipes that all have the same title although no two of them will taste the same. Someone left out the bay leaf or added a touch of sweet basil at the time of passing on the recipe—if there ever was a recipe. This goes on until only the water, meat and name remain the same. Sometimes even the meat will change.

One of the greatest soup-makers I ever knew was the owner-cook of a roadhouse on the Richardson Highway, some 150 miles north of Valdez. Her name was Nellie, and she was well past middle age when I knew her. It wasn't her cooking that first brought about our meeting—although she was an excellent cook—it was my own parents telling me that this woman always knew everything that went on within 150 miles of her roadhouse, and sometimes a lot farther away as well. It was Nellie's ear and knowledge that I wanted when I first visited her.

The third day I was on duty at the Glennallen Highway Patrol Post I had a message to call Paxson Lodge, 100 or so miles up the Richardson Highway. I knew that the magic of telephone went up that far, because there was a sign on the wall by the post telephone describing the rings necessary to reach Paxson. That tele-

GARBANZO AND RICE SOUP

I have no memory of garbanzos in my life until sometime in the 1960s. They entered my life in a 5-bean salad and a short time later I found them in a bowl of soup in Seward. My first thought was that someone had goofed and had not cooked the beans long enough. But I soon got used to finding garbanzos. I began to enjoy them and finally started to use the strange bean. Like this, for example.

1 medium onion, minced
1 clove garlic, minced
1 tablespoon butter
1 16-ounce can garbanzos
2 cups chicken stock
1/2 cup cooked rice
1/2 teaspoon dried parsley
1/3 cup tomato paste
2 tablespoons Parmesan cheese

In a 4-quart saucepan sauté the onion and garlic in the butter until translucent. Add the garbanzos and the liquid from the can, the chicken stock, rice, parsley and tomato paste. Heat just to a boil, add the cheese, and serve at once. Yield: 2 to 4 servings.

FRENCH ONION SOUP

I have been fond of onion soup ever since I was about 16 and a girl I liked invited me home for some. I've tried dozens of recipes since then and never had it quite like the soup I had at her house. I can only assume that her onion soup was spiced with something special called anticipation. But whenever I have sherry in the house I may make a batch of this soup on a moment's notice.

1/4 cup butter
6 medium onions, sliced in rings
5 cups beef or chicken stock
3 slices French bread or other white
    bread
Butter
Salt and black pepper
1 cup sherry
1/2 cup Parmesan cheese, grated

In a 3-quart saucepan melt the butter and brown the onions to a golden color. Add the stock and simmer for 20 minutes.

During this time toast the bread, cut it in quarters if it isn't French bread, and spread with butter.

Salt and pepper the soup to taste and add the sherry. Pour the soup into wide, deep ovenproof bowls. Sprinkle the pieces of toast with the cheese and float them on the soup. Place the soup bowls in a 350° oven until the cheese melts. Serve in the hot dishes. Yield: 6 servings.

phone, by the way, was interesting. You may have seen one like it on TV: a wooden box fastened to the wall with a mouthpiece sticking out front, a receiver hanging on a yoke to the left and a crank on the right.

When I figured out how to ring Paxson I lifted the receiver and found that someone was talking. Before I could take the receiver away from my ear I heard someone else mention a car over the hill and off the road, so I stood there listening.

I became so engrossed that I forgot all about not being an invited member of this conversation and asked a question. No one screamed "Wiretapping" or anything, honest. The fellow down the line in Valdez merely asked me who I was, as he didn't recognize my voice. I told him I was the new highway patrolman and he answered my questions. Then the subject matter of the call changed and I hung up.

This telephone line stretched from Valdez to Paxson, and sometimes beyond, and we were approximately at the midpoint of the line. Nellie was between us and Paxson. I soon learned that this line was a party line. So was the one that went down the Glenn Highway and up the Tok Highway. In fact, as I remember it, they were all one big party line. The wires had been installed either by the U.S. Army or the U.S. Road Commission a long time before—at least 20 years prior to my arrival on the scene. The interesting thing about the line was that according to every expert who ever saw it, the line couldn't work. We didn't argue with the experts, we just continued making our calls.

In trying to get my messages to Paxson I discovered that it definitely was difficult to get up the line that far, for you had to go

past Nellie's telephone. She never hung up her receiver. All during her waking and working hours the receiver was lying on the kitchen table in her roadhouse. She listened to everything that was said for miles around. It seemed that everyone was aware of this fact and some used her like

the answering services of today. Nellie would willingly retain and pass on a message. But to get past Nellie to the north required a special technique.

First you yelled into the mouthpiece, "Hey, Nellie, ring Paxson for me!" She would answer, "OK," and ring her phone for Paxson. When Paxson came on the line it was customary to say, "Nellie, the voice is weak. Hang up will you, Nellie?" She wouldn't hang up, but at least she wouldn't enter into the conversation.

Yes, Nellie was part of the system and helped make life interesting. She would have loved our CB radios today. I always stopped at her roadhouse and sat in the kitchen on every trip up that way. I could eat a bowl of her soup and her fresh bread and find out more about what was going on in my district than in a week's patroling.

There were those who swore that Nellie could talk to places on her telephone that were no longer connected to the wire. Twenty years of habit, they said, carried the signals through the air and the ground. I never could buy that bit of science fiction. But I'll agree that Nellie did know things that happened well off the telephone line and in places where the wire used to go.

As for Nellie's recipes, I never got one. We always had so much else to talk about.

Getting back to the days of my youth again, I remember how Dad went to a great deal of trouble to spill a pot of soup one time. Anyway, that's what the cook aboard the old *Elk* thought.

The cannery tender *Elk* was not designed to run on the Copper River Flats. She was much too deep, drawing a full seven feet when other flats tenders drew four. She had her good qualities, though. She could pull like a big tug, for instance.

On the day of this story we were running across a part of the flats known as the Race Track. The tide was ebbing slightly and we suddenly went aground. This was not unusual, as it took a normal or high tide to cross almost anything with the *Elk*. When the boat was aground the routine was to put out side braces, which kept the ship from lying down on her side, and wait for 12 hours to pass until the next high tide. Once we were settled down the cook would start a big pot of soup.

Everything would have stayed as usual that day except that the *Poppy* passed us. The little *Poppy* drew about 3-1/2 feet

of water and seemed to float on a wet sponge. Her skipper yelled at Dad, "Have you homesteaded?" For some reason this made Dad quite angry. He sat there on the rail and watched the other ship disappear in the distance.

Suddenly he smiled. In a minute the entire crew was back on the main hatch. A sling was rigged and two drums of oil rolled into the sling. Several sacks of coal were added and the sling tightened with the load. The winch took the load to the top of the boom and it was swung outboard. The *Elk* laid over on her side and came afloat. With the deep keel sticking out at about 45° on the side the *Elk* suddenly drew a lot less water.

There was a mighty yell from the galley. Out came the cook, closely followed by three gallons of soup. I have never seen a madder cook. We didn't eat for another 12 hours.

We were under way in a minute or two although the ship looked extremely different, traveling listed way over to the starboard, but she was shallow.

The topper came when we slid past a high and dry *Poppy* about five miles down the channel. Her skipper had been overconfident or had tried a shortcut. No one would have ever known if we hadn't appeared on the scene. We all stood at the side of our ship and yelled and waved. It was worth the spilled soup. Even the cook agreed, some 10 hours later.

I think I will add a few sauces to this chapter. However, as there have been great books written about sauces, I'm going

ROQUEFORT SOUP

I have been enamoured of Roquefort and other blue cheeses ever since I was a young man and ended my youthful foolishness of turning down that wonderful taste. This recipe was given to me by a man who stated, without the slightest indication of doubt, that this is the best soup ever made by man. I would not rate it quite that high but it certainly is good.

1 pound beef for stewing, cubed as fine as
    possible
2 quarts beef stock
1 medium onion, chopped
1 tablespoon basil
1 teaspoon dried parsley
1 teaspoon salt
1/4 teaspoon black pepper
2 cups egg noodles
1/3 cup Roquefort cheese, crumbled

Into a 4-quart soup pot put the meat, stock, onion, basil, parsley, salt and pepper. Bring to a boil and simmer about an hour or until the meat is tender. Add the noodles and cook for another 10 minutes. Add the cheese and stir until it is well blended.

Serve hot in deep soup bowls with oyster crackers.

SAUSAGE SOUP

When a friend's wife contracted a terminal case of cabin fever I was given 100 pounds of caribou sausage, showing how the break-up of a home can affect even people only indirectly involved.

I soon discovered that my friend liked hot sausage and this gift was the hottest sausage I ever came in contact with. It was so hot that if you didn't follow every mouthful with a half-glass of beer you would suffer painful mouth burns. Having accepted 100 pounds of the stuff I had to find a way to use it.

When all else fails, make soup. I consider that a good theory, so I set out to boil some of the fire out of the sausage in soup. It turned out to be good—a little hot, but good! It's best with beer.

1 pound hot caribou sausage or any hot
    sausage
3 quarts water
5 stalks celery, chopped
1 medium onion, chopped
1 teaspoon dried parsley
2 cups fresh or frozen cauliflower
3 eggs, beaten

Put the sausage and water into a 4-quart pot and bring to a boil. Simmer 10 minutes and add the celery, onion and parsley. After this has cooked for 15 minutes, add the cauliflower and cook another 10 minutes or until the cauliflower is done. Now, while stirring rapidly, dribble the eggs into the pot. Cook another 10 minutes.

EASY SOUP

In the last 20 years or so I must have read hundreds of soup recipes that began with, "Take a can of soup." Some of them are excellent, some good, some imaginative, but too many were just cute. But there is a really special recipe, a simple recipe, that stands out in my memory as worth repeating. Even the kids liked this. Take a can of soup. . . .

1 10-1/2-ounce can tomato soup
Water
1 teaspoon curry powder
1 tablespoon brown sugar

Heat the canned soup with an equal amount of water, add the curry powder and sugar, and stir.

Try it, then serve this at your next dinner party without comment, just to watch the response. Yield: 2 servings.

DILLINGHAM SOUP

As a rule the soups served in restaurants are designed to fill soup bowls and keep for long periods of time on the stove. There is something about making soup in quantities of 10 gallons and up that eliminates the master touch of a good cook. So when I visited Dillingham, on the west coast of Alaska, and found that the soup *du jour* in the town's only restaurant was cheese and celery, I was not greatly thrilled. I couldn't avoid being served the soup to get the dinner I wanted, so made the best of it and tasted the soup. I was delighted. I later met the cook and obtained this recipe.

2 cups celery, diced
4 tablespoons butter
5 tablespoons flour
2 cups cold water
Salt and black pepper
2 egg yolks, beaten
1/4 cup milk
1/4 pound sharp Cheddar cheese, grated

Boil the celery until tender. Drain and set aside.

Melt the butter in a frying pan over medium heat. Add the flour and mix until smooth. Remove pan from stove and stir in the cold water seasoned with salt and pepper. Stir until smooth. Mix the egg yolks into the milk and add to the mixture. Return to the heat; simmer 10 minutes.

Add the cheese and stir over medium heat until the cheese blends into the mixture. Add the cooked celery, stir, and serve. Yield: 3 or 4 servings.

to limit my efforts to those that are tried and true. Most of the recipes here are collector's items and I'm the collector. I will pass all of them on to you as I'm sure that any time you're not dieting you'll love these sauces. But use wisely or you'll all be on diets.

A rather strange recipe for sauce started me on an interesting experience. It was while I was stationed at Glennallen that I received a radio message from Tok, on the Alaska Highway. I was asked to stop and escort back to the border guard station a car containing five men. They had failed to stop at American customs after entering Alaska from Canada.

I started east along the Tok Highway toward Tok, found my vehicle and stopped it. I had observed the car coming, stopped mine, pulled my shotgun out of its rack, and stepped into the road. The vehicle stopped about 20 feet from me Five large tough-looking men climbed out of the car.

Suddenly feeling somewhat alone, I smiled and advised them that customs wanted them back at Tok. After much waving of arms, shouting, foul language and emphatic complaining they got back in their car and headed back toward Tok. I followed.

Everything went along smoothly for 10 miles, but I could see that there was a heated discussion in the other car. We were doing a flat 55 miles an hour when the car ahead suddenly made a panic stop. It had to be that the angry men were trying to get me to run into their vehicle. I didn't, just!

I motioned the driver to continue and he did, at 10 miles an hour. I know that the driver and his friends were trying to make me angry, but as long as they kept moving at all I was happy. They tried for 40 miles to irritate me and then gave up going slow · They did not try excessive speed.

At Tok they and their vehicle were searched carefully and then they were allowed to continue their trip. What they thought that they accomplished with their actions, I'll never know. They wasted some six hours of their time in going back to Tok. I worked by the month and time didn't bother me.

The most interesting thing about the incident was how the customs people detected them not clearing. The owner of a café in Tok had served the men and they were difficult enough to attract his attention. As the men were leaving he cleared off the table where they had been served. On the floor under the table was a folded piece of paper. He opened it to find it was a recipe for marijuana sauce. He jotted the license number of their car on the recipe and called the local patrolman.

The patrolman checked the border and it was discovered that this vehicle had not cleared. The border checked with the Canadian border and found that the vehicle had cleared there. The chase was on for failure to check into American customs.

No, I didn't even get to see the recipe for marijuana sauce. It was seized as evidence or something. Smoking the stuff I had heard of, as well as its use in brownies, but not sauce. That was interesting.

Enjoy what I now offer, even if I can't give you the exotic recipe for marijuana sauce.

MULLIGATAWNY

After becoming acquainted with P.K., our friend from India, I became interested in Indian cooking. As a whole I found it difficult to do because of the absence in Alaska of many of the spices that show up in Indian recipes. I was especially curious about mulligatawny soup, which is often mentioned in literature about India. This recipe for mulligatawny is good. I cannot guarantee its authenticity, only its taste.

1/4 cup butter
1 3-pound chicken, cut up for frying
2 tablespoons onion, minced
3 quarts chicken stock or water
1 stalk celery, diced
1 teaspoon turmeric
1/8 teaspoon mace
1/4 teaspoon black pepper
1 tablespoon curry powder
1/2 teaspoon dried parsley
6 tablespoons flour

Melt the butter in a 6-quart soup pot or Dutch oven. Add the chicken and onion and sauté for 5 minutes, then cover and simmer for 20 minutes. Add all other ingredients except flour and simmer for another 40 minutes.

Remove the chicken and set aside to cool. Strain the soup and return it to the pot. Debone the chicken, cut into bite-size chunks, and return to the pot and simmer for 15 minutes more.

Make up a smooth thin paste of flour and cold water and stir it into the soup until the soup thickens. Serve hot.

CONSOMMÉ ROYALE

I was stormbound in a logging camp on an island near Sitka when I first consumed this soup. It was a cold, windy day and I had stood on the beach waiting for an aircraft for some time. The cook stepped out and held up a cup, the invitation for a cup of coffee. With the coffee I got a large bowl of soup, bread and apple pie. The soup was good, so a compliment and interest got me the recipe. I've halved it and it is still a lot of soup.

1 cup elbow macaroni
1 16-ounce can peas and carrots
2 quarts beef stock
1-1/2 teaspoons cinnamon
Salt and black pepper

Cook the macaroni, drain in cold water, and set aside.

Combine the peas and carrots, beef stock and cinnamon in a pot. Boil for 5 minutes and season to taste. Add the macaroni, stir until macaroni is warm, and serve in deep soup bowls. I like to add a sprinkle of Parmesan cheese and a handful of oyster crackers.

This is a quick and filling soup that I've used to enlarge a dinner quickly when the number of guests suddenly increased.

LOWBUSH CRANBERRY SOUP

Some people might say this should be called Citrus Soup, but the Danish woman who gave me the recipe was very partial to Alaska so it's Lowbush Cranberry Soup.

1 cup lowbush cranberries or canned
    lingonberries or large fresh cranberries
    from the Lower 48, precooked
3 thin orange slices
3 thin lemon slices
2 tablespoons lemon juice
1/4 cup raisins
1/2 stick cinnamon
1 cup water
1 can grapefruit sections or sections of 1
    fresh grapefruit
1/2 cup sugar
Salt
2 teaspoons cornstarch
8 ounces heavy cream, whipped

Simmer the cranberries, orange and lemon slices, lemon juice, raisins and cinnamon for 20 minutes in 1/2 cup of water. Now add the grapefruit, sugar and a dash of salt. Bring to a boil.

Mix the cornstarch in the remaining 1/2 cup of water and add to the mixture, stirring constantly until it thickens. Check the soup for sweetness and add more sugar if needed. Remove from the heat and chill.

Serve cold on a hot afternoon, topping each serving with a gob of freshly whipped cream. Yield: 2 or 3 servings.

BÉCHAMEL SAUCE: White Sauce and Brown Sauce

This is a recipe that you should master as it is a basic sauce from which you can develop a number of variations. But use it also in its basic form.

5 tablespoons butter
5 tablespoons flour
1-3/4 cups cold milk
Salt and black pepper

To make the White Sauce, melt but do not brown the butter over a low heat. Remove the pan from the heat and stir in the flour. Add the cold milk and put the pan over medium heat, stirring the sauce constantly until it is almost boiling. Salt and pepper to taste and remove from the heat.

Brown Sauce is made in exactly the same way except that the butter should be carefully browned when you're starting out.

Having mastered White Sauce and Brown Sauce you can cook anything requiring a sauce. White Sauce can be used as a base for any creamed soup or for creamed dried beef and as a sauce for vegetables, fish, crustacea, eggs and scalloped dishes. Brown Sauce is an excellent base for onion soup or mushroom soup, mushroom sauce or turkey or chicken gravy.

HOLLANDAISE SAUCE: #1 and #2

Hollandaise Sauce is a classic for which I suppose there are dozens, maybe hundreds, of recipes. I'm sure that everyone who has a recipe thinks his or hers is the original or at least the "improved" original. I find I have 2 recipes in my files, both bearing the same name. I'll have to admit that I use the second recipe more often and I think you'll see why.

HOLLANDAISE SAUCE #1
4 egg yolks
1/2 cup butter divided in 3 portions
2 teaspoons lemon juice
Salt and black pepper

In the top of your double boiler put the egg yolks and one portion of the butter. The water in the bottom pan should be almost, but not quite, to the boiling point. Stir the yolks and butter constantly and rapidly from the first to the last moment of cooking. When a portion of butter is melted add the next until the last third of the butter has been stirred in.

Remove from the heat, still stirring. Wait 2 minutes and then slowly add the lemon juice as you continue to stir. Add the salt and pepper to taste. Return the mixture to the heat over almost-boiling water and stir until the sauce thickens. Remove from the heat and serve.

This is excellent on asparagus and eggs Benedict, besides building arm muscles.

HOLLANDAISE SAUCE #2
1/4 cup sour cream
1/4 cup mayonnaise
1/2 teaspoon prepared mustard
1 teaspoon lemon juice

Combine the ingredients in a small saucepan, place over a low heat, and stir until warm. Serve the same as Hollandaise Sauce #1. This can be simplified further by using 1/2 cup mayonnaise instead of 1/4 cup mayonnaise and 1/4 cup sour cream. Now you see?

TARTAR SAUCE: #1 and #2

The fact that there seem to be hundreds of recipes in the world all bearing the name Tartar Sauce amazes me. But then, even I have 2 that I call by that name. I'll just number them for you as I did with the Hollandaise Sauce.

TARTAR SAUCE #1
This is what I make when I have planned far enough ahead to pick up all the ingredients.

8 ounces sour cream
1/4 cup mayonnaise
2 tablespoons pickle relish
2 tablespoons green onion, minced
1 hard-boiled egg, chopped
1 tablespoon dry white wine

Mix the ingredients together, chill, and serve. Good on fish and all seafoods except raw oysters. OK, try it on them, too.

TARTAR SAUCE #2
Made when I am in a hurry and did not plan ahead.

1 cup mayonnaise
1 teaspoon onion, grated
1 tablespoon fresh parsley, minced
2 tablespoons pickle, minced
2 teaspoons pimento, minced

Mix together, chill, and serve with the same things as above.

COCKTAIL SAUCE: #1 and #2

I am very fond of shrimp or crab cocktail before dinner. The sauce on these cocktails is very important and again I have 2 recipes that have served me well.

COCKTAIL SAUCE #1
3/4 cup chili sauce
2 tablespoons lemon juice
1/2 teaspoon onion, grated
2 drops Tabasco
2 teaspoons horseradish
Salt and black pepper

Combine the ingredients in a bowl, add salt and pepper to taste, chill, and serve.

COCKTAIL SAUCE #2
1 cup mayonnaise
1/4 cup ketchup
1/4 cup flat beer
1 tablespoon prepared mustard
1/2 tablespoon horseradish
Salt and black pepper

Combine the ingredients in a bowl, add salt and pepper to taste, chill, and serve.

ALASKAN HUNTER'S SAUCE

This is another time-proved sauce. I have found it to be excellent, well worth the effort. Moose, caribou, venison, beef, hare and fowl have been touched by my mixture. Even the lowly hamburger can be made into something different with this sauce.

5 tablespoons
    butter
5 tablespoons flour
1/2 cup beef stock
1 teaspoon onion
    powder
1 4-ounce can
    mushroom pieces
Salt and black pepper
1/4 cup dry white
    wine
1/4 cup port

Lightly brown the butter in a saucepan and remove from the heat. Add the flour and stir well. Now add the stock, onion powder and mushrooms, including the liquid from the can. Return the pan to the heat, stirring and simmering the mixture until it thickens. Salt and pepper to taste. At the last minute add the 2 wines, stir well, and serve.

MORNAY SAUCE

My notes indicate that this recipe is 350 years old. The notes do not tell me where it came from or how someone knew it was that old. I can vouch for about 15 years of service and the fact that it is good on fish, fowl and some pork dishes. By all means try it on baked potatoes, too.

5 tablespoons butter
5 tablespoons flour
1-1/4 cups cold milk
1 teaspoon onion powder
Salt and black pepper
1 cup sharp Cheddar cheese, shredded
1/4 teaspoon nutmeg
1/4 teaspoon celery salt

In a small saucepan melt but do not brown the butter. Remove from the heat and stir in the flour. Add the milk and onion powder. Mix well, return to the heat, and stir constantly as the mixture thickens. Salt and pepper to taste.

When the sauce is thick add the cheese and continue to stir until the cheese is melted and blended. Add the nutmeg and celery salt. Stir again and serve.

Note: If you leave out the cheese, nutmeg and celery salt you have the makings for another sauce. Instead of adding those ingredients add 1/2 cup of white wine to the thickened mixture in the saucepan and you will have Sauce Lyonnaise, another old sauce and a reliable stand-by.

BÉARNAISE SAUCE

This sauce is excellent on almost any meat or fish and on some vegetables too.

4 tablespoons vinegar
1 teaspoon tarragon, crumbled
2 teaspoons green onion, minced
2 drops oil of anise
1 teaspoon salt
1/4 teaspoon white pepper
5 egg yolks
6 tablespoons butter

In a small enamel or stainless-steel saucepan mix the vinegar, tarragon, onion, oil of anise, salt and pepper. Cook over a low heat and stir until the liquid is reduced by a third. Remove from the stove and cool for 10 minutes. Beat the egg yolks together and slowly add to the vinegar mixture, stirring vigorously. Return the pan to the heat and add the butter. Continue stirring and cooking until the sauce thickens to the consistency of heavy cream.

This can be served either warm or cold.

Note: I have found that some people think this can be improved upon by adding, just before serving, a teaspoon of chopped green onion, a teaspoon of chervil or lemon juice, or a dash of cayenne or some fresh chopped parsley. Let your conscience be your guide.

NELSON SEAFOOD SAUCE

I think anyone who has created a sauce that has survived the test of time—25 years—is entitled to put his or her name on it, don't you? We've used this recipe on any seafood that required a sauce to bring out the taste. Shrimp, crab, salmon, halibut, red snapper and many other seafoods have all benefitted.

1/2 cup mayonnaise
1/2 cup ketchup
1/2 cup onion, minced
1 teaspoon Worcestershire sauce

Mix all the ingredients in a bowl. Big deal, huh?

Now if you feel that you've been had, add 3 tablespoons of prepared horseradish, let set for 2 hours, and name it after yourself. I claim only the 4-ingredient concoction.

ALASKA SWEET SEA PICKLES

After many years of hooking my fishing gear in kelp, losing my temper at kelp wrapped around boat propellers, and in general being of the opinion that kelp was of no earthly good, I was introduced to sea pickles.

As far as I know, you cannot go into a store and buy these; you have to make them. This is how to do it.

4 pounds bulb kelp
2 gallons and 2 quarts water
2 cups salt
1/2 teaspoon alum, usually found on a
*   grocery store's spice rack*
3-1/2 cups sugar
1 pint white vinegar
1/2 teaspoon oil of cloves
1/2 teaspoon oil of cinnamon

Kelp must be attached to the bottom of the sea to be considered alive and fresh. Use only that kind and pick strands that are from 2 to 2-1/2 inches around. Cut the kelp into 6-inch tubes for easy handling. Remove the outer dark layer with a sharp knife, then split the pieces lengthwise. Make a brine solution with the salt mixed into 2 gallons of water and soak the pieces of kelp for at least 8 hours. Keep the kelp well covered with the brine.

Remove the kelp and cut each piece into 1/4-inch slices. Wash thoroughly. Mix the alum in 2 quarts of water and soak the kelp in this solution for 15 minutes. Drain, wash, and drain again.

Now place the kelp pieces in an enameled pot, cover with water, and bring to a boil. Simmer until the pieces can be easily pierced with a fork, taking care not to let them get too soft. This will probably take 20 minutes. Drain again.

Combine the sugar, vinegar, oil of cloves and oil of cinnamon in a pan and boil for 2 minutes. Pour this over the kelp pieces and let stand overnight.

The next day pour off the syrup, heat it, and when it is boiling pour it back over the pieces of kelp. Let this stand for another 24 hours.

OK, now we are coming down the home stretch. Heat the kelp in the solution and while the kelp is hot pack it in warm glass jars, pouring the liquid over it. Seal the jars immediately, cool, and store in a refrigerator.

SALADS, SPINACH AND SEAWEED

Today the word *salad* brings to mind great green mixtures of lettuce, tomatoes, celery, onions, radishes, cucumbers and avocado, not to mention shrimp, crab, cheese and hard-boiled eggs. This wasn't always true.

The salads of my childhood were mainly potato salad and coleslaw. In fact until I was about 10 those were the only salads I was familiar with. It was cannery mess halls that first exposed me to green salad. I tasted such salad then but didn't really take it seriously for another 13 years.

Even though I lived some 25 years without green salad, I've had another 30 years to make up for lost time. It's possible to enjoy a lot of green salad in 30 years.

Back when I was much shorter, I did become involved in salad-making: coleslaw. I got to turn the crank on the food grinder while my mother put cabbage, carrots and a touch of onion into the machine. Our combined efforts made a good salad.

A few years later I graduated to both turning the crank and feeding in the vegetables. I can still hear Mother saying, "Keep your fingers out of the grinder!" I'll admit that I've said the same thing a few hundred times to six children of my own,

so memory and echo may be somewhat mixed in my mind.

The first time I made coleslaw after leaving home involves quite a jump in time. I was living the life of a young bachelor in Anchorage, just prior to World War II.

Imagine you're putting together a dinner for two, with your mind on charming the attractive creature you're cooking for. Have you found that having thoughts like that interferes with your recipes? For instance, the Nelson recipe for coleslaw includes onions. I found myself mentally debating if I should leave the onions out. Yes, when your objective changes from eating your cooking can suffer.

Did I leave out the onions? I'll have to answer that question by stating that I was young and not quite so dedicated to cooking as I am today. I was in the period of life when some activities were receiving higher priorities than food. I fear that my motive did not improve the meal.

They say it is good for you, when you have sinned, to confess. Very well, I altered a recipe without improving it. But that is the last admission of sin you're going to get out of me.

All the exciting thoughts that the above

TRADITIONAL COLESLAW

The coleslaw that I knew as a youth, and still make today, was made in a food grinder or a meat grinder with a plate for coarse grinding. I've included another coleslaw recipe but this is the real old-fashioned slaw.

1 medium-size cabbage
5 carrots, peeled and quartered
1 small onion, quartered
1/2 cup mayonnaise
Salt, black pepper and paprika

Grind the vegetables into a bowl. Mix well, add mayonnaise and salt and pepper and mix again. Turn out into a serving bowl, level the top, and sprinkle with paprika. That's it! Serve.
Note: When green peppers are in season I sometimes grind one in with the other vegetables.

MODERN COLESLAW

When we have guests and coleslaw appears on our menu this is the recipe we often use. It really isn't any better than the preceding; it just seems more suited to modern tastes and it can be dressed up easily.

3 cups cabbage, shredded
1 cup carrots, grated coarse
1/4 cup green pepper, minced
1/4 cup onion, minced
1/4 cup raisins
2/3 cup mayonnaise
Salt, black pepper and paprika

Combine cabbage, carrots, green pepper, onion, raisins and mayonnaise in a bowl and toss together. Add seasoning and paprika to taste.
Note: As an alternative try adding to the plain mayonnaise a teaspoon of prepared mustard and a tablespoon of vinegar. To this you can add 2 teaspoons of sugar or honey for another alternative.

memory brought back have also brought back my first "solo" attempt at potato salad. It was in the same period of time and on a similar occasion—with a different guest, but the objective was the same. This time, with a slight increase in confidence, I *did* put in the onions. After all if both parties to a kiss have eaten onions, kissing can still be fun. I will go so far as to report that the salad was a success, too.

A great many stories have been written about how the war interrupted men's dedicated pursuit of women. Well, listen to this one.

I was inducted into the U.S. Army in the city of Anchorage at 8:30 one morning. We departed for overseas at 8:40 a.m. the same day. I arrived overseas at Fort Richardson, A.P.O. 942, at 9 o'clock the same morning, having traveled three miles and crossed Ship Creek.

After six weeks of following old soldiers from the Fourth Infantry Division around the woods for basic training, I was back to riding a bus back and forth to my bachelor digs in Anchorage. I was able to go on making salads and other tempting dishes until the army decided it could get along without me, about 30 months later.

Shortly after the Big War my wife grew up, reaching age 18, and we could get married. Now I had a house to build, a job to work at and a few gleams in my eye. I also had a kitchen, all my own, to play in. In our back yard was a garden. My energy level was disgusting. By midsummer we had all the lettuce, radishes and onions we could eat. It was now that I really started experimenting with green salad. We enjoyed most of the results but took time only to record a very few. I had so much to do. . .

By fall our garden provided broccoli, kohlrabi, cabbage, cauliflower, peas, carrots and potatoes. In those days we were without a freezer and drove ourselves to eat up any surplus we couldn't store. By the time winter rolled around we had only potatoes, cabbage and carrots stored away in our cellar. It was back to potato salad and coleslaw for the winter.

Our next experience with limited salad-making supplies came when I was assigned to the outpost at Glennallen, 189 miles north of Anchorage on the Glenn Highway. The nearest store at the time was at Copper Center, 14 miles away, and that carried limited produce.

We finally worked out a deal with a produce company in Anchorage and the mailman to get a box of produce to us once a week. The company just sent us what was good. We had some interesting salads with what the employees thought we might like.

Several years later we moved to the Matanuska Valley and for the next five years had wonderful gardens again. It was only then that we discovered spinach and Swiss chard. These two greens have continued to be among our favorites and each year I plant longer rows. We were able to eat all we wanted and by then we could also freeze large quantities, so we continued to enjoy our garden products all winter. Today we are back in the valley and enjoying the good eating it produces.

During our years in Southeastern Alaska we were not able to have gardens. Although we missed the wonderful fresh items that a garden could supply, we had the sea.

I discovered that the ocean in that area abounded in plant life. There are cultures that enjoy seaweed and kelp but I was,

frankly, only slightly interested. The varieties of seaweed that other people find tasty are still a mystery to me. But kelp is another story. I found dozens of recipes to make this form of plant life edible and some are delicious.

Just **thinking of salads** brings many stories to mind, like the one about the old salad-maker himself, the beaver.

One evening some years ago my friend Phil and I were drifting in a boat down the middle fork of the Gulkana River. Our intention was to surprise a moose during his evening meal or drink. Instead we surprised a beaver.

On a high bank beside the river a beaver was busy eating the bark and leaves of a bush, his kind of salad. Our boat drifted to within six feet of the animal who, I'm sure, assumed there was no such creature as us within at least a mile.

Phil, who worked for the U.S. Forest Service at the time, asked, in his most official voice, "Do you have a timber permit?"

The beaver jumped straight up, looked over its shoulder, turned in the air, and dived into the river, landing in the water between us and the bank with an exceptionally large splash. It was then our turn to be startled as the splash just about swamped us. That beaver sure was a fast thinker and certainly evened the score in a hurry. I only hope that it recovered enough to put up a good stock of salad stuff for the winter.

Then there was the summer that Phil and I worked on a government survey crew out of Homer. We were in the field all

BACHELOR'S SALAD

Way back, that's *way* back, in my courting days, I created what was known then as chef's salad. My theory was that 2 young people in love were too busy to cook. So with this recipe I was able to toss a few colorful foods together to sustain me and my true love while the outside world turned without my help. It didn't work! All too soon we were hungry again, like the old joke about Chinese food. But then I never have been attracted to women with bird appetites.

Anyway, the recipe survived in my cookbook. I guarantee the flavor, but make no promises about how long it'll stick to your ribs.

1 clove garlic, halved
1 head lettuce, any kind, or a combination
2 cups cooked lean ham, cut in strips
*   1/4 inch wide*
1/2 pound sharp Cheddar cheese, cut in
*   1/4-inch cubes*
1/4 cup oil and vinegar dressing
3 hard-boiled eggs, sliced
Salt and coarsely ground black pepper

First rub the cut garlic around the inside of the salad bowl—a wooden bowl, if possible. Separate the lettuce leaves and spread them around the bottom and sides of the bowl. Mix the ham, cheese and dressing in a separate bowl and place them in the lettuce-lined bowl. Arrange the sliced eggs on top. Lightly season. Add additional dressing, if needed, and serve. Yield: lunch for 2 or 3.

WARM SPINACH SALAD

There I was with a garden full of spinach threatening to go to seed before I could eat it all. This situation was complicated by the fact that I was suddenly tired of rabbit food, as one of my friends calls salad. I needed something different and this is what developed. It wasn't quite like this the first time I made it, though, as it has improved over the years.

1 pound fresh spinach
4 green onions, chopped
Black pepper, coarsely ground
5 bacon slices, cut into 1/4-inch squares
1 teaspoon sugar
2 tablespoons wine vinegar
1 tablespoon lemon juice
1/2 teaspoon salt
1 hard-boiled egg, chopped

The spinach should be washed, the heavy stems cut out, and the leaves torn into medium-size pieces. Dry the spinach, mix in the onions, and sprinkle with pepper.

Get out your trusty frying pan and fry the bacon til it's crisp. Add the sugar, vinegar, lemon juice and salt to the pan and stir. Now add the spinach mixture. Stir and toss until the spinach is well coated and slightly wilted.

Serve by dividing the salad into individual bowls and sprinkling the chopped egg over each. You'll be back to this one! Yield: 6 servings.

KING
SALAD
SUPREME

On the afternoon of our oldest daughter's wedding a friend from Kodiak arrived at our house with 21 large cooked king crabs for the reception. It was a surprise to be long remembered. The father of the bride and the father of the groom had a busy hour between the wedding and the reception, for we were the ones who had to shell the crab while our wives made the world's biggest and crabbiest crab salad.

We took to the table 3 large platters heaped with white crab meat surrounded with crab legs. The only lettuce was in the bed the crab meat rested on. A gallon of salad dressing made of mayonnaise, cocktail sauce and minced onions was provided along with individual salad bowls and plates. That salad was well received: not one speck of crab remained when the afternoon ended. It was a once-in-a-lifetime salad. Bless you, Don!

Do try king crab salad even though today's prices put the meat of the king crab in the caviar class. Just chunk up a head of lettuce, add some onion rings, thinly sliced celery and a pound of crab meat flaked thin. To this add your favorite dressing. Decorate the bowl with tomato slices. Serve and enjoy.

summer and salads were a rare treat, made even more so by some individuals' determination to find ways to get more than their share when salads did arrive on the mess tent table.

This mess tent was a fly-catcher. Between meals the red deer flies, about the size of house flies, would collect up around the ridgepole. It was the cook's job to spray the tent before he set up the table for meals. He would brush the dead flies off the table and then set up. This made for crunchy walking, but the floor was only dirt anyway.

One of the planners, let's call him Russ, carefully collected a dozen dead deer flies and slipped them into an envelope. He had a plan. Tonight was a salad night and he would slip the flies onto the top of the salad. He would then spot the flies and yell loudly that the salad was contaminated. When everyone refused to eat the contaminated salad, he would pick the flies out and enjoy the entire bowl.

His plan worked like a charm right up to the point where he yelled that the salad was contaminated. The cook, whose name was Charlie, came rushing in from the cook tent, grabbed the bowl, and with his big spoon stirred the salad thoroughly.

There was a moment's silence until someone said, "Pass the salad." Every man except Russ took his helping and enjoyed it. It was right crunchy, as if it had croutons, and it had a particulary distinctive taste. You're right—the recipe is *not* in this book.

Shortly before I went into the army I was working for a grocery store that had a liquor store attached. A well-known Alaskan bush pilot named Chris came in one day with an interesting request. He wanted to drop a bottle of good whiskey and some salad stuff from his plane to a trapper friend up on the Skwentna River. Chris said the snow looked deep right beside the cabin and shouldn't be too crusted this

early in the season. He gave me a free hand to package these luxuries, with no limit on cost.

I started with a quart bottle of my favorite bourbon, which I wrapped in three layers of cloth. This went into an oilskin bag, which I tied tight. My theory was that even if the bottle broke the trapper could salvage the liquor from the cloth and the oilskin bag. This was before the days of plastic, but would you trust good liquor to a plastic bag?

Next I tied four empty egg cartons, the size that holds a dozen eggs, around the bottle. In the bottom of a 30-dozen egg carton I packed in dividing trays four deep,

followed by a layer of apples and oranges, and more trays. Then the bottle went in, surrounded by heads of lettuce and some celery. On top came more egg trays and a layer of carrots and potatoes. I put four more egg trays above the potatoes and then forced the top of the pasteboard box closed. The bottle was now in its nest. The box was tied shut with heavy linen halibut cord. It was ready to be bombed into the snow.

Chris picked up the rather large box, smiled, and disappeared from my life for a couple of months. Then one day he wandered in to buy something and I asked about the bombing raid.

He told me that he had hit his target with ease and his friend had found the box. When I asked about the liquor, he said, "The next day when I flew over there was a number seven and *OK* stamped in the snow. I guess he got it."

In the spring we were able to confirm our success. The bottle had indeed come through unbroken. Oh, yes! The produce came through OK too.

On the following pages are a few recipes for salads and related concoctions. I hope you'll enjoy them even if they're not dropped from the sky.

I would leave you with one thought. Never be shy when building a salad. Use your imagination. If it sounds at all like a combination of food that would make a salad, try it. Good luck!

TOSSED GREEN SALAD

Making a salad in Alaska is always an adventure. It can vary according to the season, the location or the appetites. In midsummer and fall there is a wealth of greens and other makings available. In other seasons you may find yourself limited to celery, onions and yellow-white heads of lettuce. So I'm not going to list numbers of cups of this and that, for those would be meaningless. Make your salad out of what is available, what you can afford and what you like.

Start by tearing young, fresh greens or by cutting chunks of firm lettuce into your salad bowl.

Here are some possible additions:

Tomatoes, sliced or in chunks
Onions, any kind, chopped, minced or
in rings
Radishes, sliced thin
Cucumber, sliced or in chunks
Avocado, sliced or in chunks

Eggs, hard-boiled or fried, sliced, minced
or in chunks
Cheese, any kind, sliced, crumbled or
in chunks
Meats: bacon bits, cubes of Spam, or
cooked meat such as ham, beef or
chicken cut in strips
Fish: salmon, halibut, snapper, tuna,
kippered herring
Shellfish: crab, shrimp, lobster
Fruit: oranges, apples, pineapple, bananas

As you can see the list is almost endless. Use your imagination.

Likewise the dressings for your salad make an almost endless list. A word of caution about dressings: Use as little as possible, just enough to coat the food. It's a matter of judgment, but you'll want the taste of the salad ingredients to dominate, not the taste of the dressing. Otherwise, drink the dressing from the bottle and forget the salad.

CRANBERRY RELISH MOLD

The lowbush cranberry was bound to make its way into a salad. This Alaskan berry, which is similar to a lingonberry, has been around for a long time and every housewife up here tries to find ways of using the wonderful taste. I dreamed this up on a cold winter night when we needed a touch of color at the table, but I found I couldn't eat my new invention until lunch the next day as there wasn't time in a single day to get it set. We learn from experience. Start this the day before you plan on eating it.

1 8-ounce can crushed pineapple
1 8-ounce can mandarin orange slices
1 small package cherry gelatin
1 cup boiling water
1/2 cup sugar
1 tablespoon lemon juice
1 cup celery, chopped fine
1/2 cup walnuts, chopped
1 cup cranberries, Alaskan or others,
    chopped

Open the cans, drain the juice into a bowl, and save 1/2 cup of the resulting mixture. Dissolve the gelatin in the boiling water and add the sugar, lemon juice and the 1/2 cup of fruit juices.

Chill until partially set. Then add the celery, nuts, canned fruit and cranberries. Mix well and pour into a ring mold. Chill overnight. When ready to serve, turn the gelatin ring onto a serving dish, preferably a dish covered with a bed of lettuce. Garnish with a dressing of your choice.

CUCUMBER IN SOUR CREAM

This is a simple salad that I consumed for the first time only 10 years ago. Where the recipe had been for the 45 previous years I don't know. This is equally good on a hot summer day or a cool winter evening. I rate it excellent.

1 cucumber, peeled and cut into 1/8-inch
   slices
Salt
1/2 cup sour cream
1 tablespoon vinegar
2 drops Tabasco
2 tablespoons chives or onion, minced
1 teaspoon dill seed
Black pepper

Spread the slices of cucumber on a plate, salt lightly, chill in the refrigerator for 30 minutes, and pour off any liquid that accumulates.

Mix together the sour cream, vinegar, Tabasco, chives, dill seed and pepper to taste. Spread a bit of the sour cream mixture on the bottom of a wide soup bowl.

Lift some cucumber slices from the plate and cover the layer of sour cream, alternating layers until you run out of materials. Chill for another 30 minutes before serving. Yield: 2 servings.

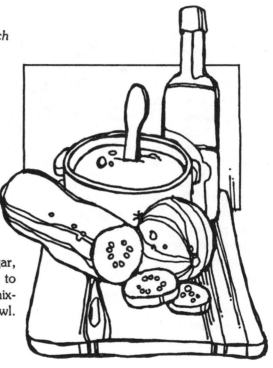

POTLATCH POTATO SALAD

I've made potato salads so small they would serve only a single eater and so big that they had to be made in a 5-gallon dishpan. I confess I do not have at this moment a written recipe for potato salad. To me potato salad is something you make out of what's available and what feels right. OK, I know that doesn't help. I'll try and write out some basic ingredients for potato salad and provide some suggestions for additions.

4 cups boiled potatoes, peeled and diced
    into 3/8-inch cubes
6 hard-boiled eggs, diced
1 cup celery, minced
1 cup onion, chopped
1/2 cup mayonnaise or salad dressing
Salt, black pepper and paprika

In a large bowl carefully mix together all the ingredients except the paprika, making sure everything is well coated with mayonnaise. Spoon into a serving bowl and level, then sprinkle with paprika. Chill for several hours before serving.

You can add any or all of these items before the dressing is mixed in:

Chopped pickles: dill or sweet pickles or
    cucumber chips
Pimento, chopped
Celery seed, 1/2 teaspoon
Dill seed, 1/2 teaspoon

Or you can add some of these to the dressing:

Prepared mustard, 1-1/2 teaspoons
Mustard horseradish, 1-1/2 teaspoons
Cayenne, 1/4 teaspoon
Chili powder, 1/4 teaspoon
Sugar, 2 tablespoons

Or garnish with a number of items:

Parsley, chopped or in sprigs
Cherry tomatoes, halved
Carrot flowers or slices
Hard-boiled eggs, sliced

Potato salad is definitely a fun food: fun to make, fun to experiment with, fun to decorate and fun to eat.

MUSHROOMS AND SOUR CREAM

If there are any foods in the world that love each other more than sour cream and mushrooms, I haven't found them. Every time I drift home from the grocery store with a wistful look, my wife says, "Mushrooms and Sour Cream?"

You can add this pair to just about anything and they will come up tasting wonderful. Try the basic recipe here and then try the suggested variations or dream up your own. Just think of me when you eat them and maybe some of that enjoyment will come my way through telepathy.

1 pound fresh mushrooms , sliced
1/4 cup onion, minced
1/4 cup butter
1 cup sour cream
2 tablespoons sherry
Salt and black pepper

Sauté the mushrooms and onion in the butter for 5 minutes. Stir in the sour cream, sherry, and salt and pepper. Heat the mixture to a point just below boiling, but be careful not to let it boil.

When this is hot you can serve it as a separate dish as is, or as a sauce on just about anything although it goes especially well with rice, noodles, mashed potatoes or broccoli. Yield: 4 servings as a side dish.

Some additions you might wish to try on the second or third time:

1 clove of garlic, minced, added during the sautéing
A dash of nutmeg, 1 teaspoon of lemon juice, 1/2 teaspoon tarragon or dried parsley or fresh chives—any of these, or any combination, added with the seasoning

BERRIES, BEARS AND MUSHROOMS

In 55 years in this great land I have made one definite decision about bears. They and I have two things in common: our fondness for fish and our fondness for berries. We've discussed fish a couple of times so now let's talk about berries.

I've mentioned the limited amount of fruit available to me as a youth. This was true most of the year, but in the summer and fall we did have berries. The variety of berries in Alaska is usually surprising to people from the Lower 48 as they think that we are a land of ice and snow.

The salmonberry is always the first berry to come to my mind. It is a member of the raspberry family and is the first berry to ripen in the summer. I can still remember these big succulent berries of my childhood. We would find them in both their red and golden phases. Both were good, but those golden ones melting in my mouth especially stayed in my memory.

Then the other varieties would come: strawberries, blueberries, red huckleberries, gooseberries, currants, raspberries and cranberries.

I remember the yearly trips the entire town of Cordova used to make to Strawberry Point. When the strawberries were ripe on the sand dunes of nearby Hinchinbrook Island, everyone took a day off. It was a day for berry-picking and picnicking.

Many of the fishermen would take friends on their boats, but a big portion of the townspeople went on a barge owned by the local canneries. This barge, hauled by two cannery tenders, would carry about 85 percent of the town's population. We'd leave early in the morning and about two hours later, at high tide, the barge would be pushed ashore on the sand of Strawberry Point.

I don't remember just how big the sand dunes were, but I do remember that no matter where I stood I couldn't see the end of them. The passengers from the barge and ships would vanish into the dunes, which were covered with strawberry plants full of berries. We would eat ourselves sick and fill buckets with strawberries.

When the next high tide was due, in about 12 hours, the people would come staggering back loaded with berries and board the barge and boats for home. The much anticipated day was over for another year.

I understand that the people of Cordova no longer make the trip to Strawberry Point as a community project. Something special may be gone forever.

LOWBUSH CRANBERRY LIQUEUR

During the long winter nights the people of Alaska have had some great inspirations. I'm sure this is one of them. Lowbush Cranberry Liqueur is one of the outstanding liqueurs in the world. The trouble is that you have to make your own to be able to try it — unless you visit Alaska and are invited to enjoy someone else's.

3 quarts lowbush cranberries
1 fifth 190-proof alcohol
6 cups sugar
3 cups water

You will need a 1-gallon stainless-steel, glass or earthenware pot.

Crush the berries in the pot and let stand for 24 hours. Add the alcohol, cover, and let stand for another 24 hours.

The next step is critical. Separate the juice and alcohol from the bery pulp. Put the solution through a sieve and then into a bag made up of 3 layers of cheesecloth. Take your time and get every drop of that liquid. Discard the pulp.

Now cook the sugar in the water to make a clear syrup. Skim the surface of any scum that appears during the cooking. Cool the syrup.

Mix the syrup and alcohol solutions together, stirring well. Bottle the liqueur, cap, and set aside to age for a minimum of 3 months.

This recipe should give you 3 fifths of liqueur to set aside and just a small amount to taste right away. Ah!

When picking berries in Alaska you can often find yourself in competition with a bear for a particular berry patch. It is not an experience that encourages berry-picking. But don't let this danger stop you. There are a number of things you can do to reduce your chances of an unexpected meeting in a berry patch.

I have found that the best method is to acquire a small yappy dog that will be scared all the time and make enough noise about it to let the bears know where you are. Most bears are somewhat antisocial and will avoid the noisy dog and, in so doing, avoid you.

Wearing a bell around your neck, or tying to your belt a can with a few rattling rocks in it, will also provide enough noise to discourage a bear from joining you. If nothing else, you can sing, whistle or talk to yourself. Take a friend along and yell back and forth a lot.

There is one other point to keep in mind. If a cute little bear cub shows up in the berry patch, remember that it will always have a mean mother around. Do not play with the cub! Do not stay in the game! Remove yourself from the berry patch after looking carefully around so as not to run over a mamma bear.

I met a bear in a berry patch many years ago. Looking back on it now, I know that I scared the bear nearly as badly as the bear scared me. We were both unaware of each other until we suddenly came face to face beside a blueberry bush. The bear was less than four feet from me.

I was terrified. Even a couple hundred pounds of black bear look awfully big when

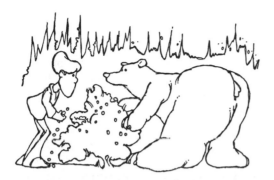

you're 10. My starter worked rapidly and I was off and running toward the trail. Looking back now, I'm sure that it was only an accident that the startled bear started running in the same direction as I did, and only a couple of blueberry bush lengths behind me.

All I remember for sure is that when I hit the trail I caught sight of the bear entering the trail a few feet away. I did a rapid 90° turn and made the next mile in record time. To this day I cannot answer my dad's question. "Did he chase you?" Friend, I was not sparing any energy in neck turning; I was dedicated to straight-ahead running. I do believe that I covered ground faster that afternoon than I ever did before or after.

There is nothing so suspect in Alaska as a bear story. Everyone has a good one, or two. Some, I imagine, are just plain fiction. Others are borrowed from those they happened to or who claim they happened

to. A few might even be true experiences of honest men and women.

If you are going to tell a bear story it helps to have a witness who saw it happen. A nice unbiased witness, like a mother-in-law. Certainly not a friend who everyone knows would support you in any wild story you told.

So once upon a time—no, that sounds phony! Let's start over. One day Dad and I were anchored in a sheltered bay waiting for a storm to blow past. We ran out of drinking water so I was elected to go ashore to get some. I launched the skiff and rowed ashore to a small creek.

I carried the two two-gallon water cans up the creek to get above the high tide mark. I found a spot where a great three-foot-wide tree had fallen across the creek. The water flowing over the log had formed a nice cool pool below it. I knelt down, with my left arm on the log for support, and began filling the cans. It takes some time to fill a couple of cans through one-inch holes in the tops. With the cans full it was time to stand up.

As I raised myself up from behind the front of the log, there was a bear standing on the other side. Neither of us had known that the other was anywhere around. The bear was quicker to react than I was. The bear swapped ends, reached up past its head with its hind legs, and started off like a hot-fuel dragster. But the traction in the black mud was not good. The bear threw that black stinking mud all over me. There was also another bit of evidence of bear fright lying around, contributing to the stinking.

Berries, Bears and Mushrooms   *149*

Suddenly I had a bear story to end all bear stories. Damn! No witnesses! How could I prove it? Well, there was always the evidence. That was the answer. So I slid a piece of bear stool onto a piece of bark to take back as evidence.

I pulled up alongside the boat with the skiff and Dad met me to take the water cans. Then I placed the piece of evidence by the ship's rail and climbed aboard to describe my experience.

Dad listened carefully to my story without immediate comment. He looked at me sharply and then at the evidence. His face was reflective as he looked back at me and said, "Who did that? You or the bear?" But all was not lost; he did believe there had been a bear.

It would seem time to switch from bears to berries again. Two varieties of cranberries must be considered. They are highbush cranberries and lowbush cranberries. Remember the highbush and lowbush moose? Well, there is no connection except names.

The Alaskan highbush cranberry grows five or six feet off the ground and is not a true cranberry. But it looks like a small cranberry, cooks like a cranberry, and makes excellent jams, jellies, and beverages.

Likewise, the Alaskan lowbush cranberry isn't a true cranberry, either. It's more like a lingonberry, and grows very close to the ground. It is tiny and prolific, will do anything a cranberry will do, and has some advantages the cranberry doesn't have. Lowbush cranberries keep very well just as they come off the bush if put in a cool place. Or they can be dried, or packed with sugar in a crock, or frozen unsweetened. They make excellent jam, jelly, syrup for pancakes, sauce for the turkey and, with a little alcohol, an outstanding liqueur.

I've been familiar with both kinds of cranberries for years, but recently I find myself preferring the lowbush kind. I always try to keep an adequate supply of lowbush cranberry liqueur in the house and a few of the berries themselves in the freezer.

Hunting the wild mushroom is a new sport to me. It has only been in the last few years that I have entered into this activity. This type of hunting does not provide me with the quantity of food that meat-hunting provides but it is interesting, is good exercise, and produces some excellent eating.

It is not mushroom-eating that is new to me—just the hunting and gathering. But for a friend who became interested in this kind of hunting, I guess I would have gone through life thinking that mushrooms could only be found in a produce market or in a can. Way back in my youth someone told me that all those toadstools in Alaska were deadly poison. I suppose it was to protect me from danger, but it also kept me from some good eating for 40 years.

My interest can be traced directly to a steak dinner several years ago. Served with that steak was a gravy made from puffballs picked behind my house about an hour before. The taste was excellent, and I seriously started mushroom-hunting soon afterward.

After talking to many people about mushrooms I was usually impressed with how little most of them actually knew about the subject even though they were busy picking and eating mushrooms. I made up my mind to study the subject to some extent before going off to hunt these delights.

After several years of reading, hunting, examining, comparing specimens with pictures and drawings, and carefully tasting the mushrooms I've found, I am comfortable with eight specific mushrooms. These I will pick and eat. I do not feel confident enough to start telling you which to pick and eat. Do your own studying, please.

While I will encourage anyone going out on a wild mushroom hunt, if properly equipped, I will offer a word of caution about feeding your finds to others. Even though you have been eating a variety of mushroom for a couple of years, don't feed it to a friend, or enemy, without telling that person what it is you're cooking. Some people cannot tolerate wild mushrooms. It can also be advisable to limit the total intake of wild mushrooms. One of our friends once found an immense patch of mushrooms of a variety that he had often eaten safely. There were so many, they would not keep, and they tasted so good. . . . He made a pig of himself and paid the price with three days of misery. No one else at the table was affected, but they had all eaten a normal amount.

So may I advise you to get out and hunt the wild mushroom, pick berries, and avoid bears with skill and daring. But if you are forced to kill a bear in self defense, the adjoining recipe may be of help.

CORNED BEAR

Here is something I found tucked away in the back of my recipe file. I can vouch for the fact that it will make good eating, but the first ingredient is not always handy when you want it.

100 pounds bear meat, boned and trimmed of fat
8 pounds salt
4 pounds sugar
2 heaping tablespoons baking soda
2 ounces saltpeter, purchased from a drugstore
1 gallon water

Another essential for this is a 20-gallon keg or stoneware crock.

Salt the meat down in layers in the keg, alternating layers of salt and meat. Let stand 24 hours.

As soon as you finish salting the meat, mix the sugar, soda and saltpeter in the water and let stand. After the meat has been in the salt for a day, pour the sugar solution over the meat in the keg. Keep the meat covered with liquid—a plate with a brick or rock on it will help hold the meat down in the solution.

After 4 days drain the liquid from the keg into a large enamel pan and bring the liquid to a boil. Strain out the blood residue by pouring the liquid through cheesecloth. Return the solution to the keg and put the plate and rock back to hold down the meat. Now store the keg in a very cool place for 4 to 6 weeks.

Use the meat as you would corned beef.

CREAM OF MUSHROOM SOUP

I know, you think it comes in a can. Well, to me that is not always true. It would seem that every time I have a large supply of mushrooms, I make Cream of Mushroom Soup. It has a very special taste that you have to experience.

2 pounds fresh mushrooms
1 small onion, chopped
6 tablespoons clarified butter (see
    page 6)
6 tablespoons flour
6 cups chicken stock
2 egg yolks
1 cup heavy cream or evaporated milk
Salt and black pepper

Sauté the mushrooms and onion in 3 tablespoons of the butter over medium heat.

In a 4-quart saucepan heat the remaining butter, remove from the stove, and stir in the flour. Put back on low heat and stir for 2 minutes. Remove from the stove, add the stock, beat with a wire whisk, and return to the heat and stir until the liquid thickens and is smooth. Now add the mushrooms and onion and simmer for 15 minutes, stirring often.

Whip the egg yolks into the cream or milk, add to this 1/4 cup of the heated stock mix, and whip. Now add the milk mixture to the contents of the saucepan and stir constantly while you bring the soup almost to a boil. Hold it at this heat for a minute and add salt and pepper to taste while stirring.

Serve immediately. As an extra bit of flavor I place a teaspoonful of butter in the bottom of each bowl before filling. Try oyster crackers with this. Yield: about 10 servings.

MUSHROOMS WITH CHICKEN LIVERS

August and September are the real mushrooming months in Alaska. Weather permitting, July and October might provide a few mushrooms, too. During the season my family eats them for every meal if they're available. In the winter months we actually buy our mushrooms. Use any mushrooms available for this recipe.

1 medium onion, chopped
1/4 cup clarified butter (see page 6)
1/2 teaspoon salt
1/4 teaspoon black pepper
1/4 teaspoon sweet basil, crushed
2 tablespoons flour
1 pound chicken livers
1/4 cup red wine or chicken broth
1 pound mushrooms

In a large frying pan sauté the onion in the butter until tender. While this is going on, put the salt, pepper, basil and flour into a small paper bag.

Shake the chicken livers in the bag until they are coated with flour, then add them to the onions in the frying pan and sauté until the livers are browned. Stir in the wine or broth. Add the mushrooms and cook until they are done. The mixture will have thickened a bit.

To serve, arrange a mound of rice in the center of a platter and surround the rice with the mushrooms and livers. Pour any extra gravy over the rice. Yield: 2 to 4 servings.

MUSHROOM HUNTER'S DINNER

After a hard day's tramping through the woods hunting the wild Alaskan mushroom, I find myself on some occasions too pooped to cook. But I'm hungry and want to eat mushrooms, so some quick, easy method of getting dinner is a must. This one fills the bill.

4 tablespoons clarified butter (see
*   page 6)*
1 pound mushrooms, any kind, sliced or
*   cut in chunks*
1/2 pound cooked ham, cut in cubes
1 16-ounce can whole or stewed tomatoes
1 16-ounce can whole kernel corn
1 16-ounce can lima beans
Salt and black pepper

Drag out that large frying pan, pour in the butter, and sauté the mushrooms until almost done. Add the ham and heat it, then add the tomatoes, corn and beans. Stir while everything gets well heated, season to taste, and serve in soup plates.

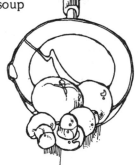

If you're not too tired to whip up a batch, homemade biscuits go good with this dish.
Yield: 4 servings.

EGGS WASILLA

One of the villages in the Matanuska Valley is Wasilla. I've spent a lot of my time in and around that area. One morning, after being out all night on a miserable case, I stopped in at a friend's house. After a single look at me, he invited me in for a wash, shave and breakfast. We had Eggs Wasilla and I had a new recipe for my notes. It's really a way to use up leftover mashed potatoes but I found myself cooking extra mashed potatoes just to have them available.

2 cups mashed potatos
6 eggs
Salt and black pepper
2 tablespoons Cheddar cheese or
*   whatever cheese you prefer, grated*

Divide the mashed potatoes into 6 balls. Put them on a greased baking sheet and flatten, then with a spoon push up the sides of each round to make a cup. Break an egg into each potato cup and salt and pepper to taste.

Bake at 325° for 20 minutes or until the eggs are set. Remove, sprinkle cheese on each cup, and return to the oven for one minute.

Serve with hot buttered toast, bacon, ham, or what have you. It makes a filling breakfast. Yield: 2 or 3 servings.

MATANUSKA BOILED EGGS

When I first lived in the Matanuska Valley the local dairy cooperative had its creamery in Palmer. It made excellent cottage cheese. I learned to love cottage cheese and was always hunting for new ways to use it. This is a method worth passing along.

2 hard-boiled or soft-boiled eggs
2 heaping tablespoons cottage cheese
1/2 teaspoon onion, minced
Salt and black pepper

Shell the eggs, chop them fine, and add the cottage cheese and onion. Mash the ingredients together with a fork and season to taste.

Eat this right out of the bowl or spread on slices of hot buttered toast. Or mix up a batch and spread it on crackers with a thin slice of radish on top for an entirely new taste in hors d'oeuvres.

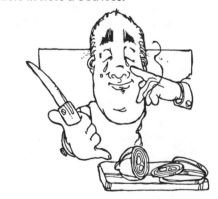

BOAT EGGS

In my early days all produce came to Alaska via steamship. This was true of eggs as well. Eggs were kept in cold-storage compartments in Seattle, aboard ship, and after arriving in Alaska.

I know from my reading that the Chinese claim to have aged eggs for hundreds, even thousands, of years. Being acquainted with "old" eggs, I'll pass. There was no way for us Alaskans to know how long an egg had been in cold storage; it is possible I have already eaten the oldest egg in the world.

In those days cold-storage eggs were referred to as boat eggs. Not because we expected them to hatch into boats but because they came to us by steamship. The weekly ship was referred to simply as the boat, hence the saying, "He's missed too many boats," for a person who was beginning to act a bit odd.

The age of a boat egg was always suspect, as it could be only a month old or over a year, depending on the care in handling, stock rotation and honesty of the dealer. We learned to live with boat eggs because they were all we had.

I'll admit that we younger folks had one advantage over other people in that we had never eaten a fresh egg. We had nothing to compare our boat eggs to. I'll have to be honest about it: only a couple of times in my life have I found a really spoiled boat egg, one that was too far gone to eat.

About the end of World War II a new word was added to the Alaskan vocabulary: *airborne*. It had nothing to do with paratroopers, although Alaska had many young men in that service. To us *airborne* referred to produce, eggs and even meat that had been brought to the territory by aircraft. As I remember it, food started to arrive by air when the number of ships coming north was reduced. I might have the sequence backwards. In any event the practice is still going on today.

Airborne eggs were expensive at first and I don't remember eating any from those early shipments. I was probably still in the army, where even a boat egg would have been a treat. We had something called powdered eggs. That was the greatest dirty trick anyone ever thought up to do to an egg but I'm not going to get sidetracked onto that. If I did my language would rapidly become unfit for publication, even in this enlightened time. Let us return to nonmilitary eggs.

My first memory of eating airborne eggs

was while I was on leave from the army in 1945. For a special treat my mother served ham and fresh eggs on my first morning home. I can remember that I was on the telephone, trying to line up a date, when Mother called me to breakfast. By the time I was ready to eat, my eggs were cold and my mind was elsewhere. Mother asked how I liked them and that is the only reason I remember eating them.

I got out of the army in 1946 and married Connie, who was Alaskan and therefore well acquainted with boat eggs. We continued to use these eggs in our cooking and eating. By that time the eggs were reaching us fairly fast; some were now less than a month old.

In fact, all too often the airborne eggs and boat eggs were so nearly the same age on arrival that there was little difference between them, although several of my friends refused to believe that.

Take a dozen eggs that have been in storage in Seattle for a month and fly them to Anchorage in 12 hours. Ship another dozen that have also been stored for 30 days and get them to Anchorage in five days by ship. Eat an egg from each shipment on the day of arrival. Your boat egg will be 35 days old while your airborne egg will be 30-1/2 days old. Not really much difference for a cold-storage egg. The boat eggs were half the price of the airborne eggs. I rest my case.

In 1955 my transfer took the family to the Matanuska Valley and the city of Palmer. After a month in an apartment, I found a house to rent. I remember that when I told Connie I had rented the house

she said, "Oh, good; now I'll go to the hospital and have this baby while you move." I thought she was kidding until 2 o'clock one morning when she woke me up. "Let's go. It's time!" she said. She was right, it was time; she did and I did.

On the second day in our new house there was a knock on the door. I opened it to find on the porch a pleasant-looking woman with a dozen eggs in her hand. She said, "I'm the egg lady. I can spare a dozen a week for now and two dozen a week when the new hens start laying." With this positive approach I signed up for her service. For the next five years two dozen fresh laid-in-the-morning eggs were delivered to our home each week.

The other reason I remember that day, beside it being our middle daughter's birthday, was that I ate the first fresh egg of my life. I had fried a pair of the egg lady's eggs in butter and slipped them onto a plate. I first noticed how the white stayed together and how the yolks stood high and proud in the frying pan.

I cut the eggs with my fork and lifted a piece to my mouth. My first impression was that it was tasteless. After 25 years of boat eggs I found these very mild. Before I was half through my taste buds had adjusted. The delicate freshness was coming through. I quickly fried two more eggs to permanently imprint that taste on my memory.

During those years in Palmer the matter of eggs was nothing to get excited about. We ate fresh eggs and enjoyed them. Then one day came an assignment in Naknek on Alaska's west coast.

The first morning in Naknek I had a rude awakening to remind me that I was still in Alaska. Ah, you guessed it. I found two boat eggs on my breakfast plate. Real old-fashioned boat eggs that had been in cold storage for an undetermined period of time. The only saving grace was that they had been cooked with loving care in butter. Believe it or not, I enjoyed them. My taste had to make quite a drastic adjustment, but the old memories were still there. Not that I would willingly go back to eating them as a steady diet but I know I could.

Years later, while we were living in Juneau, I had occasion to visit Palmer on business. Thinking of those wonderful fresh eggs, and knowing that I was going straight back to Juneau, I went out and picked up four dozen fresh eggs from our former egg lady.

Within two hours I was at the airport ready to fly home to Juneau. Out there on the field was one of my favorite planes, a Constellation. You remember that old plane with the bent back and the blackened engine mounts, dripping oil? They were good aircraft. I had almost as many hours in them as most of the pilots, although mine were passenger hours.

I was unaware that the summer schedul-

CREAMED EGGS ON BUNS

In our house we always add a teaspoon of vinegar and a few drops of food coloring to the water in which we hard-boil our eggs. Green is my favorite because the eggs look so pretty in the egg rack of the refrigerator. This way we can always tell the hard-boiled eggs from the fresh ones. Easter all year long.

When we are not dieting I love hard-boiled eggs in sauce. Try this some Sunday morning.

6 hamburger buns or English muffins or
    12 pieces of bread
Butter
6 hard-boiled eggs, peeled and chopped
1 can corned beef spread or chicken
    spread
1 cup White Sauce (see page 131)
Salt and black pepper
Paprika

Toast the bun halves, butter them and cover with the corned beef spread. Lay on a plate and cover with chopped hard-boiled eggs. Top with warm White Sauce. Sprinkle with paprika and serve. Yield: 6 servings.

WHIPPED EGGS

I mentioned the cold-storage boat eggs of my youth. In those days many recipes were developed to conceal the taste of the eggs. This may be one of those, as it came from my mother's recipe file. It works equally well with fresh eggs, I'm happy to say.

2 eggs
1 teaspoon lemon juice
2 tablespoons onion, grated
1 teaspoon Worcestershire sauce
Butter and toast

In a mixing bowl beat the eggs lightly, stir in the other ingredients, and let stand for 5 minutes.

Place a small, lightly greased frying pan over a low heat. Pour the mixture into the pan and cook slowly until the top of the mixture appears done.

Return the egg mixture to the bowl, beat it lightly with a fork, and spread on hot buttered toast.

I have also successfully added to the mixture (before cooking) cooked shrimp, flaked fish, ham or mushrooms. Any one of these at a time.

We have also used this to make hors d'oeuvres by spreading it on crackers or toast squares. Each covered cracker can be topped with a small whole shrimp or a small cross-cut section of king crab leg, making an appetizer that is out of this world.

CUBE EGG SOUP

I'm not sure where this recipe should be placed in this book. It's a way to make good soup and also a way to cook eggs. I have used it at home, on the trail, while dieting or when I was tired of eggs cooked the usual ways. This recipe is a single serving for me, maybe 2 servings if eaten before a meal.

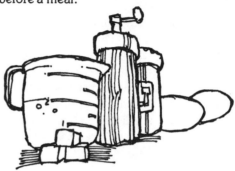

1 vegetable bouillon cube
2 beef or chicken bouillon cubes
2 cups water
2 large eggs
Salt and black pepper

Add the bouillon cubes to the water in a saucepan and set on the heat to boil.

Beat the eggs in a container with a spout. When the bouillon is boiling, stir it rapidly with a spoon and dribble the egg mixture into it. Cook for 5 minutes, salt and pepper to taste, and serve.

I have had people puzzling over the "noodle" in the soup for years. The eggs seem to lose all identity as eggs, but are delicious.

ing had ended and this was to be a milk-run flight. The plane would stop at both Cordova and Yakutat before feeling its way into Juneau.

The takeoff from Anchorage was normal, which means that we squeezed out between a flight to Tokyo and a polar-route flight to Copenhagen. We climbed to altitude, flew a few minutes, and started the let-down into Cordova.

The airport at Cordova is located out on those flats I mentioned before. From the air it appears to be extremely short. It appears the same way on the ground, too. The strip is paved but that doesn't make it a bit longer. Looking down I could see the wind whipping the water off the puddles on the Copper River Flats. The wind was coming directly across the runway, and I guessed it was 30 knots at least. We would go on to Yakutat without landing, no doubt.

I was wrong. The Connie made a long straight-in approach with much wobbling of the wings in the crosswind. As the pilot started that final I'm-going-to-set-her-down action, the wind lifted the left wing, the runway markers flashed by, and the throttles were chopped. It was at this point I wondered if I would even get to deliver those fresh eggs.

The pilot had fought the plane almost level when we reached the point of touchdown. I use the term *touchdown* incorrectly, as we came down like 100 tons of bricks. There was a bit of a tail squiggle which unlatched a couple of storage cabinets, but the most exciting part was the sound of the engines. Those four big engines, with their props reversed, were trying faithfully to stop the aircraft while there was still runway under the wheels. I wish to report they did. The right wheel of the plane fell off the end of the pavement while the pilot was turning us to taxi back to the terminal, but the touchdown itself was on the pavement. A good landing.

We were on the ground only 30 minutes and then we were off to Yakutat. On takeoff I was sure that the right inboard engine was running awfully ragged for a takeoff on full power. But it seemed to smooth out nicely at cruising altitude. The Copper River disappeared into the clouds, and we droned our way to the next stop.

We reached Yakutat in clear skies and made a normal landing, except for that moment just before touchdown when the pilot added a bit more power to lift onto the pavement. The same engine was running ragged again. After we landed I noticed that the two pilots and a fellow in white coveralls had wandered out to look at my worrisome engine. Now there were at least four of us who knew something was wrong.

I have a theory about flying. That guy up front in the captain's seat is *not* going to take off unless he thinks the aircraft will fly nor is he going to fly deliberately into a cloudful of rocks. You know—where he hits first, and such nonsense. If the captain will fly so will I. True, there are some pilots that I trust more than others, but the captain out there looking at that engine was one of the best.

Within a few minutes the Connie was bouncing down the runway with all four engines ticking over. Then came the turn onto the runway, full power, and we were flying. When the wheels came up I looked out the window to see that again my engine was not running. The propeller was standing feathered while the other three did all the work.

The approach to Juneau is down through or over some mountains, across a bit of water and some islands, over a medium hill, and then into a dog-leg turn at a 10° angle to line up with the runway. I imagine that it requires a certain amount of concentration on the pilot's part, too. If you add a crosswind, blowing clouds, heavy rain or an icy runway, you can figure out the cause of those distinguishing gray hairs that cover the senior pilots' heads.

Our pilot already had his share of gray hairs, but he surely added to his collection that day. When the aircraft was about a half-mile from touchdown and committed, something started banging on the port side. I couldn't see what. I had only seconds to consider the probabilities of egg delivery. There was a slight yaw in the aircraft's attitude followed by a right turn just before the touchdown. This was all there was to show that my friend up in that captain's seat had lost another of his engines back there a way.

My own Connie, my wife, met me at the terminal. After a kiss, I handed her the four dozen eggs and explained just how hard a certain pilot and I had worked to get them to her.

Just the word *egg* can bring many experiences to mind. The first time I crossed Egg Island Bar, for instance. I was aboard the cannery tender *Billy*, out of Cordova. We had been over to Martin River to pick up a load of fish. Because of the tides my brother Ken, the *Billy*'s skipper, had elected to avoid the Copper River Flats. We were actually out in the Gulf of Alaska.

The disadvantage of this route was that we had to cross what was known as Egg Island Bar to get back into the channels on the north side of the flats. This was a treacherous piece of water, where the entire Pacific Ocean came in and piled itself in huge breakers against the island and its surrounding sand bars. Egg Island itself was not much more than a high sand pile.

To add interest to the area, people were always talking about the ships and boats that had tried to cross the bars and been lost.

So, for the moment, sit beside me on a bunk across the back of the *Billy*'s crowded pilothouse. Ken stands straddle-legged amidships, holding the wheel. As always when I am with him, he is talking to me in a running commentary on what he is doing. This is part of my education and is the way that Dad had taught Ken.

"Now, kid, we've run one hour and 30 minutes from our sighting of Puffin Island on a course of west-northwest. According to our log on other runs this should put us right on the channel across the bar in five minutes. I wish I could get a sighting off Hinchinbrook Island but it's blacker than hell over there. We'll just feel our way across. Hey, Sam," (Sam was the deckhand) "take a line forward and stand by with it! Okay, kid, here we go!"

At this point he brings the *Billy* around to starboard and heads her in toward a solid line of white surf breaking in the distance. We are now riding a deep ocean swell that lifts and drops us eight to ten feet. The *Billy* moves slowly toward the surf.

"Sam, give me a reading!" Ken shouts out the wheelhouse window. Sam heaves the line far ahead of the ship and lets it sink until it's straight up and down. "No bottom!" comes his yell.

Several minutes go by with Sam throwing the lead line every few minutes. Suddenly Sam yells, "Six fathoms." He quickly pulls up the line and looks in the tallow pocket, which is a little indentation in the weight. "White sand!" he yells.

Ken reduces the engine speed down to the slowest possible. "Let's study the surf a few minutes."

All I can see is white water. A solid wall of white water. Then Ken's pointing finger moves a little to the left of straight ahead. "There's the hole! Can you see it?" I cannot and say so. Ken answers, "You'll see it as we approach and go through it."

The *Billy* jumps ahead on her two big engines and we cross through the line of surf. Gradually I see the dark flat spot that is the channel. We slip through the channel and across the bar with ease. How Ken was able to hit the hole is just due to the kind of navigation he had been taught.

My last memory of Egg Island is the cabin of a long-ago lost ship that we passed to starboard that day. Someone who had not found the hole.

I **don't know what memories** the word *egg* brings to your mind but I hope they are pleasant. So wherever you live—in the far corners of the world on boat eggs or on farms with fresh eggs—I hope you find a recipe here to add to your enjoyment of the *egg*.

EGGS TRAITOR

I'll admit that Eggs Benedict was the grandfather of this recipe. I had a refrigerator full of newly smoked salmon at the time I dreamed it up. An egg-poaching pan is nice for this dish; those pans make such nice round poached eggs.

3 English muffins or hamburger buns or 6
*   pieces of bread*
Butter
1/2 pound smoked salmon, sliced thin
6 eggs
Hollandaise Sauce (see page 130)

Halve the muffins, toast and butter them, and cover with the smoked salmon. Poach the eggs, put them on the fish-covered muffin halves, pour warm Hollandaise Sauce over the eggs, and serve.

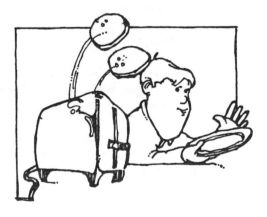

PICKLED EGGS

While traveling around the state in my official capacity I've been in many bars, saloons and cocktail lounges. Setting on the back bar in many of these establishments will be a large jar of pickled hard-boiled eggs. Eating these eggs can be an experience. In remote outposts, pickled boat eggs can have a lot of flavor. The safest test is to find out if the owner or the bartender will eat an egg. Then I'll try them.

I love pickled eggs, so I had to learn how to make them. For some good eating try pickling your own fresh eggs. I have 2 recipes and usually alternate between them.

PLAIN PICKLED EGGS
2 cups white or cider vinegar
2 tablespoons sugar
1 teaspoon salt
1 teaspoon pickling spice
1 large onion, sliced in rings
12 hard-boiled eggs, shelled

In an enamel or stainless-steel saucepan combine the vinegar, sugar, salt, pickling spice and onion rings. Bring to a boil and simmer for 5 minutes.

In a glass jar big enough to hold a dozen eggs, alternate layers of eggs with layers of onion rings until you have all the eggs in. Pour the pickling spice into the jar, making sure all the eggs are covered. Add extra vinegar if necessary.

Refrigerate for 24 hours; then you can eat the eggs. Kept in the refrigerator they should last 2 weeks, but they will not if anyone around your house likes pickled eggs.

Note: For a dash of color add some yellow food coloring to the pickling liquid. Do not use green, even on Saint Patrick's Day. Green eggs are a bit much—for me, anyway.

FANCY PICKLED EGGS
1 16-ounce can sliced beets with juice
2 tablespoons sugar
1 teaspoon salt
2 cups white or cider vinegar
1 cinnamon stick
1/2 teaspoon ground cloves
2 bay leaves
1/2 teaspoon celery seed
1 large onion, sliced in rings
12 hard-boiled eggs, shelled

In an enamel or stainless-steel saucepan combine all ingredients except the eggs. Bring to a boil and simmer for 5 minutes.

In a large glass jar alternate layers of eggs, beets and onion rings until you are out of material. Pour the heated liquid into the jar, making sure all layers are covered. Refrigerate for 24 hours before serving.

These little jewels come out of the pickling spice a nice purple color with a reddish tinge. They are excellent, and also make colorful decorations for potato salad or what have you. The beets and onions, of course, are delicious, too.

EGG FOO FISH

Whenever we had a fish fry in the evening the kids hoped for leftovers so that we could have Egg Foo Fish for breakfast. To date I have yet to find anyone who doesn't like this or is uninterested in seconds.

2 cups any leftover fish or contents of 1
  tall can of fish
6 eggs
1 small onion, minced
Salt and black pepper
1 cup fresh or canned bean sprouts
1/4 cup clarified butter (see page 6)

Break the fish into small pieces and remove any bones, skin or dark fat.

Break the eggs into a medium-size bowl and beat. Add the fish, bean sprouts and minced onion. Mix thoroughly and salt and pepper to taste.

In a frying pan over medium heat melt 2 tablespoons of the butter. With a large mixing spoon add enough of the mixture to the frying pan to form a pancake about 5 inches across. Cook until the bottom is firm, turn, and cook until the other side is firm. Continue this way with the rest of the mixture, serving each portion right from the pan with stacks of buttered toast. I usually provide as accompaniment soy sauce, oyster sauce, cocktail sauce and whatever else the family likes.

Note: When I'm short on fish, or long on people, I stretch the mixture with a couple more eggs and a cup or so of cooked rice. Or throw in some mushrooms. It's a flexible recipe. Yield: 4 servings.

IMAGINATION EGGS

The shirred egg is baked, usually in a small individual baking dish, and served in the same container. The possibilities for variety are just about endless and limited only by your imagination.

For just plain shirred eggs: Into an individual baking cup or dish place 1 tablespoon of cream or evaporated milk and break in an egg, being careful not to break the yolk. Sprinkle lightly with salt and pepper. Set the cup or cups in a shallow pan and pour about an inch of hot water into the pan. Bake at 325° for 20 minutes or until firm.

VARIATIONS:

Place 1/2 strip of cooked bacon around the inside of the cup before adding the cream and egg.

Sprinkle 2 tablespoons of grated cheese over the egg about 5 minutes before it is done.

Add 1 tablespoon of cooked spinach or 1 tablespoon of cooked minced ham, or 2 cooked shrimp to the cup before the cream and egg.

Add whatever your own imagination suggests.

DUNKING DOUGHNUTS

The real old stand-by of the mug-up has always been doughnuts. Everyone used to make them and they are not too difficult. Try this recipe.

3 tablespoons butter
1 cup sugar
3 egg yolks
1 egg white
1 cup mashed potatoes, made from a mix
 if you prefer
1/4 can evaporated or fresh milk
2-3/4 cups pastry flour or all-purpose flour
3 teaspoons baking powder
1/2 teaspoon salt
1/2 teaspoon cinnamon
1/2 teaspoon mace
1/2 teaspoon nutmeg
Grease, vegetable oil or fat for frying

In a large bowl combine, in the order listed, all ingredients except the grease. Stir well and turn out on a floured board. Flatten the dough down to about 5/8-inch thick. Cut out the doughnuts with a doughnut cutter.

I have assumed that at this point you have a French fryer full of hot grease. If you do, drop the doughnuts into the grease until they're brown on one side, turn, and brown on the other side. Don't forget to cook some of the little center doughnut holes for the kids.

If you're without a French fryer heat enough vegetable oil or fat in a small frying pan to float a cooking doughnut. Watch the temperature so that the grease never gets over 380°.

The cooked doughnuts should be set on paper toweling to drain and cool. To sugar them, shake in a paper bag with some powdered sugar.

Serve at your next mug-up. Yield: about 2 dozen doughnuts and some holes.

MUG-UPS

There is an old Alaskan term, also a seamen's term, that I seem to be hearing less and less each year. The term is *mug-up*.

What is a mug-up? Well, the term basically involves hospitality. To invite people to mug-up is to tell them one of the following: you like them, you think they are interesting, you think you would like to talk to them, they look like they would benefit from your fire and food, you are lonesome and need company, you have the only place in sight to get warm, or you are proud of your place and want them to see it. The fact of the matter is that for the price of a little coffee you can acquire a captive audience.

What do you get when you accept an invitation to a mug-up? In most cases you get warm. You step into a house and dining area out of the cold, wind, rain or whatever is out there. In a field camp mug-up may only mean a spot next to the fire, out of the wind, but you'll feel the warmth. Next you'll be offered something to drink, usually in a coffee mug. The liquid may be coffee, tea, cocoa or even a royal—coffee or tea with a touch of liquor—but it too will be warm.

Most mug-ups also go a step farther and include something to eat—cookies, cake, pie or even a bowl of soup or chili.

If the conversation is stimulating and you hit it off with your host a mug-up might just be stretched into a dinner invitation. If you're in no hurry this could result in some fine eating.

I first heard the term *mug-up* aboard one of the boats of my youth. I seem to remember the Chinese cook on the *Billy* saying something like *mulg-mp* which was followed by everyone gathering in the galley for coffee and doughnuts. I got cocoa as I was just a little fellow.

But mug-up really started for me aboard the *Smile*, where I was a crew member, a deck hand in all but salary. That first season the *Smile* had a cook that made the best dried-apple pie the world has ever seen or tasted. The crew wanted apple pie at every mug-up. As there were mug-ups at any time of day, it required a lot of pie.

Aboard the *Smile* the mug-up rules were made by the cook. When he was asleep, which was from midnight to 6 in the morning, he would have coffee on the stove and pie in the icebox. You were free

CHARLEY'S APPLE PIE

I know that Charley, the cook on the *Smile,* used dried apples for his pies, but that was all he had available. Today we have things like pie crust mix, fresh apples and good Cheddar cheese. Wouldn't you rather make a modern pie and just remember Charley? I would! To make an apple pie for your mug-up try this.

Pie crust mix for a 2-crust pie
1/2 cup brown sugar
1 teaspoon cinnamon
1/4 teaspoon ground allspice
1/8 teaspoon ground cloves
2 tablespoons butter
1 cup Cheddar cheese, shredded
4 cups apples, peeled, cored and sliced
1/2 cup white sugar
1 tablespoon flour

Combine half of the pie crust mix with the brown sugar, cinnamon, allspice and cloves. Cut in the butter until the mixture is crumbly. Now stir in the cheese and set aside.

Mix the remaining pie crust dough as indicated on the box to form a pie shell. Roll it out and line a 9-inch pie pan.

Arrange the apple slices on the crust. Mix the white sugar and flour together and sprinkle evenly over the apples. Then top with the cheese and pastry mixture.

Bake at 375° for 45 minutes or until the apples are tender.

Serve hot or cold, but do invite a friend in for a mug-up.

to quietly help yourself. From 6 in the morning until midnight the cook was in the galley and he was boss. You were either invited in for a mug-up or a meal, or you did not enter his kitchen at all. The cook was the sole ruler of that 9' by 11' space aboard the ship. He did an outstanding job of feeding the hungry crew of four and me.

Of course Charley was so warm-hearted that if anyone appeared at the galley door he got attention. If Charley was making pies on the dining table, you got a cup of coffee and were told to go somewhere else to drink it. But bring back the mug. If the table was not in use you would be invited in for a mug-up of pie and coffee. If you were really hungry and had missed a meal for a good reason, Charley could have two eggs, hash browns and ham or bacon in front of you in 10 minutes. In the winter he worked ashore as a short-order cook.

If you happened to be sitting at the table when he was ready to use the table to prepare food or make pies he would let you know. He'd jar you with, "Get your ass the hell out of my galley!" While you were still in shock and hadn't had time to react to his attack he would start slamming things like 25-pound cans of lard, meat cleavers or sacks of flour onto the table. These all acted well as starters to get us out, and the crew scattered.

As a result of Charley's yells and such, we soon learned to spot signs and anticipate him just a little. We assumed that we could frustrate him a bit if we all got up and walked out about 15 seconds before he planned to yell at us. Smart cook, wasn't he?

Many times since, I have sat down to a mug-up or just a cup of coffee and remembered the mug-ups aboard the *Smile* and that apple pie.

The mug-up as an established institution was always useful to me as a policeman. It opened locked doors and locked minds and helped create a sudden rapport with strangers. It allowed me to help people and may have even saved my life on at least one occasion.

Picture for a moment this scene. You are the only trooper or policeman for 50 miles in any direction. You are five miles off the main highway and you've rowed a boat across a lake, and as you near the shore a bullet smacks the water beside you. Somewhere up there by that cabin near the lake is a man with a rifle hiding from you.

Yes, you know who he is; he's the man you came to see. Just an elderly, lonesome man whose mind is not what it was even a few years ago. He is now sure that "they" are out to get him. I have just traveled up here to see if he is all right because he has not been to town lately.

I stop rowing and stand up in the boat so he might better see the uniform and especially the trooper hat that is so well known in Alaska.

A voice comes across the water, "You'll never get me! Get out of here!" It appears that he has slipped some more mentally or has had a recent unhappy contact with someone. So I yell back, "Hey, Pete, it's Nelson. I just came by for a mug-up!"

There is a full three minutes of silence while this thought is being considered. Suddenly Pete stands up from behind a woodpile, very carefully lays his rifle on the wood, and motions me to the shore. His voice comes clearly across the water. "I'll put the coffee on." A lifetime of hospitality and the institution of mug-up have broken through his thoughts and fears.

Pete makes good coffee and we have a long talk. I think I'm able to leave him just a little more at ease with the world.

On another occasion the institution of mug-up nearly killed me. I flew from Anchorage to Cold Bay and then on a Grumman Goose to King Cove, a bit south of Cold Bay. I had about 30 minutes of important police work to do and then I would be ready to leave. The pilot of the Goose said he would go on down to Sand Point and pick me up when he returned.

By the time my business was finished and the Goose came back, two hours later, there was no way the pilot could land that plane. The wind had shifted and was blowing onto the shore and there was a 12-foot sea breaking on the beach.

I stood on the cannery dock and watched the Goose fade into the rain. I was not to see that plane again for five days. The cannery radio operator told me that the pilot sent his regrets and that he would return when the wind went down or shifted.

The cannery superintendent offered me a room in the executive bunkhouse and led me to the mess hall for (you guessed it) a mug-up. This cannery mess hall brought back those wonderful memories of the can-

nery mess halls of my boyhood. The policy of the King Cove mess hall is worth explaining. A notice on the door indicated the following:

Breakfast	7:00 a.m.
Mug-up	9:30
Lunch	12:00 Noon
Mug-up	3:00 p.m.
Dinner	6:00
Mug-up	9:00
Mug-up (night crew)	11:30
Mess hall closed	12:00 Midnight to 7:00 a.m.

How did these people stand it, with no eating between midnight and 7 in the morning! To make this schedule even more unbelievable, the food was excellent. The cannery had a special baking crew that did nothing but turn out bread, rolls, pies, cakes and lots of other good things.

For the next five days I did not miss a meal or a mug-up. Six or seven times a day I marched from the bunkhouse to the mess hall and back. Once a day I walked through the village and talked to people, but that in no way began to wear off my calorie intake. There just wasn't anything else to do except mug-up. I had to go to the mess hall to find someone to talk to, as everyone was busy working the rest of the time.

I gained nine pounds in five days. If that storm hadn't ended and the Goose hadn't come for me, I know that I would have eaten myself to death. What a way to go!

Then there was the time that the mug-up almost led me to the well-known

MUG-UP CAKE

This is the most successful recipe that the Nelson family has ever had. Both my wife and my oldest daughter won ribbons at the Alaska State Fair with this cake. We have also given away more copies of this recipe than of any other in our notes. This cake has made many mug-ups something to remember.

2 cups flour
1 cup sugar
1/3 cup cocoa
1 cup Miracle Whip salad dressing
2 teaspoons soda
1 teaspoon vanilla
1 pinch salt
1 cup water

There is nothing complicated about this. Just put all the ingredients into a bowl and mix well. Then pour the mixture into a 9-inch-square baking pan.

Bake at 350° for about an hour—until a toothpick comes out clean.

Cool and serve. You can frost it if you must, but why bother—it's wonderful right out of the pan.

FINNISH OVEN PANCAKE

Some years ago I was invited in for a mug-up with a couple living way back in the bush. The coffee was good and so was the treat. I was served a bowl containing a kind of cake that had been heaped with strawberry jam. The couple had grown and picked the strawberries and made the jam themselves. The cake, they said, was Finnish and came from the wife's mother's recipe file. The recipe was so simple, and the results so tasty, that I had to add it to my notes. We've used it often for mug-ups and in school lunches, too.

4 eggs
4 cups milk or evaporated milk and water
2 cups flour
1 teaspoon sugar
1/4 teaspoon salt
4 tablespoons butter

Mix the eggs, milk, flour, sugar, salt, and 2 tablespooons of butter in a large bowl. Melt the remaining butter to grease a large cake pan, something near 10" by 20" by 1". Pour the batter into the well-buttered pan.

Bake at 450° for about 15 minutes. The pancake should be crisp and brown.

Serve hot with jam or syrup, cold as a cake, or hot or cold with any topping you can dream up, including ice cream.

I can testify that it makes a good mug-up base.

MRS. SMITH'S LEMON PIE

After our ill-fated mug-up I couldn't very well ask Mrs. Smith for the recipe for her pie, could I? To be on the safe side I described the pie to my wife, as well as the experience. I'm fairly sure she believed my story as she went right into the kitchen and made me a pie with the recipe below. True, she wanted me to use a different name for it. She suggested Flaming Miracle or Opportunity Lost Lemon Pie. But I settled for giving it the fictitious name of the woman involved.

When I asked Connie where *she* got the recipe all she did was smile.

Prebaked 9-inch pie shell
1-1/3 cups sugar
4-1/2 tablespoons flour
Salt
1-1/4 cups water
3 eggs, separated
2 tablespoons butter
1/4 cup lemon juice
2 teaspoons lemon rind
1/4 teaspoon cream of tartar

Make the filling by mixing 1 cup of sugar with the flour and a pinch of salt in the top of a double boiler. Add the water and the lightly beaten egg yolks. Cook over boiling water, stirring constantly, until the mixture thickens. Then cover and cook 10 minutes, still in the double boiler. Add the butter, lemon juice and lemon rind and pour into the pie shell.

For the meringue, beat the egg whites with the cream of tartar until the whites will hold soft peaks. Gradually add the remaining 1/3 cup of sugar and beat until stiff and glossy. Pile the mixture on top of the pie and bake at 350° for 10 minutes or until the meringue is golden brown.

This is bound to make a success of any mug-up.

fate worse than death. Again I was traveling and that's all I'm going to say about where, when and who. I arrived in a small community by air and reached shore by boat and by wading. Again I had less than an hour's work but I had a day to wait for a plane to lift me out again. I have spent a lot of time doing this.

When I arrived I was met by a delegation: the curious, the troubled and those wishing to help me. Within a few minutes I had a dinner invitation, a bed for the night and a late mug-up date. The people of Alaskan communities are usually helpful and hospitable to everyone. As a trooper I used to find this doubly true, as we were considered "their" troopers, and we were.

After I finished my work I had dinner with one family and visited several others, ending up at what was known as the government building for a mug-up with the Smiths. The name is phony as you will understand.

I was met at the door by Mrs. Smith, who escorted me to the kitchen and coffee. Then she brought out a beautiful lemon pie. The absence of a husband around began to bother me so I asked where he was, only to find that he had been gone for a week and would be gone still another week.

After the second cup of coffee, Mrs. Smith excused herself and left the kitchen and disappeared down the long hall toward the rear of the building. A long 10 minutes passed and I was becoming worried that I had said something to offend the woman. Then there was a loud crash toward the back of the house.

I jumped up and ran down the hall because I envisioned Mrs. Smith falling off something. Halfway down the hall I came

to the open door of the master bedroom. I looked in to see if I could help Mrs. Smith. She was there all right, smiling at me, not needing any help, and was in a state of what I guess is dishabille. The fact is, she was lying naked on the bed, raising a hand to me. I stood there, I suspect with my mouth open, for a long count of five.

I was to be saved by duty. Before I could either say anything or react in some other way, there was a pounding on the front door. I opened it to find a neighbor, who reported that he had just run his old truck into the back of the building. Oh, yes! The crash I had heard earlier. As I was the only accident investigator in town I had to go investigate the accident.

While I was poking around in back of the house I was joined by a fully dressed Mrs. Smith. When my work was finished I did not get invited back in the house to finish our mug-up. A moment of my life was gone forever.

Would you join with me in trying to save this old custom of the mug-up? Let's see, you could bake a pie, cake or some doughnuts. Invite your neighbor over for a mug-up. So what if you have to explain it to him or her. Sit down and drink coffee or a less expensive beverage together. Tell the neighbor about the tradition of hospitality called the mug-up. Suggest he or she try it too.

OK, let's spread the word. Here are some recipes to help the cause.

LOWBUSH NUT BREAD

This is another recipe that I picked up when I was invited in to have a mug-up and I can proudly say that Connie and I have returned the favor several dozen times by serving it at our own mug-ups. The flavor, with Alaskan lowbush cranberries, is distinct but try it with any cranberries.

1 orange rind, grated
1 cup sugar
3 cups flour
4 tablespoons baking powder
1-1/2 teaspoons salt
1/2 cup walnuts, chopped
2 eggs
1 cup milk
4 tablespoons butter
1 cup lowbush cranberries or any other
   kind

Combine orange rind, sugar, flour, baking powder, salt and nuts. In another bowl beat the eggs and combine with the milk and butter. Mix the dry and wet ingredients together and fold in the cranberries. Pour into a greased loaf pan and bake at 350° for an hour.

Serve either hot or cold with lots of fresh butter.

TONI'S BREAD PUDDING

My mother's nickname was Toni and my middle daughter was named after her. This recipe came out of the original Toni's recipe notes and has been a family favorite for years. The biggest problem has always been finding enough dry bread for making it. We've had to plan to have dry bread sometimes just so we could make the pudding. Any old bread you have around, white or brown, can be used.

2 tablespoons butter
1 quart milk or evaporated milk with water
3 eggs, beaten
1/4 teaspoon salt
1 teaspoon vanilla
1/2 cup sugar
3-1/2 cups dry bread, cut in 1/2-inch
   cubes

In a large 4-quart saucepan melt the butter in the milk. Add the eggs, salt, vanilla and sugar. Stir over a gentle heat until the sugar is dissolved. Then stir in the bread cubes and pour into a 9" by 9" baking pan.

Bake at 375° for 50 minutes.

Serve the pudding hot from the pan with ice cream for a topping. Or try it cold with whipped cream. Today you are having a mug-up. You can diet tomorrow!

NELSON BAKED ALASKA

This really isn't a mug-up recipe but I know that no one outside of Alaska would believe that a book on Alaskan cooking would be complete without a baked Alaska. There's no reason why you couldn't plan an extra special mug-up for new residents of the state and surprise them with this recipe. It's such a good idea, I may just do it myself. For the look on people's faces it will be worth the fussing.

1 quart vanilla ice cream
1 cup fresh strawberries, sliced
2-1/3 cups Bisquick biscuit mix
3 tablespoons sugar
2/3 cup evaporated or fresh milk
4 egg whites at room temperature
1/2 teaspoon cream of tartar
1/4 cup sugar
1/2 teaspoon vanilla

Soften the ice cream, fold in the strawberries, and pack the mixture in a bowl 7 inches in diameter. Put in the freezer and freeze hard.

Several hours later or the next day combine the Bisquick with the sugar and milk.

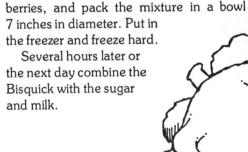

Pour this into a well-greased cake pan 8 inches in diameter. Bake at 450° for 15 minutes, remove from the pan, and cool.

Cover a baking sheet with aluminum foil, lay the cake on the foil, remove the ice cream from the freezer and center the ice cream on the cake. Put the baking sheet, cake and ice cream back in the freezer.

When you are ready to put things together heat the oven to 500°. While it's heating make up the meringue. Beat the egg whites, gradually adding the cream of tartar, until they are foamy. Beat the sugar in a little at a time, add the vanilla, and continue beating until the mixture is stiff and glossy.

Take the cake and ice cream out of the freezer and cover completely with the meringue, right down to the foil. Bake for 3 to 5 minutes—until nicely browned.

Remove the baked Alaska from the oven and slide the foil off the baking sheet onto a serving plate. Trim or fold the foil to the edge of the meringue and serve immediately. It works, and tastes great. It would certainly make a memorable mug-up.

CUSTARD DE CORN

My mother, one of the world's best custard-makers, made many custard pies during my youth. People came to our house just to try her pies. It might have been that memory, plus our kids' love for creamed corn, that triggered this.

1 16-ounce can creamed corn
1 cup milk
1 cup bread crumbs
3 eggs, well beaten

1 pinch dried parsley
1/2 teaspoon salt
1 tablespoon onion, minced
1 tablespoon green pepper, minced
1 tablespoon clarified butter (see page 6)

Combine all the ingredients in a bowl and mix well. Pour into an ovensafe dish and set the dish in a pan of water. Bake at 350° for 40 minutes. Serve hot right from the cooking pan.

PARTIES, FUN FOODS AND OTHER RECIPES

All my life I've enjoyed parties. Big parties to celebrate elections or governors' birthdays; medium parties like open houses, wedding receptions and even wakes; small parties for all your friends and neighbors; intimate parties with two to four couples. And private parties, just you and the one you love.

Living in my parents' home was often like living in a party. During a great deal of my growing up we had people living with us or visiting for a few days, or coming to play cards or just dropping by. It wasn't a bad way to grow up. You sure learn to recognize people for what they are and not for what you would like them to be.

I know that one of Mother's happiest times was when she was running a boarding house in Kodiak from 1939 to 1942. There was a pinochle game in the living room from the time four people arrived home from work until midnight, seven nights a week. That was before TV, you know. The players would change as different people had different things to do, but the game went on. There was no money involved, just a lot of fun.

It is no wonder that when I acquired a home of my own and eventually collected six kids, we ran our home in a similar way. We always seemed to have room for extras, drop-ins and overnighters.

Another factor, the tendency for policemen and troopers to group up and entertain each other, came into our lives. We hosted and cohosted many a party over the years—birthdays, promotions, transfers, welcomes for new men and their families, or just easy get-togethers. These parties were all B.Y.O.B. (bring your own bottle) so we could have lots of them.

There are two parties that especially stand out in my memory. One was the party we threw in Juneau where the order of the day was to dress like hippies. I had seen some colorful hippies prior to the party, but they all seemed positively "establishment" after some of the characters that turned up at the party. Several men went to the beauty parlor to have their hair done right. My, the wild rumors that generated. Then at midnight every policeman in the area stopped by to mug-up with the ones who were already

ORIENTAL COLESLAW

On a patrol on the Glenn Highway I found a young Asian man with automobile trouble. If I remember right he had lost a water pump on his engine. Anyway, I drove him to a service station where he could make arrangements for his car to be fixed. During our ride I discovered that he was well educated and an interesting talker. When it became evident that he would be stranded for some time, I invited him home with me for dinner.

We had a discussion and finally arrived at this decision: He would accept if we allowed him to make and provide the salad. So we bought the makings and that evening our new friend made us this salad. We enjoyed both his visit and his slaw. We still do, every time we use this recipe. I hope you like it too.

3/4 cup mayonnaise
2 teaspoons soy sauce
2 teaspoons sugar
1 teaspoon salt
1 medium cabbage, shredded
1/2 cup green onions, chopped
1 8-ounce can water chestnuts, sliced thin
1 8-ounce can bamboo shoots, diced
2 tablespoons pimentos, chopped

In a large bowl whip together the mayonnaise, soy sauce, sugar and salt. Add the remaining ingredients and toss the mixture until the cabbage appears to be well coated. Chill for an hour and serve. Yield: 6 servings.

there. Of course the late arrivals arrived in a bunch, with sirens growling. It excited the entire neighborhood.

The other memorable party was one we just threw because we wanted to. But we had live music for dancing. One of our sons and his musical group played for us far into the morning. We had dancing, eating, drinking and good fellowship at their best.

The food served at these parties was brought by the people attending. Nothing very fancy. Well prepared, ample and neatly presented was the rule. As the host and hostess Connie and I would do something like bake a salmon, prepare a batch of smoked salmon, or roast a ham or turkey.

None of our parties were tightly planned and dress was casual. I hate ties under all circumstances and dislike shoes when I'm in the house, and this does tend to informalize our parties.

I also used to take part in hunting parties; about six people were right. Too few to act like an army camp, but enough to divide the work so no one was overworked. Besides, it's nice to have lots of help packing out moose. Moose are big animals. A party this size is big enough to bother with tables and chairs, gas stoves and working space for the cook. I hate to cook while kneeling on the ground and with smoke in my eyes.

The horse is still the best means of getting way back from the world to hunt. I don't necessarily mean riding a horse for the actual hunt, but for carrying you and your duffle to the base camp. Also to pack out the game. With heavy work transferred to the horse, a man can enjoy the hunt and companionship.

All this is without the rattle and exhaust of the internal combustion engine. With luck, the horse will live off the country and the exhaust is biodegradable.

But **trail horses** can result in fall-out at times. On a survey party one year we had a dozen plugs and Red. Red did not like a pack saddle to slip or pinch. In fact he was known to make his dislikes known by taking violent action.

One afternoon we were moving camp and working our way up a side hill. Red was just in front of me. Something must have slipped or pinched him. Red turned and started running straight down the hill. When he hit the flat at the bottom he really turned it on, kicking with both hind legs, bucking and twisting. It was then that things started coming loose from the pack.

First there was a fine white dust floating

SAUSAGE SUNBURST

This recipe came to us from another family, but I remember eating something like this as a child. The first time we tried it on the kids it was an instant success. It's a fun food.

1 pound pork sausage in links
1 cup white flour
4 teaspoons baking powder
1/2 teaspoon salt
1 cup yellow corn meal
1/4 cup sugar
1 cup milk
2 eggs
1/4 cup shortening

Fry the sausages in a 10-inch cast-iron or ovensafe frying pan. Pour off the grease, arrange the links in a sunburst pattern in the pan, and set aside.

Into a bowl sift the flour, baking powder and salt. Stir in the corn meal and sugar, then add the milk, eggs and shortening. Beat with a spoon or your mixer for 1 or 2 minutes until smooth. Pour the batter into the pan, being careful not to destroy the sunburst design.

Bake at 425° for 25 minutes. Turn out onto a plate so that the sausage pattern will show.

Serve hot with butter and syrup. This also is good with a pork sausage gravy.

Note: I've made this in camp by crumbling bulk sausage into pieces and adding them to the batter before baking in a Dutch oven. This ends arguments over who gets the most links.

in the air. The wrangler said, "There goes the flour!" Then the air was filled with metallic things, sparkling in the sun. "Oh, oh. There go the knives, forks and spoons," the cook commented. Then a larger white object or two arched skyward. Dishes, no less.

After 10 minutes of this Red stood head down, totally beat, in the middle of an acre of assorted camp essentials. Fifteen men worked two hours to find what was still usable in the fall-out.

When Red was repacked we were on our way again toward the next camp. An hour later we were in the process of crossing a river. Something pinched Red again but he was too tired to jump, buck or twist. He seemed to have just one good kick left in his body and figured now was the time. He reared up and placed both hind feet right on the side of another horse's pack load. This tired old mare, known as Old Swayback, promptly fell down in the river. She landed flat on her back with all four feet sticking straight up and still running like crazy. Her head kept dropping back under water.

Five men waded out to try and save the horse and the camp gear. Did you ever stand waist-deep in an ice-cold mountain stream, trying to keep the head of an upside-down horse out of the water? Not to mention the fun of trying to dodge four steel-shod horse's feet, while untying a diamond hitch under water. We had to get that pack off her before she drowned all of us. We were mean, stubborn and very wet when we managed to get Old Swayback to her feet.

So you see it is not without some serious consideration that I recommend horses for going into the woods to hunt.

The fishing party, now, should always be limited according to the size of the boat. I think two men and their wives are about right on anything smaller than 50 feet in length. But pick your fishing companions with care. Even being out over a single night with some couples can be a long time. The couple that you love dearly and can have a wonderful time with at home or when out dancing can be pure agony aboard a boat.

Living aboard a small boat for hours, or days, requires the ultimate in courtesy, tact, willingness to work and an honest desire for everyone aboard to have a good time. All too often I've watched one sorehead spoil a weekend for three other people.

Yes, I say for fishing aboard a small boat rate your friends and choose your fishing companions only from those having excellent ratings. You can enjoy the other friends, those with poor boat ratings, in other ways and on shore. Do this even if it means that you lose a weekend during the summer fishing season.

On the subject of fun food I would expound a bit. Until I was grown and started raising kids I didn't know such things existed. My mother did, though. As I was experimenting and creating things with food to encourage reluctant children to eat, the memories came back to me. It was as if my mother was standing beside me chuckling.

Little things, like a few drops of food coloring to make a glass of milk into something different—a green brew for Martians, maybe. Or a gingerbread man made out of biscuit dough, complete with raisins for eyes.

Really, all fun food consists of is any well-prepared food attractively served, placed in interesting surroundings or served in good company.

A dozen young people standing in the kitchen get their fun food by dishing up heaping bowls of beans and chili sauce right from the pot and eating it with giant slices of bread. All the while having so much fun in conversation and giggling that no one wants to leave the kitchen to sit down in the dining room. That's fun food.

Or four adults, standing around a steaming pot in that same kitchen, just waiting for those right-out-of-the-pot fresh steamed clams to dip in a dish of melted butter and pop into their mouths. Seasoned with good conversation and fellowship, that's fun food.

Then there was the day that four families gathered on the beach for a crab feed. Two young men went diving right off the beach to catch the crab to put in our pot of boiling water. The dads were in charge of cooking. Talk about fresh crab! I never counted the crab shells but we went through two cases of good beer. That, too, was fun food.

Now one of the things that made that crab feed such a good time was the fingers-only rule. No one could eat with anything except fingers. We had one paper cup to hold the Nelson Seafood Sauce (see page 141). Oh, those juicy Dungeness crab pieces, dipped in that sauce! It was food fit for a king; Henry VIII would have loved it.

HOMESTEADER'S HONEY

I first tasted this honey in 1940, when I was a young man on a survey crew in the Homer area. We were working hard and I was always hungry. One weekend I was visiting a local family and for Sunday breakfast we had sourdough hotcakes and this honey. Now, even though I'm trying to limit the sugar in my diet, I still make a batch of this once in a while.

10 cups sugar
2-1/2 cups water
1 teaspoon powdered alum, found on the
    spice rack of a grocery store
30 white clover flowers
18 red clover flowers
18 fireweed flowerets or rose petals

Put the sugar, water and alum in a 3-quart saucepan, bring to a boil, and remove any scum. Boil for about 10 minutes. Remove from the heat and add the flowers. Steep for 10 minutes. Strain the syrup into jars, cover, and cool.

That's it! You have now joined the bees in making honey, or at least Homesteader's Honey. Use it just like the real stuff.

SPAMANIA

From 1942 to 1946, as a member of the U. S. Army, I was assigned "overseas"—in Alaska. I joined the thousands of soldiers who had the chance to become acquainted with pork luncheon meat or, as you may have heard it called, Spam. I liked the stuff the first time I ate it but the mess halls certainly did serve it often, and after my discharge in 1946 I didn't eat much Spam. But by 1951 I could stand to taste it again. We men struggling with low wages and new families learned to enjoy things like Spamania toward the end of each month when money was always short. I still like it once in a while.

2 cans Spam or other pork luncheon meat
1/4 pound bacon
1 small onion, chopped
1 cup cracker crumbs or bread crumbs
2 eggs
1 cup tomato juice
Salt and black pepper

Grind the Spam and bacon together in a food grinder. Add to the resulting mixture all the other ingredients and mix well. Add extra juice if the mixture seems too dry to make a meat loaf.

Put the mixture in a well-greased loaf pan and bake at 350° for an hour.

Serve with potatoes or rice and a vegetable. It fills those empty stomachs. Yield: 6 to 8 servings.

COOKED LETTUCE

Every time I have a garden I end up growing a lot more lettuce than we can eat in salads. I certainly hate to see it go to waste but I find I can't give it away fast enough. So I learned to cook lettuce as a green vegetable. Have a go at this recipe.

3 pounds green lettuce
1 cup water
1 cup celery, sliced thin
1 small onion, cut in rings
2 tablespoons butter
Salt and black pepper

Cut up the lettuce. Pour the water into a 6-quart pan and add the celery, onion rings and 1 tablespoon of butter. Pack the lettuce into the pan, cover, bring to a boil and simmer for 20 minutes. Drain and place in a serving bowl. Add the remaining butter and salt and pepper to taste.

Serve with the vinegar bottle, since some people like this best with vinegar sprinkled over it.

KETCHIKAN OYSTER FRY

My wife was born in Ketchikan, but I've spent very little time in the area. Long enough, though, to find out that the world's best oysters grow somewhere around there. I've never actually seen those luscious oysters growing in the ocean but I've eaten them, and that's enough.

On one of my official trips to Ketchikan I was introduced to the Ketchikan Oyster Fry, my hostess's version of the San Francisco hangtown fry. It was a delightful eating experience, and my raving about it earned me this recipe.

12 fresh oysters
Cracker crumbs for coating
8 eggs
1 small onion
1 clove garlic
8 ounces ham, chopped
Salt and black pepper
2 tablespoons butter

Roll the oysters in the cracker crumbs. Beat the eggs in a large bowl and grate the onion and garlic into the eggs. Add the ham, salt and pepper and mix into the eggs, then slide in the oysters.

Heat the butter in a large frying pan and pour in the contents of the bowl, distributing the oysters evenly in the pan. Cook slowly until the eggs are done. Slide onto a warm plate and serve with celery salt and Tabasco sauce. Yield: if the oysters are large, up to 6 servings.

HONEYMOON CASSEROLE

This recipe was Lazy Bride's Delight in my mother's recipe notes. But I was a bit more polite and came up with a new name. With another name change, and doubling or tripling the quantities, this might be a good thing for a working mother to ask her teen-age kids to make.

1/2 pound thin bacon, diced
1/2 pound boiled ham, diced
1 16-ounce can cut-up tomatoes
1 16-ounce can whole kernel corn
1 16-ounce can green lima beans
1 4-ounce can mushrooms
1 16-ounce can spaghetti in tomato sauce
1 tablespoon flour mixed with enough juice
*   from a canned vegetable*
*   to make a thin paste*
Salt and black
*   pepper*

Fry the bacon in a casserole and pour off the grease. Add the ham, drain the vegetables and mushrooms, and add them. Mix well, add the spaghetti and sauce and the flour paste, season, and stir again.

Bake at 350° for 30 minutes. Serve in the casserole. Yield: 2 generous servings.

INSULATED PIGS

Some fairly wild ideas seemed to appear whenever my kids and I started inventing fun foods. The kids always liked these foods, though, no matter how wild they became. This was a favorite.

3-inch potatoes, 1 for each sausage
1 pound pork sausage in links
1/4 cup butter
1 tablespoon Worcestershire sauce
Garlic salt
Cornflakes for coating potatoes
Paprika

Peel each potato and make a lengthwise hole in it with an apple corer. Boil the potatoes for 5 minutes in salted water. Drain and set aside. Boil the pork links in the same water for 10 minutes. Then insert a sausage in each potato.

Make a sauce of butter, Worcestershire sauce and garlic salt. Crush some cornflakes and roll the potatoes in the butter mixture and then in the cornflakes. Dust with paprika.

Put the potatoes on a rack in a pan and bake at 375° for an hour. Baste the potatoes with the drippings halfway through the baking.

Serve hot from the oven; your kids will love them.

DEEP-FRIED POTATOES

French-fried potatoes are an American favorite. It is getting to the point where they are served with everything. And I have to admit that there are 1 or 2 restaurants that make them so I can eat them. But every time I'm in such places I wish I had the makings and was home to have some of the recipe below. This makes potatoes for 2.

If you do not have the second ingredient you can't make these fries. Oh, you can try with vegetable oil, but I'll not recommend the results.

2 large potatoes, peeled and cut in
3/8-inch strips
Beef fat (see page 27)
Dry mustard in a shaker

Pile the potato strips on paper toweling and dry carefully.

Bring the temperature of the beef fat to 380°. Put 1/2 the potato strips in the wire basket of the deep-fat fryer and cook for 8 minutes. Now lift the basket and set it so the fat will drain off the potatoes and back into the fryer; meanwhile, the fat in the fryer should be rising again to the high temperature. Then put the basket back in the fat for an additional 2 minutes or until the potato strips are nicely browned. Shake while frying.

Drain the potatoes and turn out onto a serving plate. Sprinkle powdered mustard over them and serve. You'll find none better anywhere.

Parties, Fun Foods and Other Recipes   *183*

JUNEAU MULTI-BEAN SALAD

While I was polishing off a bowl of this salad a woman named Sandy gave me the recipe. Basically all you need is a can opener to make it. Note, however, that it's a large-family or take-to-a-potluck type of salad. You will need at least 8 good eaters to finish it, or plan on it for 2 days.

1 16-ounce can red kidney beans
1 16-ounce can garbanzos
1 16-ounce can yellow wax beans
1 16-ounce can green lima beans, large
   Norfolk beans if possible
1 16-ounce can cut green beans
1 large onion, sliced in rings
1/2 cup cider vinegar
1/4 cup salad oil
1/4 cup sugar
Salt and black pepper

Open the cans, drain, and place the vegetables in a large bowl with the onion rings. Stir the vinegar, oil and sugar together and pour over the beans, carefully mixing everything together until the beans are coated. Salt and pepper to taste. Chill in the refrigerator for at least 2 hours before serving.

KODIAK *NAWTET*

Way back in 1941 I was living in Kodiak and had an opportunity to attend a Russian Orthodox wedding. Let me say that the ceremony was impressive, as it required 5 hours to tie the knot joining the bride and groom, but the reception was outstanding. It lasted for 5 fun-filled days.

Such eating and drinking I never experienced before or, for that matter, since. It was at this reception that I first tasted Kodiak *nawtet*, a liver dish that required a month of research before I could find out how to make it.

1 pound beef, moose or calf liver
1/2 pound chicken livers
1/2 pound butter
2 tablespoons onion, minced
Salt and black pepper

Boil the pound of liver until tender. Drain and set aside. In a fresh pot of water boil the chicken livers. Drain the livers and save the liquid. Put both kinds of liver through a meat grinder several times, using the plate for the finest grinding.

Warm the butter, and cream it into the liver and onion. Add the bouillon drained from the chicken livers until a good spreading consistency is reached. Season to taste and pack into a small buttered mold. Chill for 5 hours.

Serve as a sandwich spread or on crackers. This is an excellent spread for hors d'oeuvres.

MEATLESS CABBAGE

I imagine you know that cabbages grow big in the Matanuska Valley. Fifty-pounders are not uncommon and I understand one in 1972 went to 78 pounds. Forget the big ones; the best eating is the little early cabbages. I first tasted this recipe while visiting an old and confirmed bachelor who was meatless at the time because he hadn't shot his winter's meat yet. He said it was still too early for hunting and anyway he was busy with his garden.

2 small cabbages
4 tablespoons butter
1 tablespoon curry powder
1/4 teaspoon paprika

Boil the cabbage until tender. Cut the heads into quarters and drain in a colander for 15 minutes.

In the pot that held the cabbage melt the butter and mix in the curry powder and paprika. Drop in the cabbage and stir until each piece is well coated. Serve with salt and pepper if needed

This is an excellent diet item as 2 chunks of cabbage total only 75 calories, in spite of the butter. I should add that I've tried this recipe substituting Brussels sprouts and found it just as good.

Leftovers

LEFTOVERS

Browsing in my past while looking for incidents for this book was like turning over a rock on the beach. Ideas and thoughts went scurrying in all directions.

Taking each incident firmly in hand, I briefly outlined it and fitted it to the other stories that I wanted to tell. I'll admit to eliminating some really wild tales and a few merely tall ones as I worked a reasonable number into each chapter.

Just now I looked around and discovered I had some leftovers. Stories, not food. It seemed that every stirring of my old memory loosened more stories.

As I was writing about my mother's bean soup and drop-in guests in Cordova, the saga of Dr. Jones filtered its way down to the front of my mind.

The doctor spent a winter building a sea sled. This was an interesting idea in boat construction in the 1930s. A big wide hull, a shovel bow and a tunnel stern combined with a large high-speed engine gave you a sea sled.

In the spring the town turned out to the launching of the craft. She floated proudly, although not deeply, in the sea. It was some time, about a week I think, before the mechanics could unscramble the wiring job Doc had completed and get the engine

started. The boat was equipped with a new V-8 engine, the best available.

For the next few weeks the doctor spent evenings blasting around the bay in front of the town. The critics sat on the rails along the dock and discussed the craft. She was fast, they agreed, maybe 20 knots. She didn't seem to steer too well, as all Doc was able to do was make great wide turns. She sure did make a fuss going through the water. So it went, on and on. Everyone liked Doc and was interested in his new boat.

Then the good doctor decided that he wanted to make a trip out on the Copper River Flats. This was why he had built the shallow-draft boat: to get around out there during the waterfowl season. He asked both my dad and my brother to go with him to act as guides, but this was outfitting time for the canning and fishing season, so no one could spare the time to help him play with his new toy.

After a few days Doc showed up at the house for a mug-up and some talk. He said he was going to the flats anyway, and would Dad and Ken draw him a chart. They did, putting all their knowledge and seamanship into the effort. It was a masterpiece of a chart. Every channel and every mud or sand bar was plainly marked. On the margins were the notes on tides necessary to cross the bars and a wealth of other information. Doc was pleased.

Two days later the doctor was off to the flats, fully loaded with fuel and supplies for a week's cruise. The weather turned sour about the time his sea sled disappeared around the point.

It rained steadily, the wind blew, and the weather was cold for the entire next week. We had no first-hand communication with Doc, but several tender captains reported seeing him on different sand bars way off in the distance. We knew he was at least moving around and was likely all right.

Just eight days later, almost to the hour, the doctor's sea sled banged into our dock. A dirty, tired, bearded, wet, miserable old man crawled out of the craft.

My God! It was Doc! Dad grabbed one of Doc's arms and Ken the other, and they started for the house. I climbed aboard the sea sled to secure it. What a mess! Everything that could come loose had come loose and was either sunk in or floating in the bilge water, which reached a foot over the floorboards. I pumped her out and secured her to the dock.

Meanwhile, Dad had Doc sitting in a tub of hot water. Mother was cooking. A half-hour later the doctor was sitting at our kitchen table, clean and shaved, but still looking awfully tired. Dad's clothes were much too big for him, and he looked shrunken in them. Mother got two big bowls of her bean soup, three eggs and some bacon into him. He was asleep in the spare bed inside of 10 minutes. He had not said how he had enjoyed his trip. He slept 18 hours.

Later, rested and awake, Doc was a dif-ferent man. He had decided not to tell us about his trip. He mentioned being here and there as he and Dad talked, but no details. The closest thing to a complaint was when he said, "You know that chart you made me, the one with all the sand bars marked? Well, you were correct. I found every one of them. I spent a tide on most of them."

I just had to ask about his boat's condition. He looked long and hard at me and then, just because of my age, I guess, he answered. Just a mile from the dock, around the point, one sea had broken over the sea sled and caused all the damage. He went on to say that if he could have stepped out of the boat at that moment he would have left it forever.

Mentally, I think, Doc did just that—left the boat forever. He did it right there in the kitchen as he talked to me. We ended up towing it to town and I'm sure he sold or gave it away, if possible, without ever looking at it again. The next time I saw the doctor he had taken up a new hobby. It seems to me that it was cooking, but I might be wrong.

Other stories fell out as well back there when I was telling about Pete V.'s interesting way of punching the white part out of the bread. Or did I mention his name before? Anyway, it was Pete V. because no one could either spell or pronounce his last name. Pete was all man, though, and didn't mind his last name being shortened to just V. What he *did* mind was the idea of being cheated.

It had always been that when you delivered a king salmon to a cannery tender it was counted as one fish. It didn't matter if it weighed 10 pounds or 50 pounds. The pay was the same. Incidentally, the price was 75 cents at the time. A fish, not a pound.

One spring an efficiency expert at a desk in Seattle decided to change this, in the cannery's favor, of course. The new cannery policy was that a king salmon had to weigh over 25 pounds to be "one" fish. Anything under 25 pounds was counted as half a fish.

The fishermen fishing company boats were forced to go along with this latest gimmick. But Pete V. owned his own boat and gear. He could be as independent as he wanted.

The first time he threw a 15-pound king salmon up onto the tender's deck, the counter shouted, "Half a king!"

Pete stopped pitching fish, climbed up on the tender's deck, looked at the fish he had just thrown aboard, and said, "That was a whole king, see?"

So the argument started between the fish-counter and Pete. It went on and on. Boats were piling up behind the tender waiting to unload, the tide was dropping, and Pete was still arguing that he had delivered a whole fish, not a half.

The skipper of the tender finally made a decision, shouting, "A king is a king!" His voice rang out so loud that 20 fishermen heard him. So much for that idiot at a desk 3,000 miles away. Pete V. became even more popular.

When I was writing about my little trolling ship back there a way, I couldn't help but recall one of the hazards of fishing in Juneau in the summer: the large whale population. In the spring and again in the fall we would see the killer whales, which are about 25 feet long, but during the summer the larger whales, humpbacks and grays, would be around with their young.

The last summer we lived in Juneau two boats ran over or into whales. One boat was traveling at nearly 25 knots when it hit a whale. The boat flipped completely over lengthwise and landed upside down. Luckily, all five people in the boat survived. They were wearing life jackets at the time.

Whenever I am out in my boat I look for two things: drift logs and whales. They even look similar at times. Over the years we have dodged dozens of whales and a few drift logs as well. I always make it a point to give the big old whales a lot of room and all of the right of way.

My closest encounters with them have been when I was anchored or drifting with the engine off. There was one time when I was anchored, relaxing with my feet up, beer in hand and a line over the side. There was a sudden blowing sound just outside the boat, and a foul wet smell settled around me. Looking over the side I discovered that a whale had just surfaced and blown about five feet from the side of the boat. He had rolled and exhaled practically in my face. Talk about bad breath! His presence could be smelled long after he was gone.

On another occasion I was anchored. I was standing on my cabin top, casting into a profitable-looking tide rip, when a whale surfaced. My cast was already in the air and I bounced three ounces of lead off the whale's back. For one horrible moment there I thought I might hook the whale.

Can you picture having such an animal on your line? What a fish story that would have been, but the hook didn't hook into the whale.

Whales have the habit of jumping straight up out of the water and coming down with a splash so big that it can be seen for miles. They seem to go down deep and come up fast. I have watched this form of play from a distance and that is close enough. At times I have been close to one when it dived and then I had to wait around and wonder where it was going to come up. The feeling must be akin to Russian roulette. But there are about five chances out of ten that you'll never see the whale again, as whales swim out of the area underwater.

One of our friends had one shoot out of the water and splash down alongside his anchored boat. It caused quite a commotion in the water and, for that matter, in the boat. There were a number of splashes: the sea, coffee, beer and soup, for starters. He had visitors aboard at the time and they were thrilled, scared and emotionally upset. They voted to move at once. Three of the votes were for the middle of Texas.

Another friend of mine tells of watching a killer whale come right up on the beach in front of her Ketchikan home and grab a king salmon for lunch.

There had been a bit of a surf rolling in on the beach that day. My friend saw a wave bring in a large king salmon and strand it on the beach. The next wave brought in the whale, who picked up the salmon and went back out with the same wave.

The salmon no doubt had been swimming for its life and ran right out of ocean. It found a beach, but not safety.

The story of flying from Cordova to Valdez pushed another flying memory to the surface. On one occasion I left Cordova en route to Valdez aboard a Widgeon Aircraft. That's the small cousin of the Grumman Goose, and also an amphibian. I knew the pilot so rated the left front seat.

We flew across the northern edge of Prince William Sound while the weather turned into low clouds and fog. We tried the west entrance to Valdez Arm, but the water and clouds met in there in a white wall. The pilot pulled a 180° turn and we flew back the way we had come. He said, "Let's try the east side of the island."

He was flying, so I was willing. As we proceeded up the channel the clouds and water met. Very soon we were flying along at just flying speed, about eight feet in the air, with everything solid behind us.

At this point I was glad that I was in an amphibian. We could always land on the water. But we did not, for suddenly we spotted a rock with a light blinking at us. There was a slight argument between the other two passengers, both fishermen, over which light it was. We were much too late getting their agreement, and the light was long gone. We were turning up the arm, we hoped.

We were still down low, flying slow, when without warning there was the excursion boat out of Valdez. It was broadside to us and only 200 yards ahead. We were too close to drop onto the water. Over was the only chance, and the pilot made up his mind in time. We were lifting under full power. The plane had just cleared the ship's masts when I felt a stall start. Down went the nose of the aircraft and we flew back into the fog, who knows how low.

When everyone was able to take another breath a few words passed back and forth. Only the pilot and I had even seen the ship. Seen it! I looked right in the eyes of the man at the ship's wheel and watched them widen as we flashed past. I know that he had not known of our presence until that very moment. Our eyes locked together for a microsecond. Talk about ships that pass in the night. Try it in a fog at 100 knots. No! I take it back! Don't!

In the days when passenger steamers used to ply the Alaskan waters one of the stops was always at the Columbia Glacier, on Prince William Sound. The main act of the visit was for the ship to blow its big deep steam whistle. The vibrations would cause giant chunks of ice to break off the glacier, falling into the ocean with monstrous splashes. It was a grand, spectacular sight. I saw this happen from the decks of the old *Yukon*, many years ago.

The next time I saw the glacier was from the decks of a smaller ship. At the end of the seining season we went to the face of the glacier to show a crew member from the Lower 48 the sights. He had a great time taking pictures of ice.

As we started to leave the skipper remembered the horn-blowing act of the big ships. He reached up and pulled the lanyard on his ship's power foghorn. The sound was satisfactorily loud and echoed back from the glacier. Then a deep bass rumble began to reach us across the water.

We looked up in time to see what looked like the entire face of the glacier starting to fall outward. I can't even begin to estimate how many thousands of tons of ice were falling. It seemed to take forever for the ice to reach the water. Then the ice disappeared into the sea and a great splash came into being.

The splash and the wave from the impact of the ice ran toward the ship at an unbelievable speed. I can thank God that the seine boat had its great wide stern to the wave.

I could feel the lift of the stern long before the crest of the wave reached us. The stern was very high when the wave hit. There was white water over the stern all the way to the forward cabin. The bow of the ship was driven completely underwater. I honestly believe that for a long second only the top of the cabin and the masts were out of the water.

Anyone standing on the deck would have been lost. It happened, by chance, that all of us had been standing on top of the cabin by the upper control station.

The great wave rushed on by us and dissipated in the distance. We found ourselves in a sea of broken chunks of ice, and many were banging into the hull in the disturbed waters. Back on the after hold were three large pieces of ice that I would estimate weighed two or three hundred pounds each. I'm sure that they had bounced off the seine net piled up on the deck and rolled to where we found them. Any one of them, hitting the hatch, could have sunk us.

Oh yes, I almost forgot to mention the angry engineer. He had the door to the engine room hooked open because of the nice weather and not all the wave that came aboard had gone back into the sea. He claimed that a thousand gallons had come down into his engine-room and landed on him.

After we all got our breathing settled down to normal we held a short election. Those in favor of *never* blowing a horn at a glacier won by a landslide. I almost said by an ice fall!

D**o you like bear stories?** I've got hundreds of them. You realize that I am not the person they all happened to. A bear story in Alaska becomes community property after a very short time. You might as well tell it as if it happened to you; it'll be suspect anyway, so tell it as your own.

The summer I worked on a survey crew we had a man named Ole, who was from California, working with us. Ole was a chainman, one of the two fellows who measure distances.

One hot day in July the crew reached the Kenai River with their survey line. A process known as triangulation was required to measure the width of the river, and that would take some time. The delay found Ole all by himself on one side of the river. He figured a little nap would be nice, so he curled up against the bottom of a spruce tree and went to sleep.

Ole awoke to find himself eyeball to eyeball with a brown bear. When Ole started, the startled bear turned and ran off a way. Ole decided to climb the tree. As he started up, the bear came back and pranced about a bit like a puppy who wanted to play. Ole didn't want to!

As Ole reached what he thought was a safe height, the bear stood up against the tree and bit a chunk out. Ole thought that a bit more height would be a good idea, and reached for a higher limb. His groping fingers found a dead branch and when his weight came on it the branch broke. Ole fell out of his tree and landed on the bear.

Momentarily startled, the bear again ran off a little way, thought it over, and started the puppy business again. Ole still was not interested in playing even though his first efforts had entertained the bear. He was busy getting back up the tree.

Ole had not quite reached a point of safety when the bear reared up against the tree a second time. This time the upward-reaching paw hooked Ole's boot and pulled Ole loose from the tree. Down he went again, landing on the bear a second time.

Thinking this was great fun, the bear danced away again, did his puppy act, and started back. Ole was now practiced in tree-climbing and went straight to the top, touching only an occasional branch. There he was in the top with his arms wrapped around the tree.

Ole's bear was still having fun bouncing around down at the base of the spruce. The bear seemed quite disappointed that Ole didn't want to play any more. So disappointed that he reached up and once more bit a chunk out of the tree, 10 feet from the ground.

The rest of the crew talked Ole down from his perch an hour or so later. He walked right to camp, packed his gear, caught a boat to Kenai, flew to Anchorage, and went back to California. It is reported that he kept saying over and over, "I've used up my luck, I've used up my luck!"

You know, maybe he was right.

I **now have a message** for the youth of today. Respect your elders and you may live to join them. A little lady of 97 pounds and a year for every pound brought this fact home to me.

I first met Mrs. B. about 45 years ago, or so my folks told me, but I didn't get to know her until some 20 years ago. She was an old lady then, although she was still actively operating a hotel at the time.

For a period of five years I was often in contact with Mrs. B. and we had many talks. Circumstances then prevented me from seeing her again for some time.

In fact, 15 years went by until Mrs. B. visited Juneau in 1971, shortly after I was promoted to colonel. I called her daughter, who was traveling with her, and asked if it would be possible to call on Mrs. B. It would be fine.

I was in full uniform, with eagle wings on my collar, when I called on her some hours later. She greeted me by name and as warmly as during those years before. We talked for several minutes before she commented, "I see you are still in the Highway Patrol."

Then out of the blue this lady spoke a few words that changed the whole meeting. She said, "I'm glad to see that there are a few of us old-timers still around." In her mind I had finally joined her generation. I was no longer a child she once knew, or a young man among many, but an old-timer like herself. The fact that she was twice my age no longer mattered between us.

The last time we two old-timers visited was an enjoyable time for both of us, I'm sure. I'll never have another chance to talk to her in this life because she is gone.

We come to the end of the leftover stories for now. If I were to follow the format of other chapters in this book there would be a few good recipes for leftovers right about here.

You won't find any, though, as most of my leftover recipes I just included as I went along.

Could it be that I like to tell stories even more than I like to cook?

INDEX